The Campus History Series

PENN STATE ALTOONA

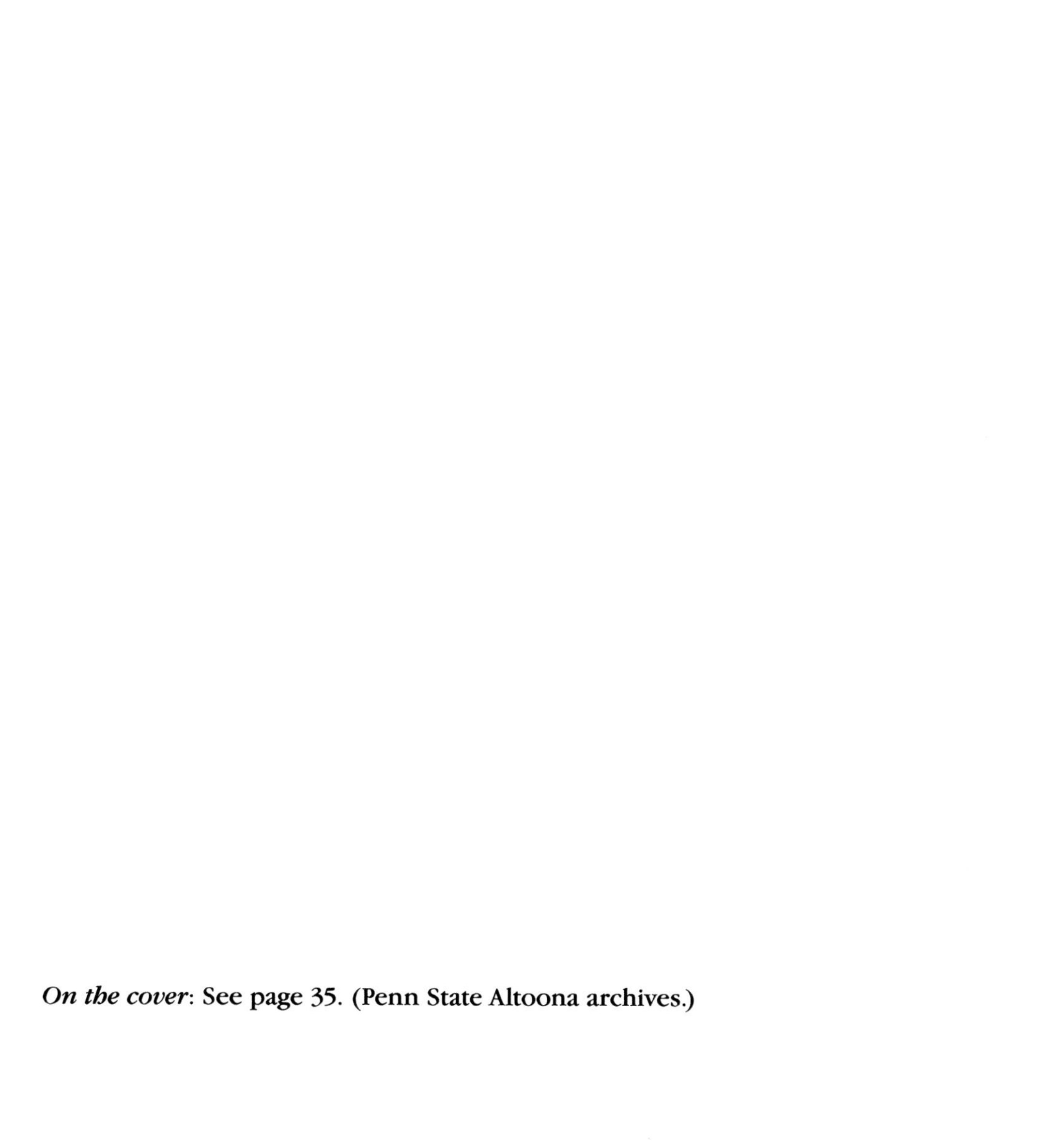

On the cover: See page 35. (Penn State Altoona archives.)

The Campus History Series

PENN STATE ALTOONA

LORI J. BECHTEL-WHERRY AND KENNETH WOMACK

FOREWORD BY ROBERT L. SMITH

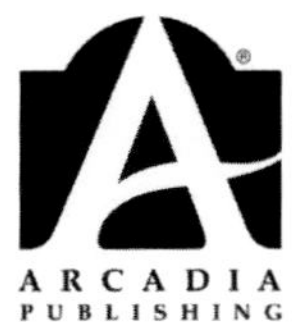

ISBN 978-0-7385-6599-6

Published by Arcadia Publishing
Charleston, South Carolina

Printed in the United States of America

Library of Congress Control Number: 2009922500

For all general information contact Arcadia Publishing at:
Telephone 843-853-2070
Fax 843-853-0044
E-mail sales@arcadiapublishing.com
For customer service and orders:
Toll-Free 1-888-313-2665

Visit us on the Internet at www.arcadiapublishing.com

For Athleen J. Stere in celebration of a lifetime of teaching, research, and service.

Contents

ACKNOWLEDGMENTS

This volume would not have been possible without the efforts and support of a host of colleagues who unselfishly shared their time and memories. We are grateful to Gary Baranec, Margaret Benson, Alison Bonsell, Carole Bookhamer, Marissa Carney, Sen. John Eichelberger, Bill Engelbret, Richard Flarend, Paula Ford, Marc Harris, Chyrl Harshbarger, Cherrie Henry, Mark Hoover, KT Huckabee, Dave Kimmel, Norm Knaub, Carl Larsen, John Lennox, Tom Liszka, Sherri McGregor, Maggie McNulty, Cindy Mighells, Dana Miller, Nick Miskovsky, Dinty W. Moore, Jacki Mowery, Judy Paul, Sandy Petrulionis, Bob Quinn, Robin Reese, Shari Routch, Tom Russo, Brigid Sheedy, Peter Shull, Megan Simpson, Jack Sinclair, Tim Slekar, Molly Slep, Athleen J. Stere, Denny Stewart, Valerie Stratton, Andy Vavreck, Anna May Very, Nancy Vogel, Sam Wagner, Mike Weiner, Tim Wherry, L. A. Wilson, Jim Winsor, Sue Woodring, and Annette Zalanowski.

The compilation of this photographic history of our college has benefited from the groundbreaking archival work of Mila Su, as well as from the generous assistance of Drew McGhee, Jonathan O'Harrow, and Roseanna Shumskas, whose talents and expertise resulted in many of the illustrations included in this volume. We are also indebted to Cindy Baney, John Kazmaier, Peg McCartney Smith, and Carson Veach for sharing their memories about Penn State Altoona.

We owe a special debt of thanks to Michele Kennedy for her indefatigable efforts on behalf of this volume. We are especially grateful to our editor, Erin Vosgien, who provided encouragement and advice throughout this project, as well as to Jeanine Womack, whose watchful editorial eye kept us on the straight and narrow throughout the duration of this book's production.

Unless otherwise noted, all images are from the Penn State Altoona archives.

FOREWORD

It began as a vision in June 1929, when 15 men from the Altoona Works of the Pennsylvania Railroad began taking evening courses at the local public high school through Penn State Extension. At the time, Altoona was a prosperous railroad town. Higher education was associated with economic affluence, a luxury rather than a necessity. Most people were not interested in attending college nor did they find a need for such an institution in the community. Yet a number of visionary individuals knew that the key to the future—a future of new industry, higher wages, quality of life—was higher education. The dream of Penn State Altoona began with the local residents, as they launched their campaign to bring an undergraduate center to Altoona.

By 1938, enrollment in evening classes had increased from 15 to 175, and more space was desperately needed. A plea to Penn State president Ralph Hetzel was made to establish a junior college campus in Altoona. In the spring of 1939, approval was granted for a one-year freshman school. Support from the local community was there from the beginning, just as it is today. A committee led by chamber of commerce chairman Ted Holtzinger launched a campaign to raise money to renovate an abandoned grade school for the new college. Within two months, more than $5,000 was raised to renovate the old Webster elementary school at Lexington Avenue and Tenth Street—a school that would accommodate 119 freshman students and 9 faculty members when it opened its doors on September 13, 1939.

Yet the greatest achievement of the campus came on July 1, 1997, when it officially became designated as a four-year, degree-granting college. No longer to be known as the "Altoona campus," the official name of the college became the Pennsylvania State University, Altoona College, or Penn State Altoona, as the college is widely known today. And with its designation as a four-year college, Penn State Altoona joined the National Collegiate Athletic Association, competing at the Division III level against other four-year institutions.

Penn State Altoona continues to grow and flourish thanks to the dedication and support of our faculty, staff, and generous community. To those of you who are just experiencing Penn State Altoona for the first time, we welcome you and invite you to join us as we continue the realization of the dream that began way back in June 1929.

—Robert L. Smith

INTRODUCTION

Come walk with me around the pond of memory,
And we will teach the beauty of learning.
—Peg McCartney Smith, "A Poem for September"

Founded in 1939, Penn State Altoona began its life as the Altoona Undergraduate Center, owing its genesis to an inspired local citizenry who built, financed, and nurtured the college through the economic woes of the Great Depression, an enrollment collapse engendered by World War II, and the rise and fall of the region's railroad fortunes. The lifeblood of Penn State Altoona finds its origins in the Altoona Undergraduate Center's enterprising Citizens Committee, which petitioned Penn State University to open a junior college in Altoona on a trial basis. With the university's support in hand, the committee raised $5,000 for the renovation of the old Webster School building in downtown Altoona. Under the leadership of school director Robert E. Eiche, the Altoona Undergraduate Center enrolled 119 students and employed 9 faculty members during its first year of operation. Having quickly outgrown the Webster School, the Altoona Undergraduate Center expanded in 1940 to the nearby Madison School building.

Yet with the advent of World War II, the Altoona Undergraduate Center's growth spurt came to a sudden halt. Having rechristened itself as the Citizens Advisory Board, the institution's unflagging civic and administrative leadership staved off the Altoona Undergraduate Center's imminent demise by enrolling a robust and growing female class through its 1942–1943 "New War-Time Academic Program." As the war came to a close, the Altoona Undergraduate Center earned widespread praise for the ambitious "Altoona Plan" designed to assist servicemen as they transitioned into life stateside. With the emergence of the GI Bill, the postwar years brought new energy to the college. The Citizens Advisory Board responded to the region's increasing hunger for higher education by seeking out a larger, permanent facility in which to house the Altoona Undergraduate Center. Having raised $36,000 from private citizens and local industry, the board purchased the abandoned 38-acre Ivyside Recreation Park, which had been a thriving amusement park from 1927 to 1945, only to be felled by the Great Depression and World War II.

The decaying property featured a roller coaster, a Ferris wheel, a bowling alley, a tunnel of love, a carousel, and a shooting gallery. The park's crowning feature was its massive swimming pool, nearly 121,000 square feet in size with a capacity of some three million gallons of water. At the time, it was renowned as the world's largest concrete pool, complete with a tree-laden island in its center. Known as "Bathhouse U." because of the bathhouse that served as its primary classroom building, the Altoona Undergraduate Center enrolled some 900 students at the former Ivyside Recreation Park in 1948. Over the following decade, the institution continued to expand, transforming the former amusement park's various attractions into the trappings of a college. The key feature was the construction of the E. Raymond Smith Building during the late 1950s.

The American postwar educational boom saw the Altoona campus enjoying a similar rise in good fortune. Over the ensuing four decades, enrollment increased dramatically, while the advisory board continued to expand the Ivyside Recreation Park facility by purchasing adjacent acreage and engaging in a host of building and renovation projects. Penn State Altoona experienced remarkable degrees of change throughout the 1960s. Recognizing the need to finance the growth of the campus's facilities, the advisory board raised some $400,000 from 3,400 contributors, while also securing university-backed loans. In 1964, the Altoona Campus Student Commons was completed, affording the institution a focal point for its growing social and educational activities. In addition to popular ROTC and homecoming events, Penn State Altoona students established annual traditions involving freshmen initiation rites and Campus Spring Week. The professoriate also continued to evolve. In 1965, music professor Hayden C. Oliver earned the college's first university-wide teaching award, and in 1968, Ernest Dejaiffe became the first Penn State Altoona faculty member to earn the coveted rank of full professor.

By 1966, Penn State Altoona's enrollment had grown to nearly 2,000 students, and more than 4,000 donors pledged $1.1 million in capital gifts in order to meet the challenge of expanding the college's facilities. The end of the decade saw a flurry of construction that virtually transformed the campus, including the building of such key academic spaces as the Robert E. Eiche Library, the science building, the J. E. Holtzinger building, and the Learning Resources Center. In January 1969, Penn State University president Eric A. Walker dedicated a replica of the Nittany Lion Shrine in the alumni lounge of the Altoona Campus Student Commons.

Throughout the 1970s, the college's facilities continued to expand, with the completion of the Edith Davis Eve Memorial Chapel, which afforded the campus and the community alike with an all-faiths chapel for area weddings. By 1971, Penn State Altoona's enrollment had soared to 3,400. The construction of the Steven A. Adler Athletic Complex provided the college with a large, multipurpose gymnasium suitable for a wide range of sporting events, commencement exercises, and speakers' series. This trend continued well into the 1980s, with the completion of the Community Arts Center, including the 400-seat Margery Wolf Kuhn Theatre, as well as the opening of the campus bookstore.

By the 1990s, the Altoona campus encompassed well over 100 acres, while also recruiting an increasingly accomplished faculty. The college's full-professor ranks began to swell accordingly, with faculty members beginning to earn national accolades through book publication and grantsmanship, including significant attainments from such agencies as the National Science Foundation, the National Endowment for the Humanities, and the National Endowment for the Arts, among a host of others.

In 1997, the Altoona campus made history of another sort when it was rechartered as a four-year college in the Penn State University system. With the necessary facilities and resources in place, including the construction of the expansive Hawthorn classroom building in 2004, the faculty began to fulfill the campus's destiny by establishing some 20 baccalaureate programs and a wide range of cultural and academic initiatives. As Penn State Altoona, the college now sports an enrollment of more than 4,000 students and employs nearly 600 people, including 160 full-time faculty. What was once the modest dream of an innovative citizenry had been transformed into a flourishing teaching and research institution of national acclaim.

One

Ladies and Gentlemen, the Altoona Undergraduate Center

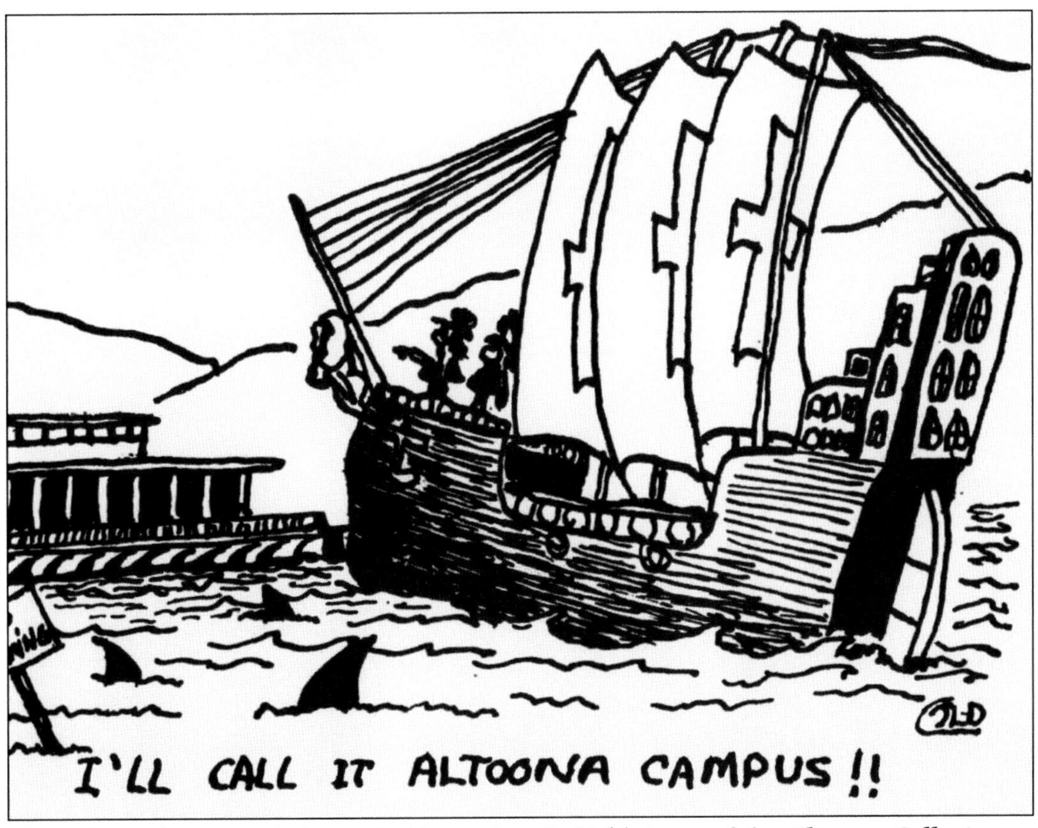

This editorial cartoon is from the December 8, 1964, issue of the *Altoona Collegian*.

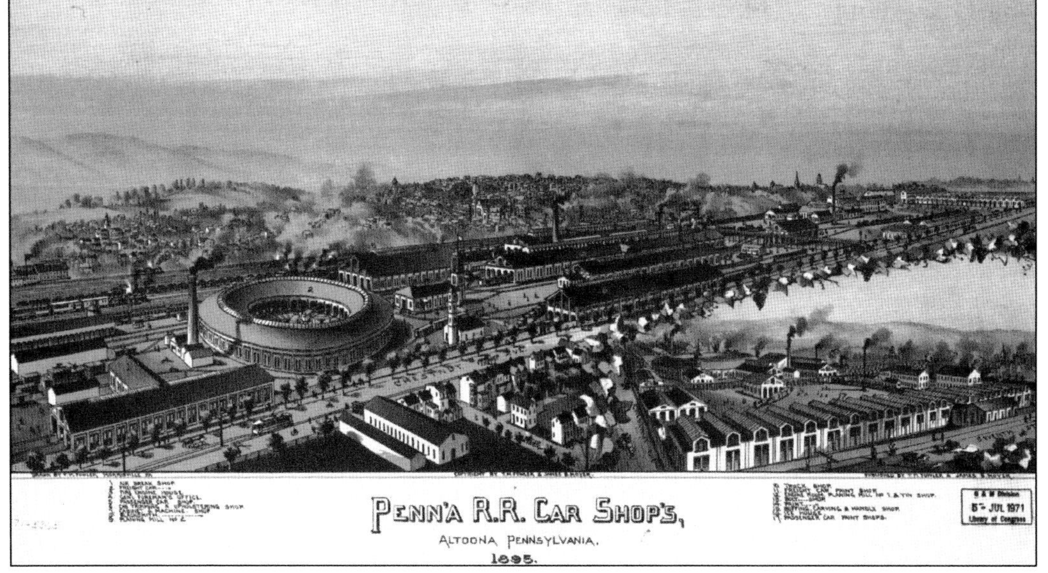

Life in Altoona around 1895 revolved around the legendary car shops that acted as the region's overarching economic engine. At its peak, the Altoona Works occupied some 125 buildings, employing nearly 16,000 people. The railroad's steep decline in the postwar years forced the region to diversify in order to improve its economic and cultural future—one of the imperatives that clearly motivated the Citizens Committee to found the Altoona Undergraduate Center. (Library of Congress.)

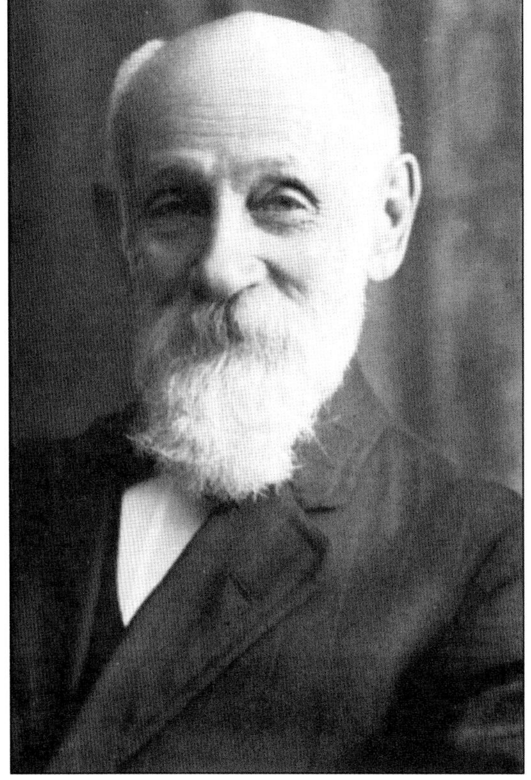

Harry E. Slep opened a printer's shop in Altoona in 1871. The following year, he founded the *Evening Mirror*, which became the *Altoona Mirror* in 1874. He served as the newspaper's president until his death in 1922. He was the grandfather of J. E. "Ted" Holtzinger, whom many credit as the founder of the Altoona Undergraduate Center. The Slep Student Center honors Slep's many contributions to the growth of the greater Altoona area.

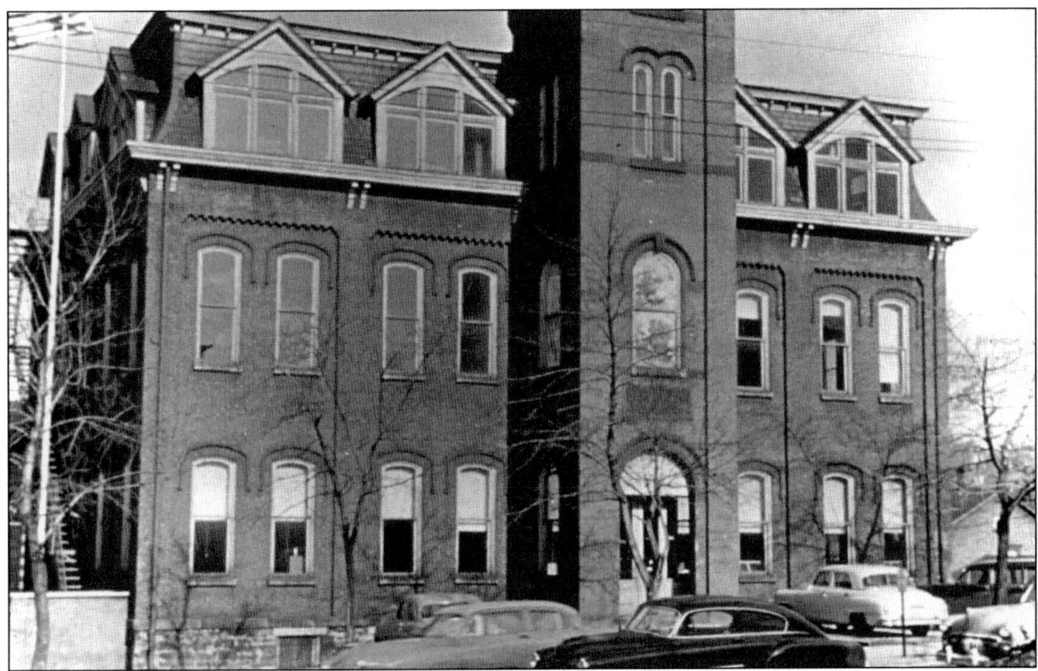

Under the leadership of chamber of commerce chairman Holtzinger, the Citizens Committee raised $5,000 to renovate the abandoned Webster School building, which was located at Lexington Avenue and Tenth Street in downtown Altoona. Rechristened as the Altoona Undergraduate Center, the two-year college opened its doors on September 13, 1939, with an inaugural enrollment of 119 students.

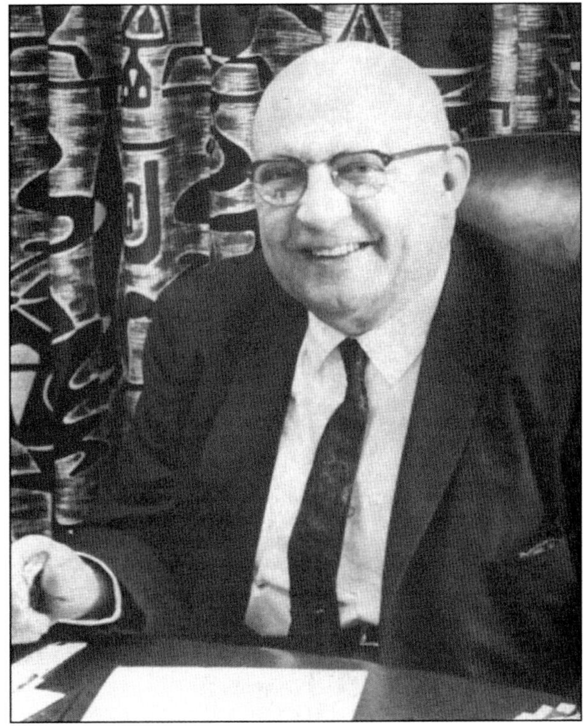

Known as the founder of the Altoona Undergraduate Center, Holtzinger served as an inaugural member of the Citizens Committee that petitioned Penn State to open a branch campus in Altoona. He later championed the Altoona Undergraduate Center's relocation to the former Ivyside Recreation Park. For many years, Bathhouse U. was referred to as "Holtzinger's Folly," given local concerns about moving to the defunct amusement park. The campus's remarkable growth in subsequent years vindicated Holtzinger's dream of establishing higher education in Altoona.

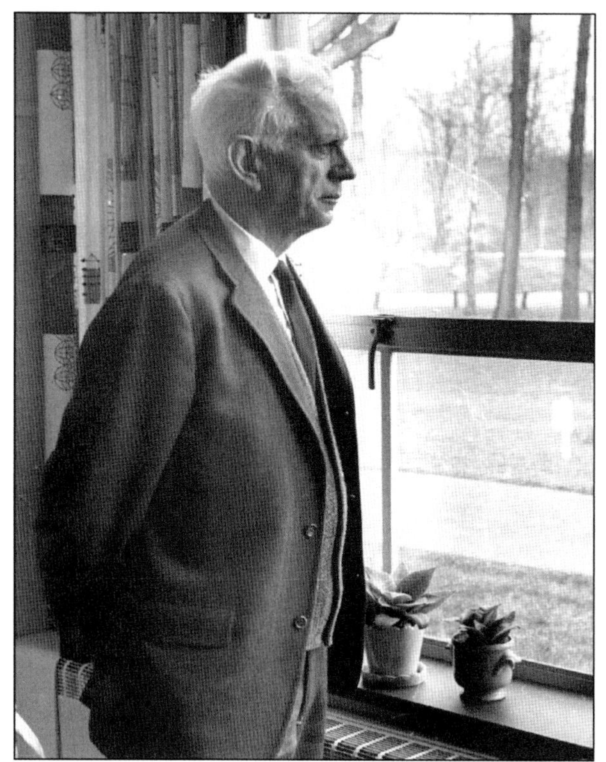

Robert E. Eiche served as the inaugural campus director from 1939 to 1968, steering the institution from its incipient days as the Altoona Undergraduate Center through its transformation into the Altoona campus of the Pennsylvania State University. David R. Pugh, director of undergraduate centers for Penn State College, recommended Eiche for the directorship. As he told the local committee, "We are sending you a man who is a builder, an educator, and a fine administrator."

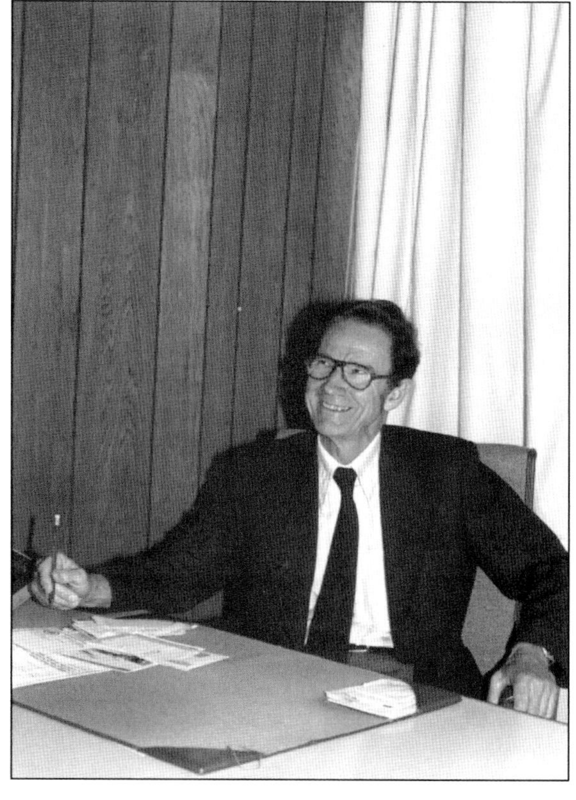

Robert L. Smith was the first employee of the Altoona Undergraduate Center, which he joined in 1939 after graduating from Penn State College. In 1948, he earned a master's degree and became a member of the faculty, teaching economics, accounting, and business administration. Over the years, Smith served as administrative assistant, registrar, financial officer, business manager, associate professor, and interim director. For 63 years, he served as treasurer of the campus's advisory board, retiring in 1983 as associate director emeritus.

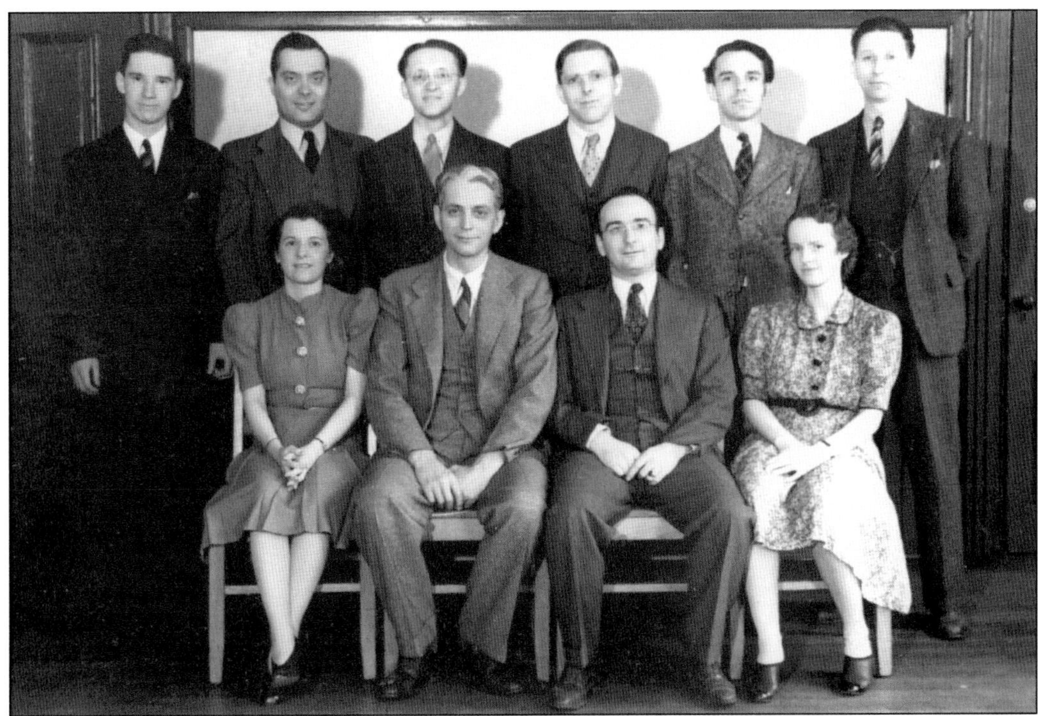

Photographed in the Webster School building, the inaugural faculty and staff of the Altoona Undergraduate Center included, from left to right, (first row) Dorothy Barnes, Eiche, T. Stewart Goas, and Mary McKenzie; (second row) Smith, Edmund Umberger, Raymond Maneval, James Miller, Charles Diehl, and George Bowman.

The first edition of the Altoona Undergraduate Center's student newspaper, the *Altoona Collegian*, was published in November 1939. In the ensuing years, the Penn State Altoona newspaper has continued to grow and change with the times. Now the centerpiece of the college's communications degree program, the paper has been rechristened as the *Altoona Collegiate Review*. Pictured is the December 19, 1958, issue of the *Altoona Collegian*.

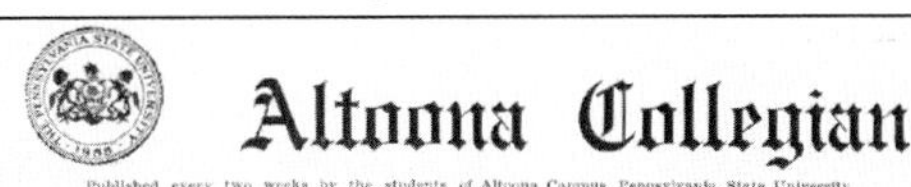

Altoona Collegian

Published every two weeks by the students of Altoona Campus, Pennsylvania State University

VOLUME I — FRIDAY, DECEMBER 19, 1958 — No. 3

Student Council Will Present Annual Christmas Party

TEX Announces New Membership

The Tau Epsilon Chi Fraternity held their formal initiation banquet Nov. 15, 1958 at McDowell's Party House. The banquet was presided over by Mr. Ernest Dejoiffe and Mr. Donald Ulrich, TEX sponsors, Eugene Hershberger, President, Dennis Snowberger, V. President, Fred Gerardine, Secretary-Treasurer. Attending the banquet were present and alumni members, Mr. Levine, McKeesport Center's TEX sponsor, and Three McKeesport students who are members of the TEX society at McKeesport.

The members who were initiated into the fraternity on Nov. 15 are as follows:

Henry C. Buterbaugh, Ludwig Campagna, Robert F. Davis, James G. Foust, Robert C. Lantzy, Donald A. Moses, Charles H. Reeder, Van S. Richards, Charles T. Wrye.

The requirement for a student to be eligible for consideration as a member in the fraternity is that he have a 3.5 or better average at the end of his first semester. A student who maintains an average of 3.0 or better at the end of his second or third semester is also eligible for membership in the TEX Fraternity.

Calendar of Events

Dec. 19 Altoona Campus Choir will present a Christmas music program.
Dec. 19 Juniata J. J. at Altoona, 8:00 p. m.
Dec. 20 Altoona at Behrend, 3:00 p. m.
Dec. 20 Christmas Recess begins, 11:50 p. m.
Jan. 5 Recess ends, 8:00 p. m.
Jan. 8 Altoona Symphony Society
Jan. 9 Behrend at Altoona, 8 p.m.
Jan. 8-9 Plays by Ivyside Players
Jan. 10 Frostburg at Altoona, 3:00 p. m.

LECTURE ATTENDED

On Friday, December 5, Mrs. Leopold, part-time teacher, Dr. Goodfellow, and Mr. Zubrod attended a lecture at main campus on "Teaching by T. V."

Rehearsals Begin

The Ivyside Players and the Theater III Class are currently in rehearsal for the January 8th and 9th presentations of three one-act plays. This will be the first actual performance of the Players this term, their earlier offering being the Penn State Players' production of "The Druid Circle".

"The Devil and Daniel Webster" Stephen Vincent Benet, a historical fantasy, is being directed by Miss Janette Burns; "The Boor" by Anton Tchekoff, a farce comedy, is under the direction of Calvin Israel; and "Time Was," an original modern serious play written by Altoona Campus' own Jack Holleran, is also being directed by that ambitious gentleman.

The January offering promises much in the way of varied entertainment and should be of interest to all students.

Campus Visited By Engineering Committee

On Wednesday, December 10, the Executive Committee of the College of Engineering visited us here at the Altoona Campus. Those who were here were the Dean of Engineering, Associate Dean, Assistant Deans, Department Heads, and the Professor of Nuclear Engineering. This was the first visit of this type to any branch campus. They visited the Engineering I lecture and talked to the Engineering Staff while here.

NEW ART COURSES SCHEDULED FOR SPRING

Two courses for the Spring semester are being offered in Art that require no previous art training and are not specifically for art students. A. A. H. 7, a history course covering painting and sculpture from 1800 to the present day, and Art 64, a class in oil painting, are being offered. The oil painting course offers the basic fundamentals in color and composition for the student interested in art for their own satisfaction.

Government Sponsors Student Aid

In an effort to aid needy students, the Federal Government has passed a bill which will create loan funds at American colleges and universities from which graduate and undergraduate students may borrow to complete their education. Penn State will participate in this program. To "assure the intellectual eminence of the United States," the law requires that special consideration be given teacher trainees for any teaching level. Students with superior academic background in science, Mathematics, engineering, or a modern foreign language will also be given primary consideration.

A maximum of $1,000 may be borrowed in one year and up to $5,000 during a recipient's entire academic course. Repayment (an essential part of any loan) begins one year after the student stops being a full-time student, and must be repaid within ten years. The interest is very low, 3 percent per year, and the principal may be reduced up to 50 percent if the borrower becomes a full-time public elementary or secondary school teacher. The reduction is 10 percent per year, up to five years. This allotment will be repaid by the Federal Government.

Who will be eligible for this award, which will go into effect by September, 1959? It is available to those students who show sufficient need and meet the academic standards determined by the University. This act is still in the stage of development and any further information will be made public by the Collegian.

STUDENTS REMINDED OF SKATING RULES

Skating at the Altoona Campus pond is by lease agreement, under the supervision of the Altoona Park and Recreation Board. This agency tests the ice and approves skating only when it is completely safe. The Recreation Board also determines the hours for skating and supervises this activity. When skating is safe, the approved hours will be posted.

CHARLIE LOCKARD TO PLAY FOR END-OF-SEMESTER DANCE

The Student Council has been busy planning for the events which will occur between now and the end of the semester. The first social function that the Council has charge of will be the Kiddie's Christmas Party for the children of the students here on Campus. This has been a custom for several years and will be continued this year. The members of the Council will decorate the Student Union Building about a week before the party, which will be held on Saturday afternoon, December 20. This will give the students a chance to enjoy the tree and trimmings before the Christmas vacation starts. Ron Houser is the general chairman for the party and Wanda Filler and Dick Carothers are in charge of gifts and refreshments respectively.

The second dance to be sponsored by the Student Council will be the end-of-semester dance to be held at the Hotel Penn Alto on Jan. 24. Charlie Lockard will supply the music, and the dancing will last from 9:00 until 12:00 p. m. The theme for the occasion has not yet been chosen, but well over a month remains in which to make the final preparations.

A very important piece of legislation was approved and passed by Student Council in our meeting on November 24. It concerns the election of officers by the student body. The Constitution of the Student Government, before the present change, stated that all officers would be elected in the fall semester, to hold office for the full year, but this method left too much time lapse between the beginning of school and the election. During this period, there was no form of student government at all. The revised paragraph in the Constitution now reads, "Sophomore representatives, including the president, shall be elected on or before May 15 of the Spring semester for the following academic year. Elections for the Freshman representatives shall be held on or before Oct. 1 of the Fall semester." The Council feels that this is a better plan because at least part of the new group of officers would be ready to act as soon as school commenced in the Fall.

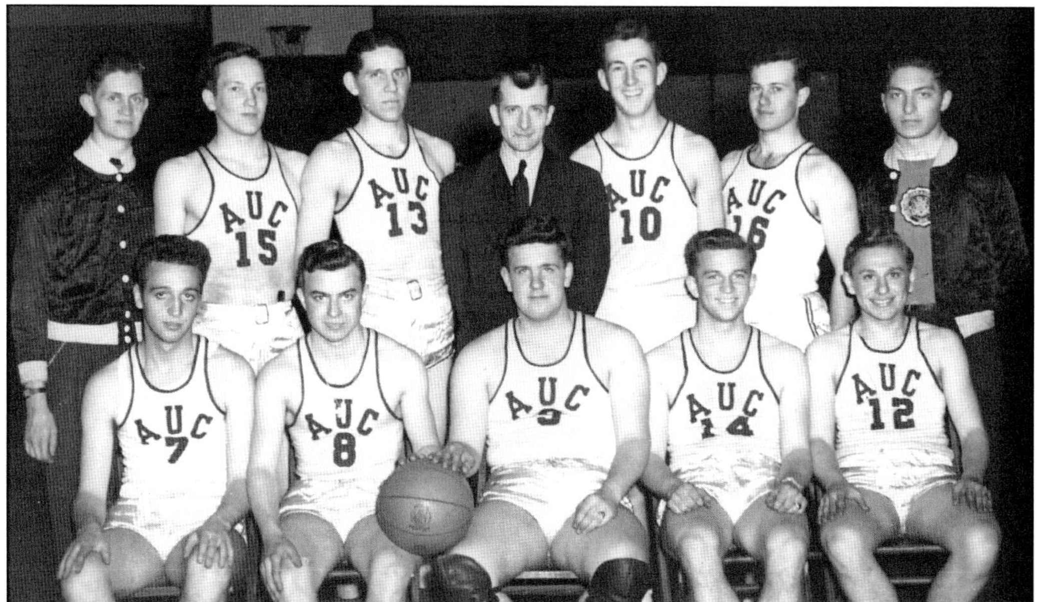

In 1941, the Altoona Undergraduate Center fielded its inaugural collegiate sports team in the form of the institution's first basketball team. In 1949, the Altoona Undergraduate Center enjoyed its first sports triumph when the basketball team won the Pennsylvania Junior College Basketball Championship. In this photograph of the 1942–1943 basketball squad, coach Steven Adler stands in the middle of the second row.

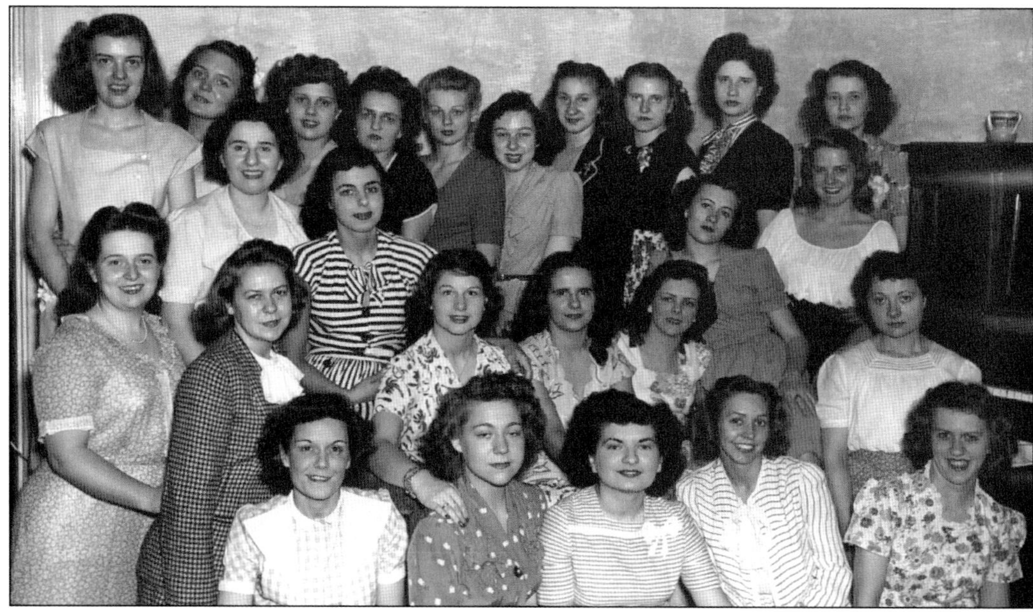

The advent of World War II nearly spelled the end for the Altoona Undergraduate Center. The Citizens Advisory Board staved off an enrollment disaster by purchasing and operating the campus's first residence hall. The Annie C. Wolf Women's Dormitory was located in a large Altoona home at 1609 Thirteenth Street. Christened as a woman's "home away from home," the dormitory allowed the campus to enroll a female undergraduate class through the New War-Time Academic Program.

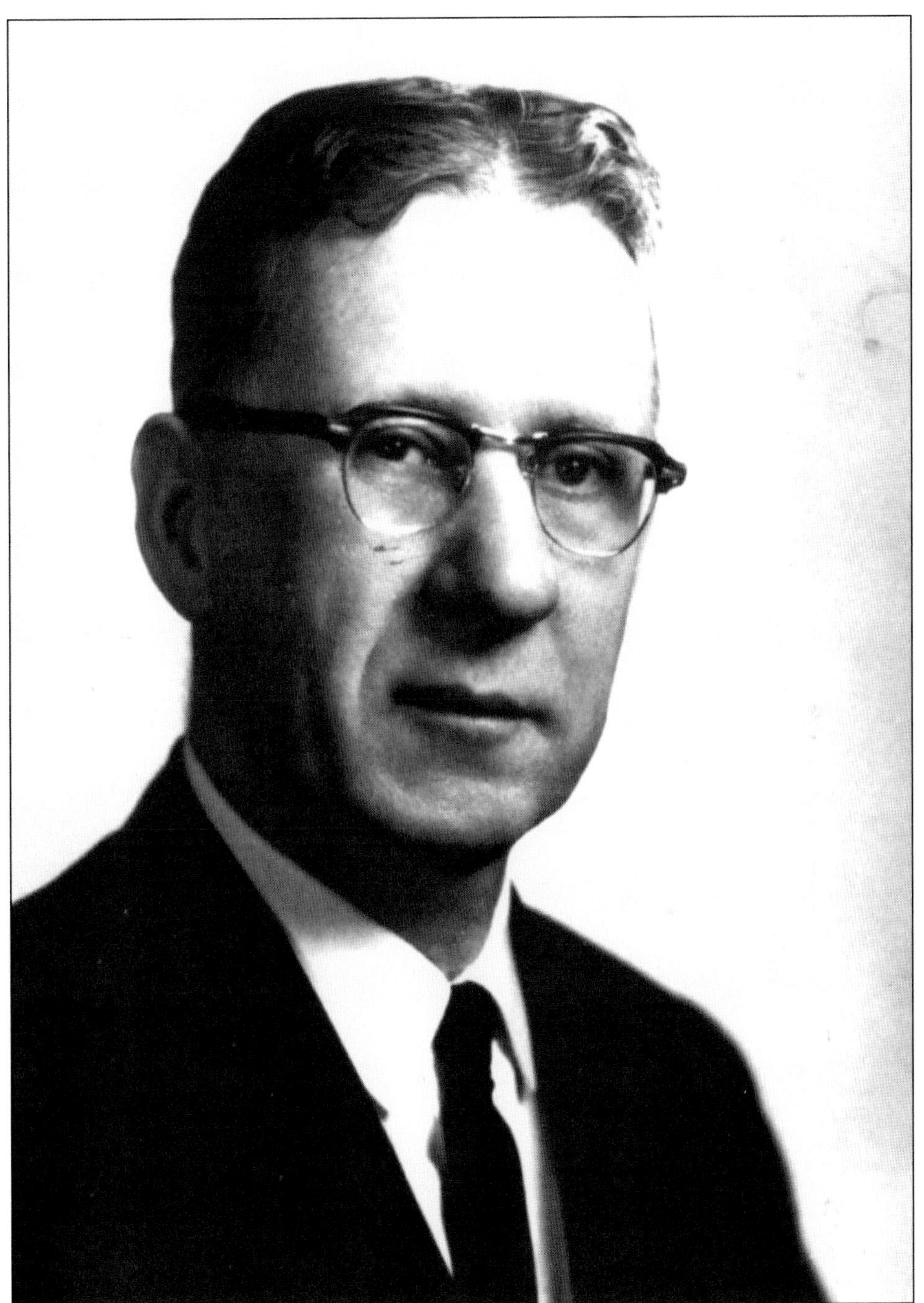

A 1932 doctoral graduate in psychology from Northwestern University, Louis D. Goodfellow attained the rank of professor of psychology at Penn State Altoona. After serving as the director of Air Force Technical Training Command during World War II, Goodfellow joined the faculty in 1946. An Altoona native, Goodfellow served the community in a variety of capacities, including working on behalf of the Blair County Mental Health Association, the Association for Crippled Children, and the Ecumenical Council. He retired in 1971 after 25 years of service.

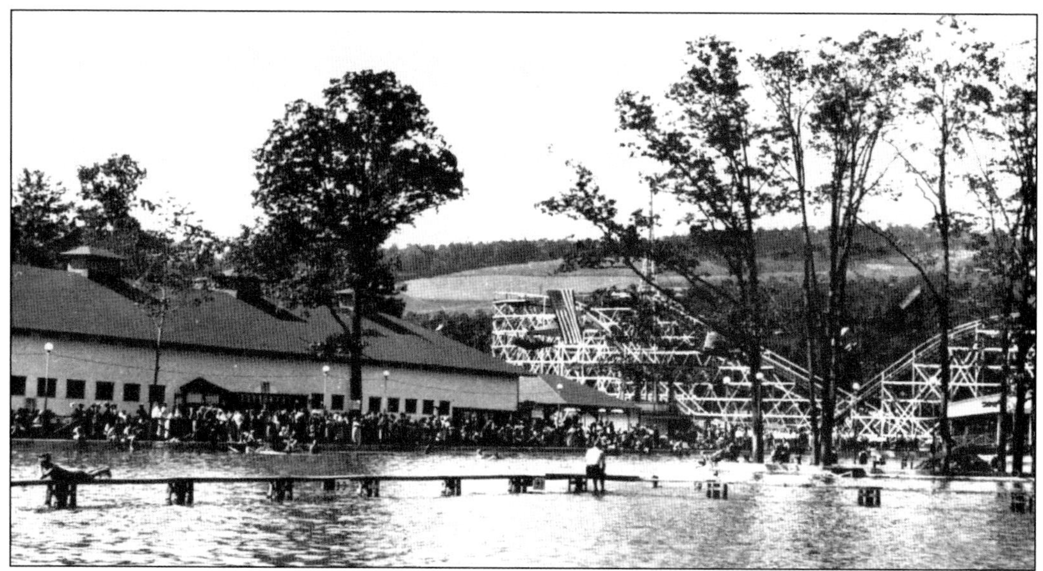

The brainchild of E. Raymond Smith and James Gwinn, the Ivyside Recreation Park was a thriving regional attraction from 1927 to 1945, eventually closing under the shadow of the Great Depression and World War II. Nestled along the Juniata Gap, Ivyside Recreation Park featured a large bathhouse that could accommodate some 3,000 bathers. During the winter months, the park's massive swimming pool was transformed into a festive ice-skating rink.

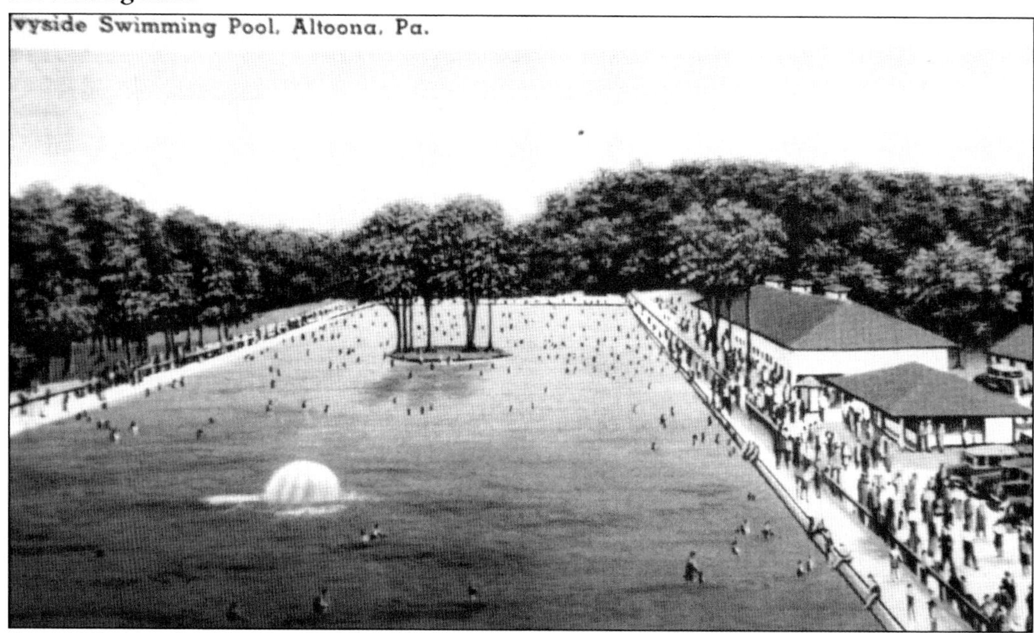

The Ivyside Recreation Park featured a wide variety of popular attractions, including a roller coaster, a Ferris wheel, a bowling alley, a tunnel of love, a carousel, and a shooting gallery. But the park's crowning feature was its massive swimming pool, measuring nearly 121,000 square feet in size with a capacity of some three million gallons of water. At the time, it was renowned as the world's largest concrete pool, complete with a tree-laden island in its center.

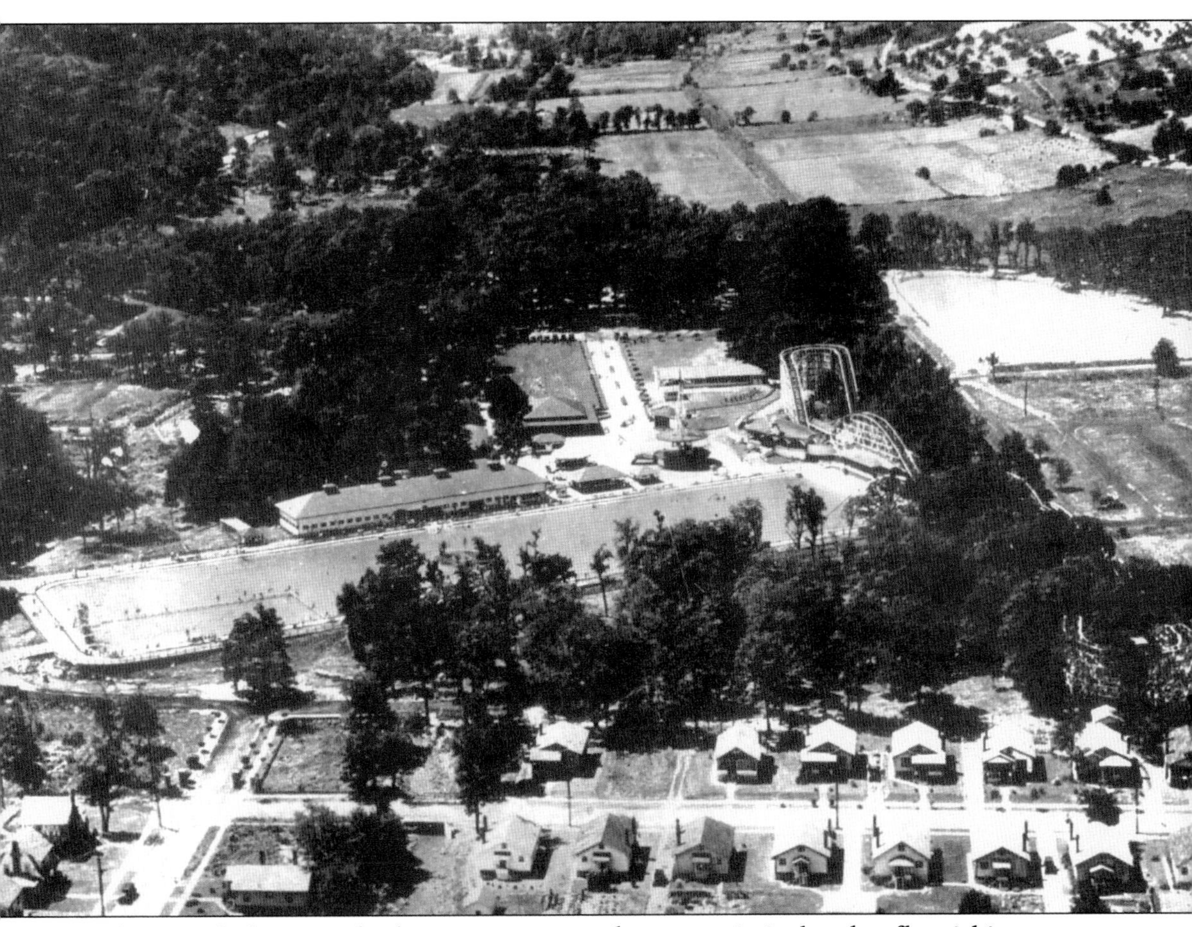

In this aerial photograph, the amusement park appears in its heyday, flourishing as one of the region's most vaunted attractions.

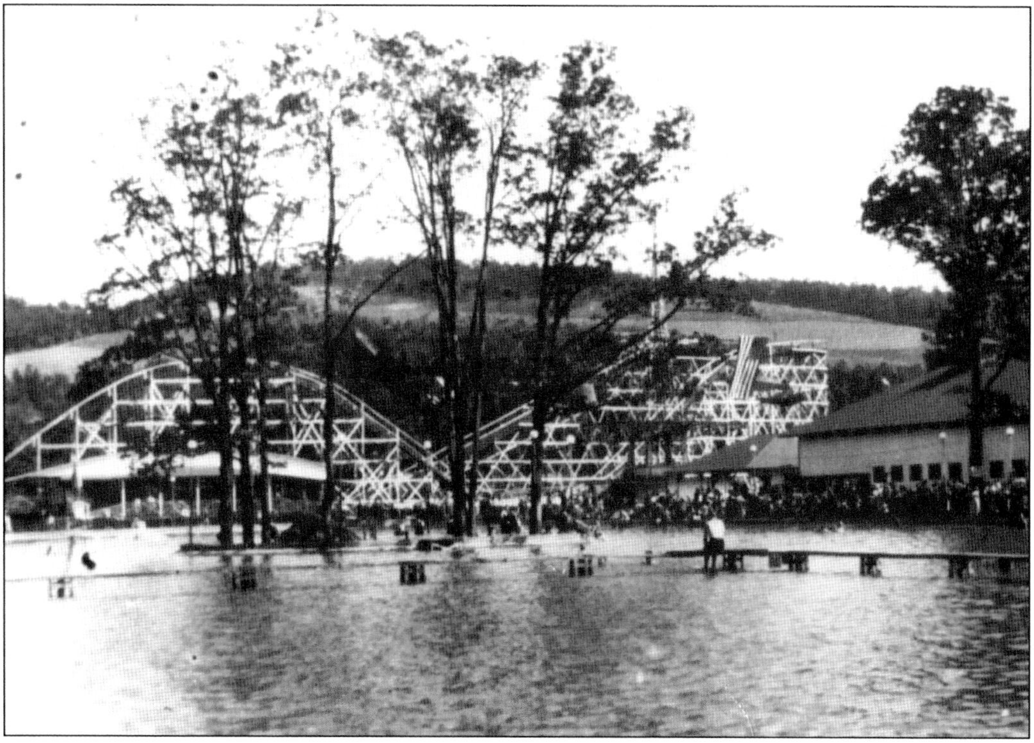

The Ivyside Recreation Park's wooden roller coaster was one of its most popular attractions. In the foreground is the swimming pool, and just beyond is the large bathhouse.

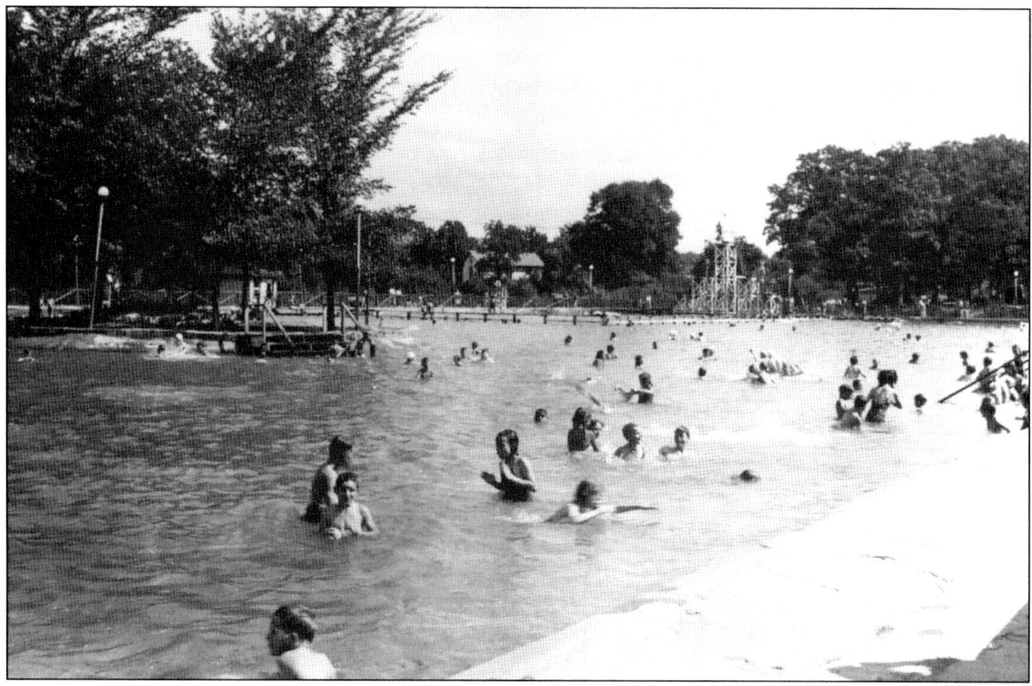

In this period photograph, the diving platform can be seen across the island at the heart of the swimming pool.

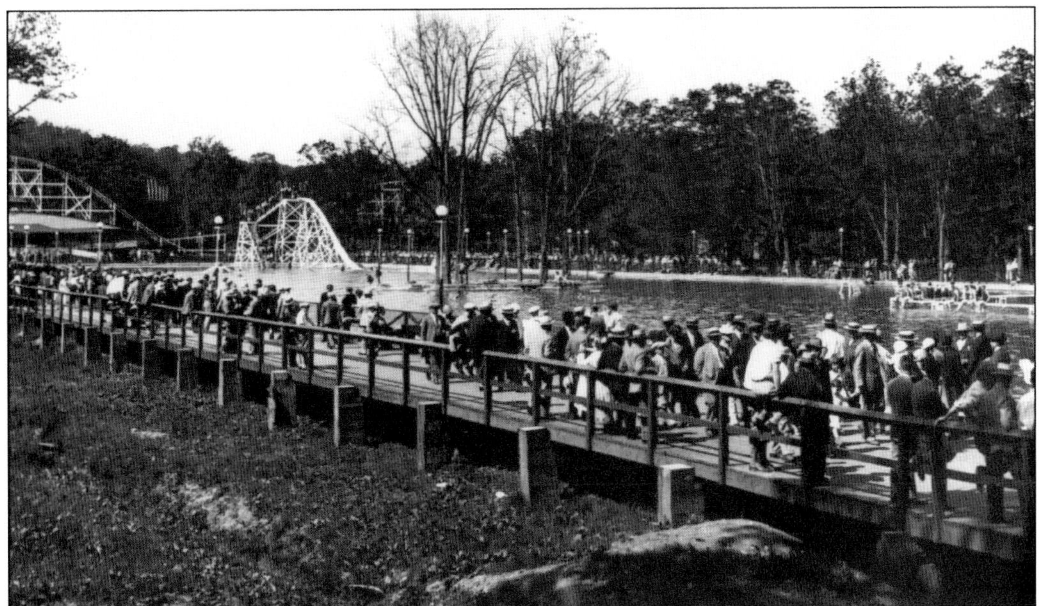

During the park's heyday, guests flocked to the old-style boardwalk, which fronted the swimming pool's western edge.

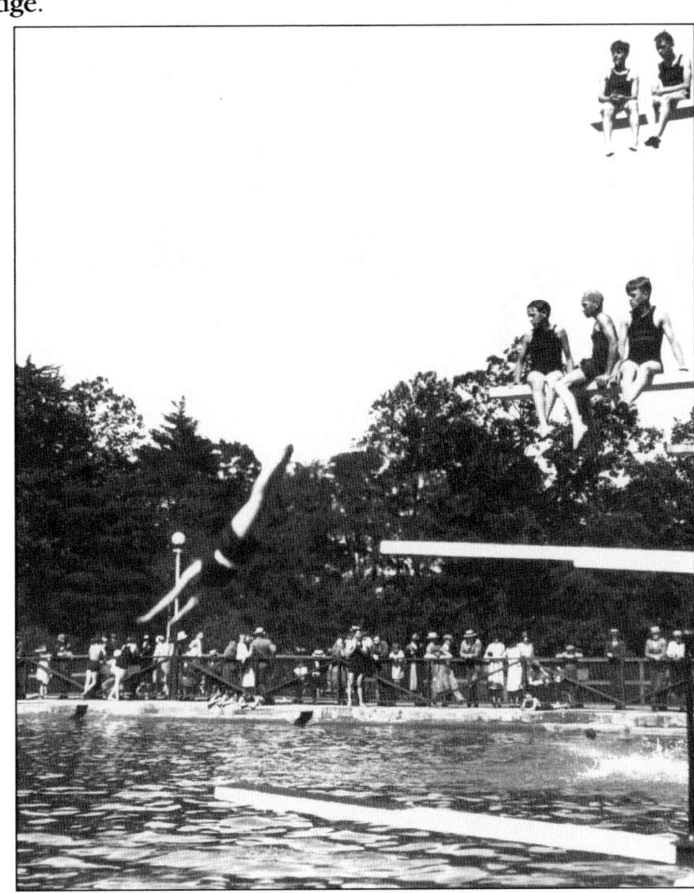

The swimming pool's southern end featured a series of increasingly higher diving boards.

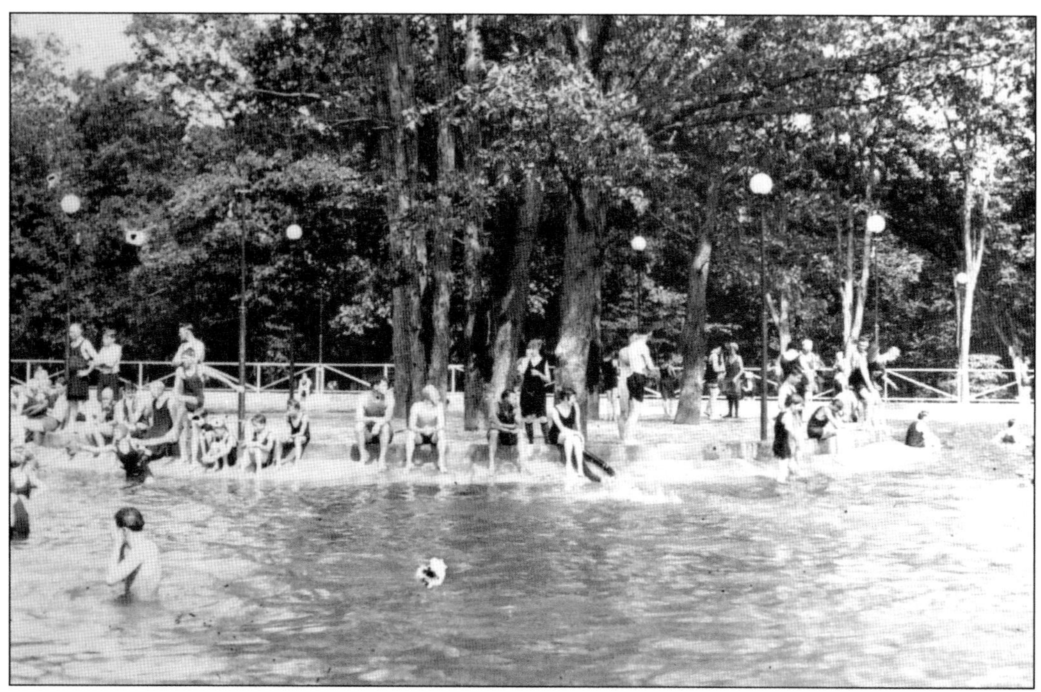

At the center of the swimming pool was a tree-laden island popular with bathers who would relax beneath the foliage and while away the summer day.

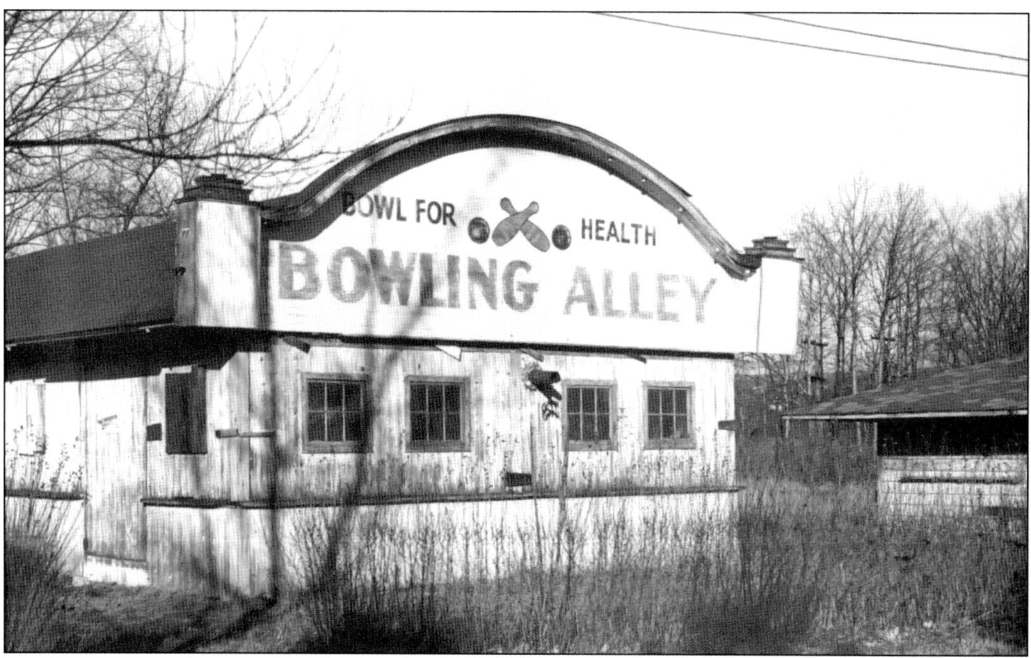

Not to be outdone, the Ivyside Recreation Park even featured a multilane bowling alley among its multitude of attractions. After the Altoona Undergraduate Center relocated to the former Ivyside Recreation Park, the bowling lanes were refinished and returned to regular usage by faculty and students alike.

The massive waterslide took advantage of the northern end of the Ivyside Recreation Park's vast swimming pool.

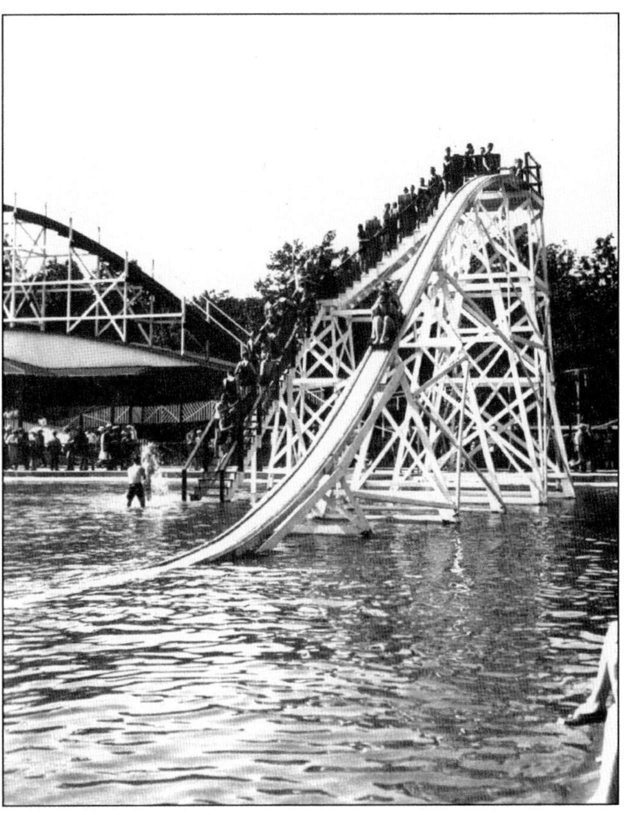

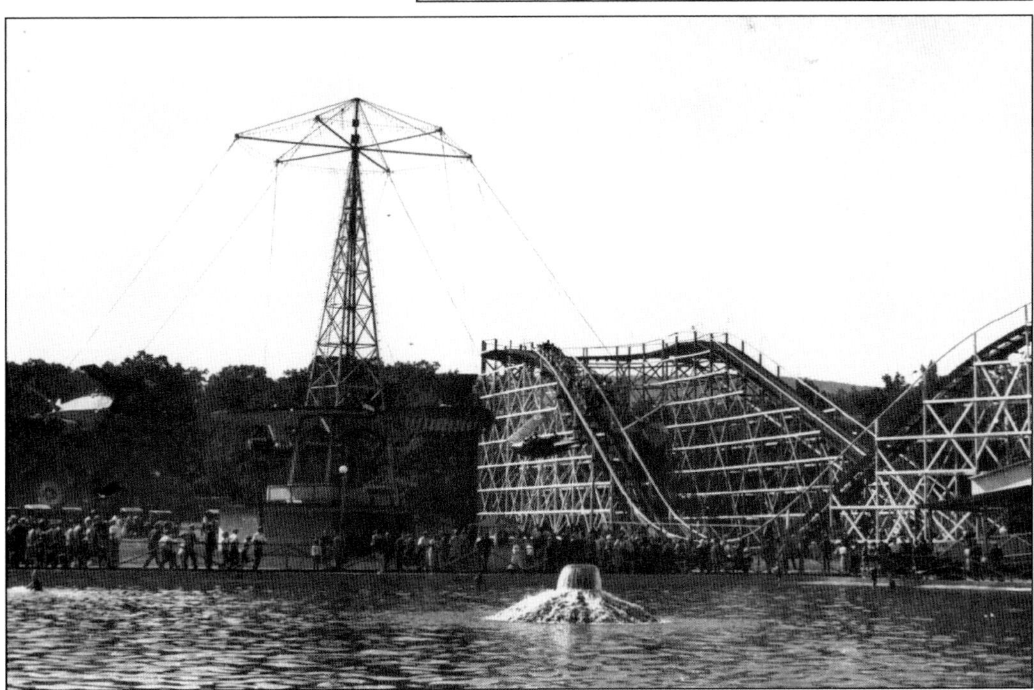

In addition to the roller coaster, one of the most popular attractions was the looming, sky-high Aeroplane Swing Ride.

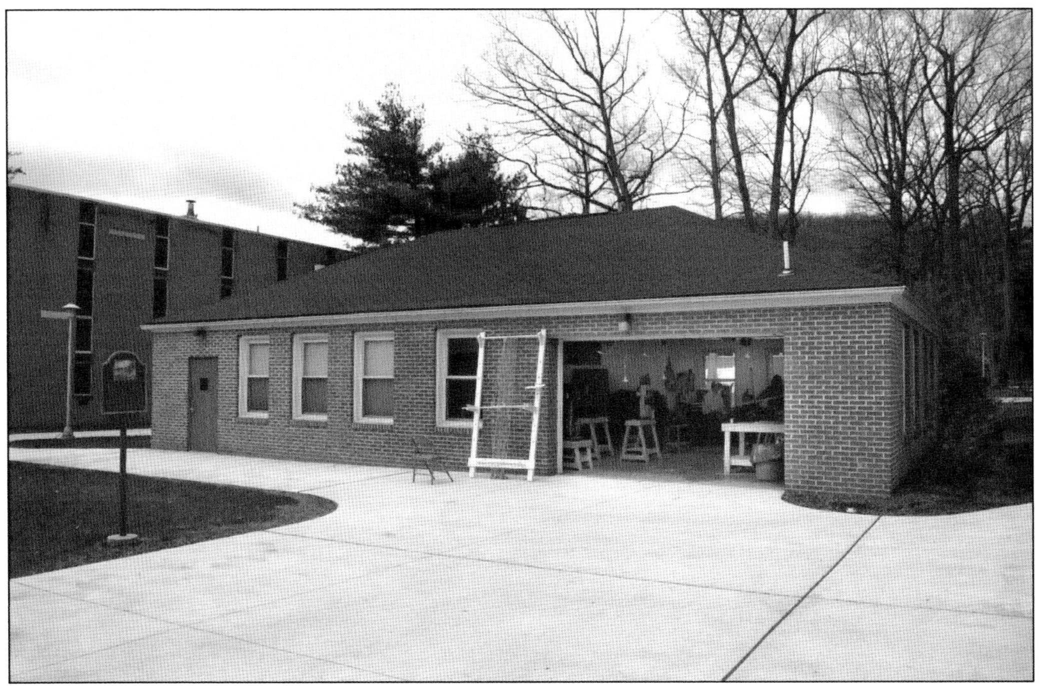

One of the last remaining structures from the Ivyside Recreation Park, the Pine Building was the home of the park's refreshment and concessions stand. The building now houses the visual art studies program's three-dimensional arts studio, as well as the communication program's computer laboratory and editing facilities.

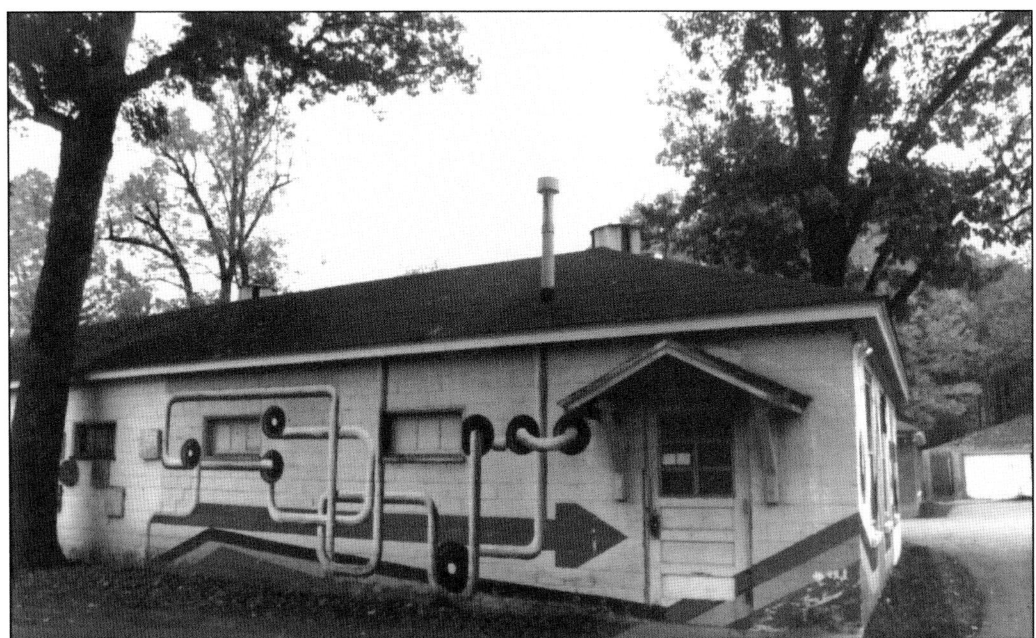

During the Ivyside Recreation Park's heyday, the Elm Building functioned as the park's shooting gallery. Over the years, students painted the building to reflect the taste and culture of the times, as seen in this early 1960s–era photograph.

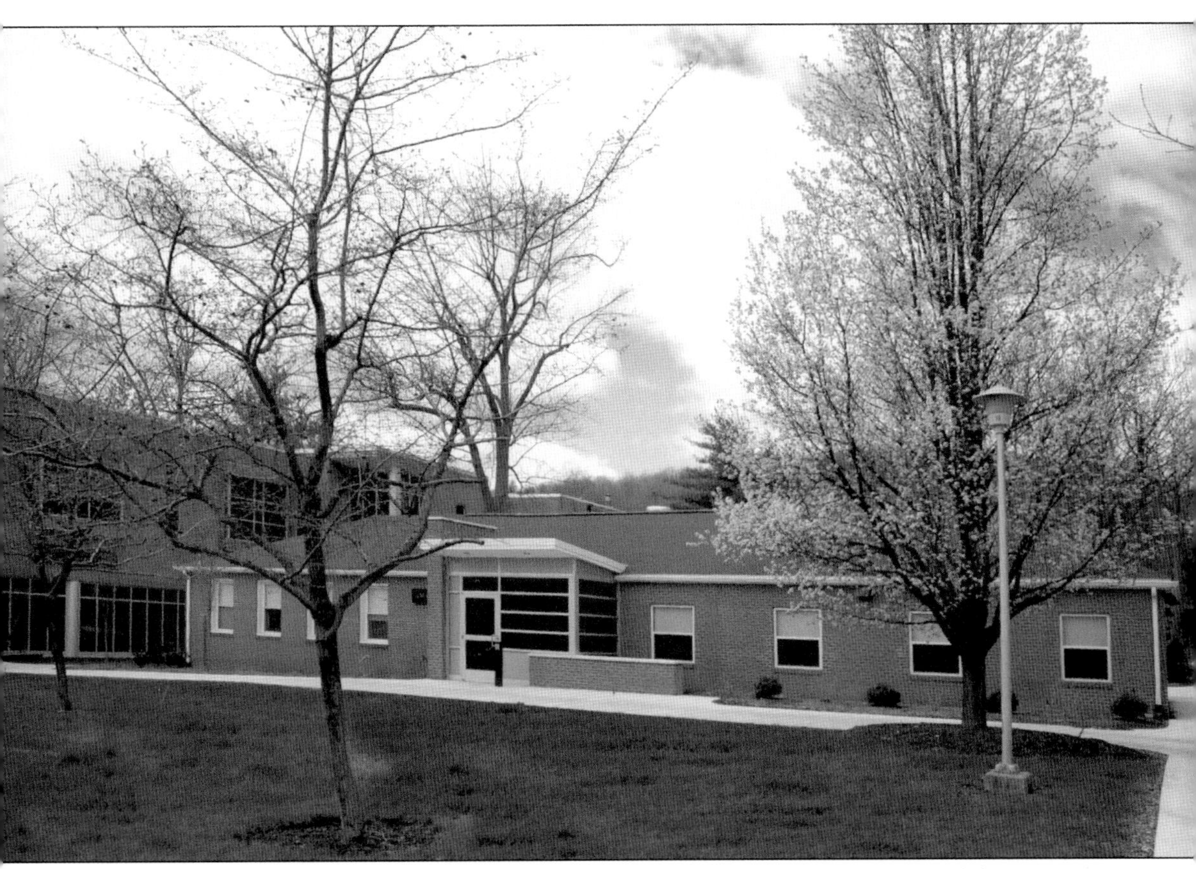

The Elm Building has housed a number of facilities, including chemistry laboratories, faculty offices, a kiln studio, and a costume shop. This 2008 photograph was taken after the building was extensively renovated in order to house the offices of the college's division heads and their supporting staff.

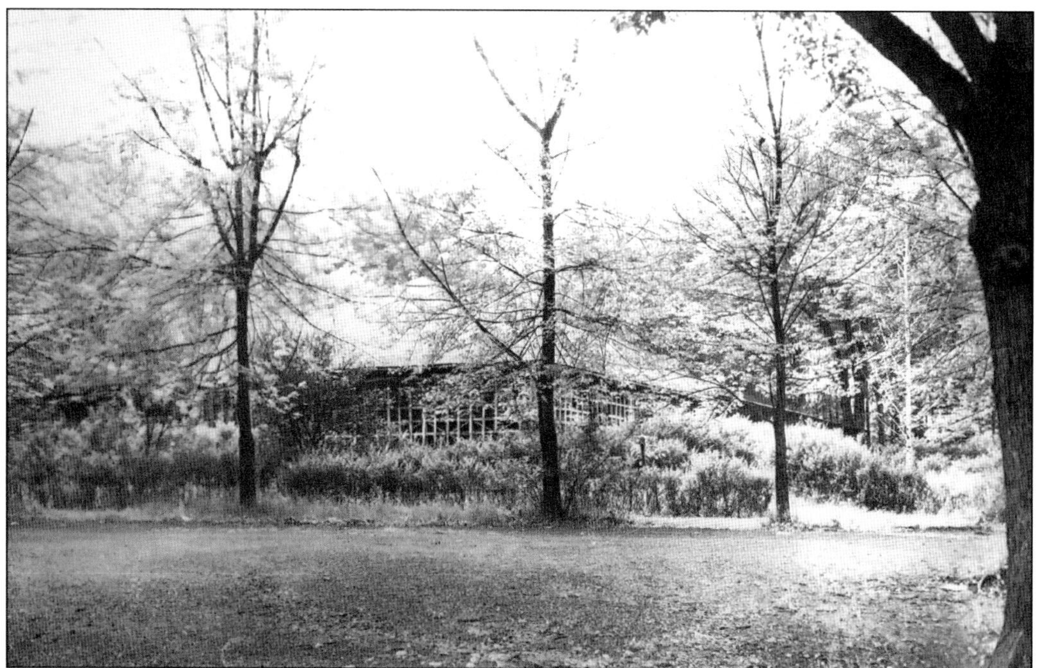

In this 1947 photograph, the abandoned Ivyside Building is already becoming overgrown in the wake of the closing of the Ivyside Recreation Park. The building originally served as an open dance hall, later being repurposed as a roller-skating rink for the Ivyside Recreation Park.

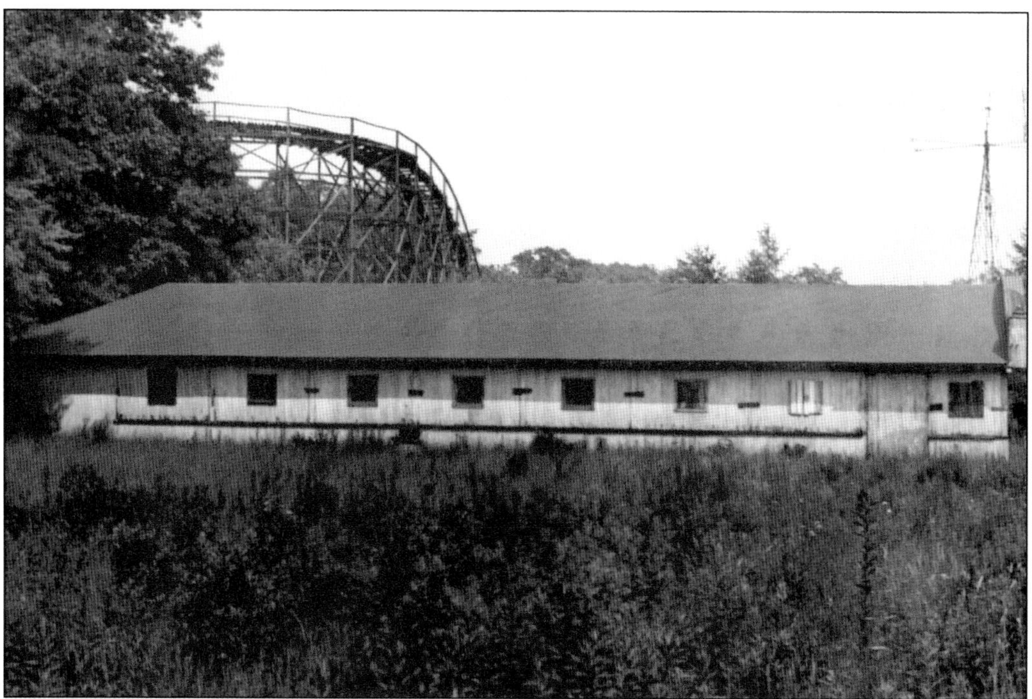

In this 1947 photograph, the abandoned arcade is pictured with the dormant roller coaster looming off to the left and the listless Aeroplane Swing Ride to the right.

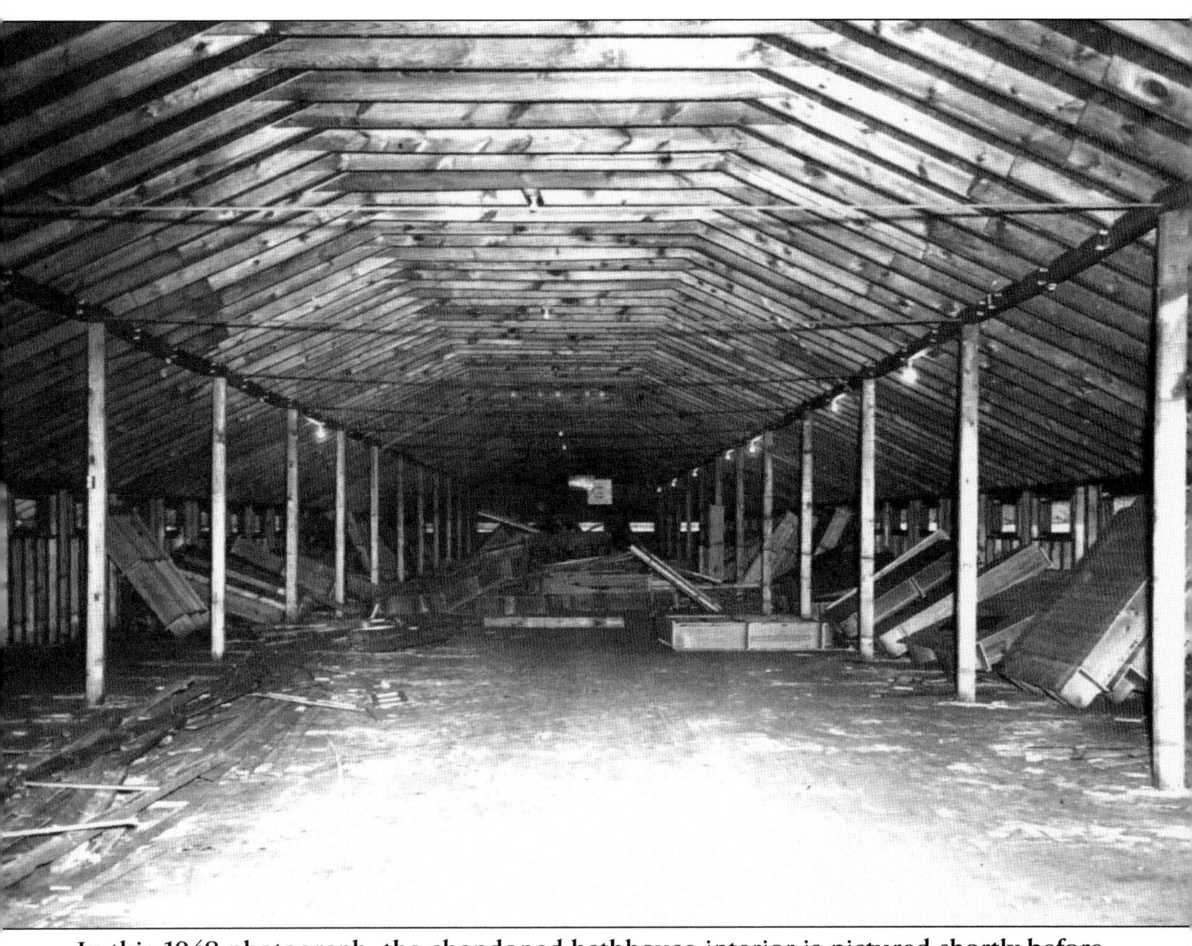

In this 1948 photograph, the abandoned bathhouse interior is pictured shortly before the amusement park's renovation under the vision and leadership of the Citizens Advisory Board.

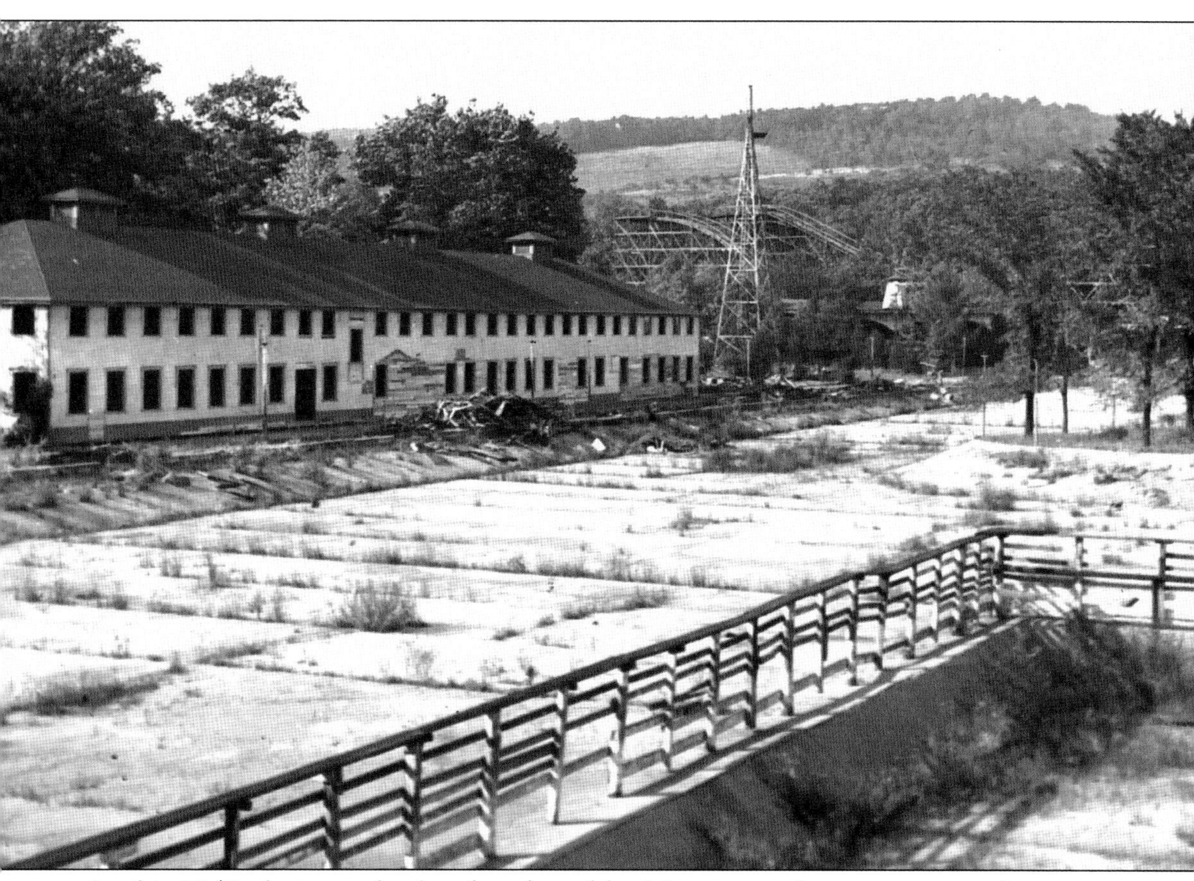

In this 1947 photograph, the abandoned bathhouse can be seen across the empty concrete swimming pool.

Two

The Life and Times of Bathhouse U.

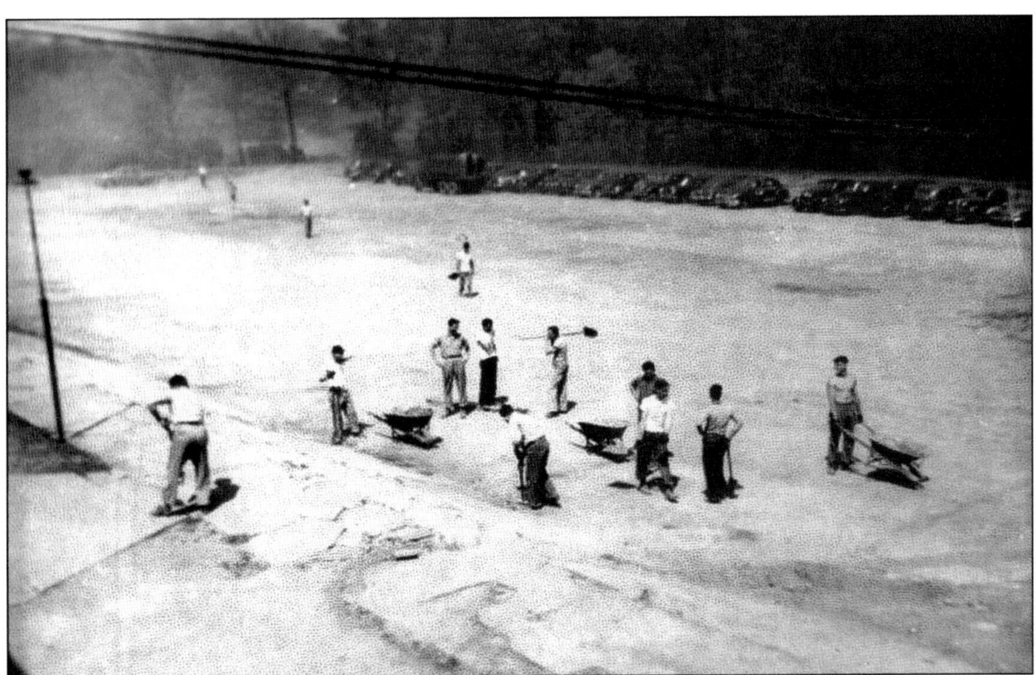

Formal campus workdays were established after the move to the former Ivyside Recreation Park. Classes were cancelled one day each semester, and students, faculty, and administration would work on various maintenance projects. After lunch, students would challenge the faculty to a softball game. In this May 1949 photograph, students break up the concrete skin of the former Ivyside swimming pool.

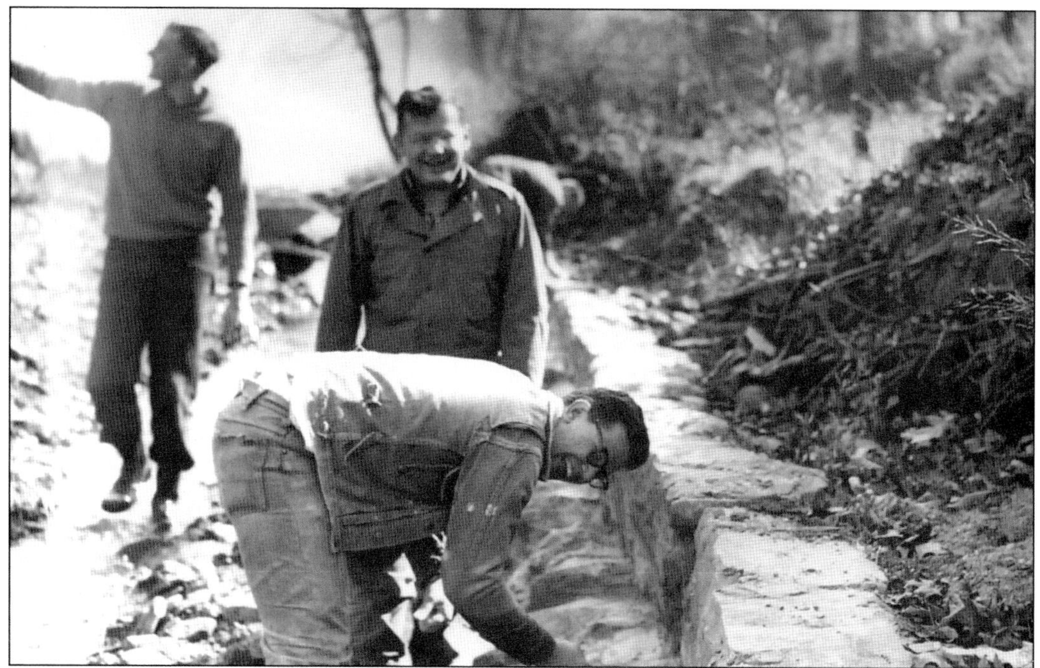

Led by associate professor of chemistry Albert S. Carney, who taught at the campus from 1943 to 1978, Penn State Altoona students erected the retaining wall that bolsters the embankment of Spring Run Creek, the narrow waterway that runs along the southeast corner of the college. Carney's Wall was constructed as part of the regular campus workday activities in which students endeavored to leave Penn State Altoona in better condition than they found it.

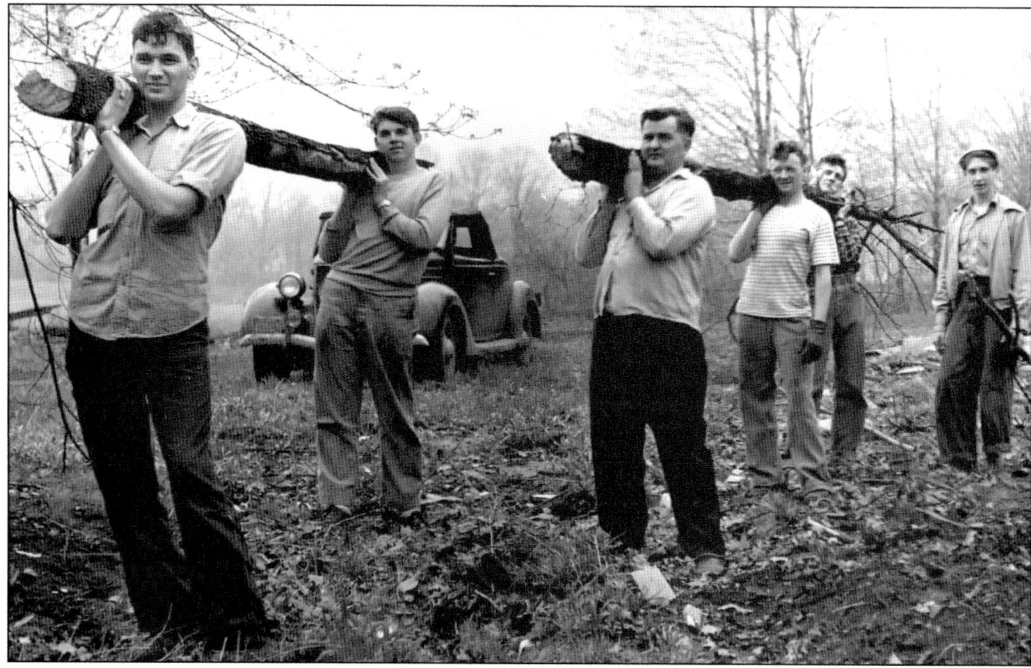

In this May 1959 photograph, students clear dead trees from the campus grounds.

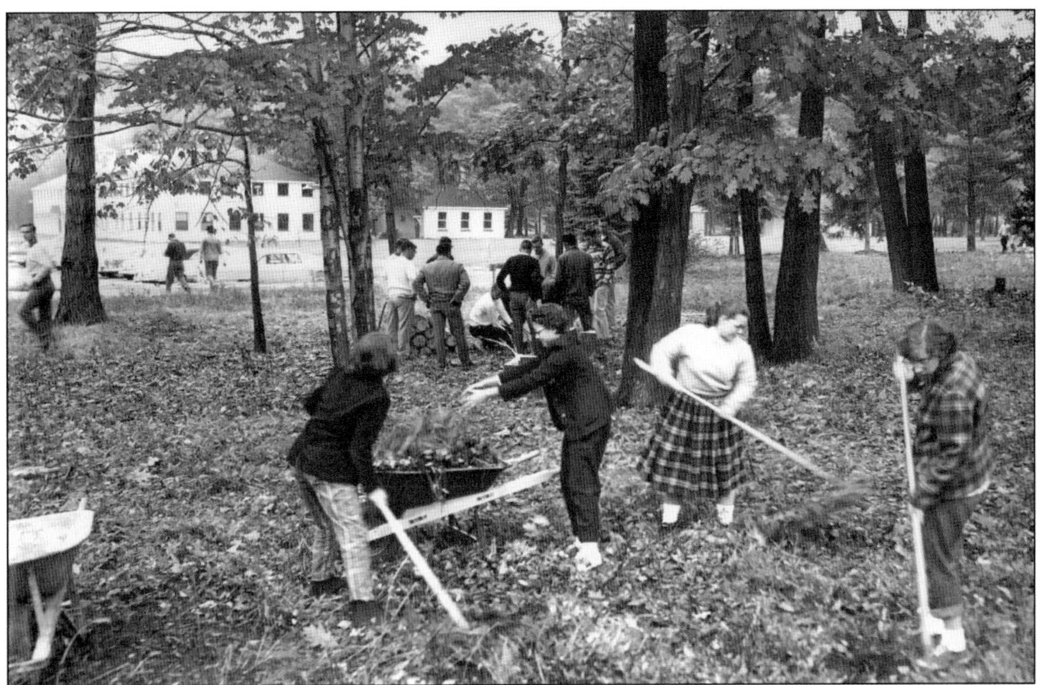

In this May 1959 photograph, students rake leaves. The bathhouse is visible in the background.

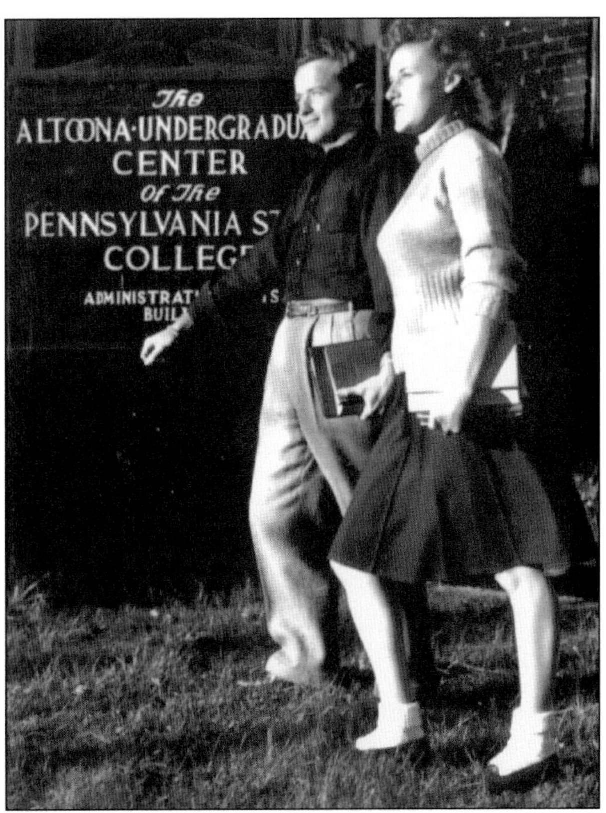

After the purchase of the former Ivyside Recreation Park in 1947, it would take another year and a half to transform the park facilities into much-needed classroom, laboratory, and library spaces. The bathhouse was recommissioned as a multipurpose classroom and office building, while the dance hall became the student union building and cafeteria. While the shooting gallery was renovated to become the college's first chemistry building, the amusement park's famous swimming pool was drained and converted into a large parking lot.

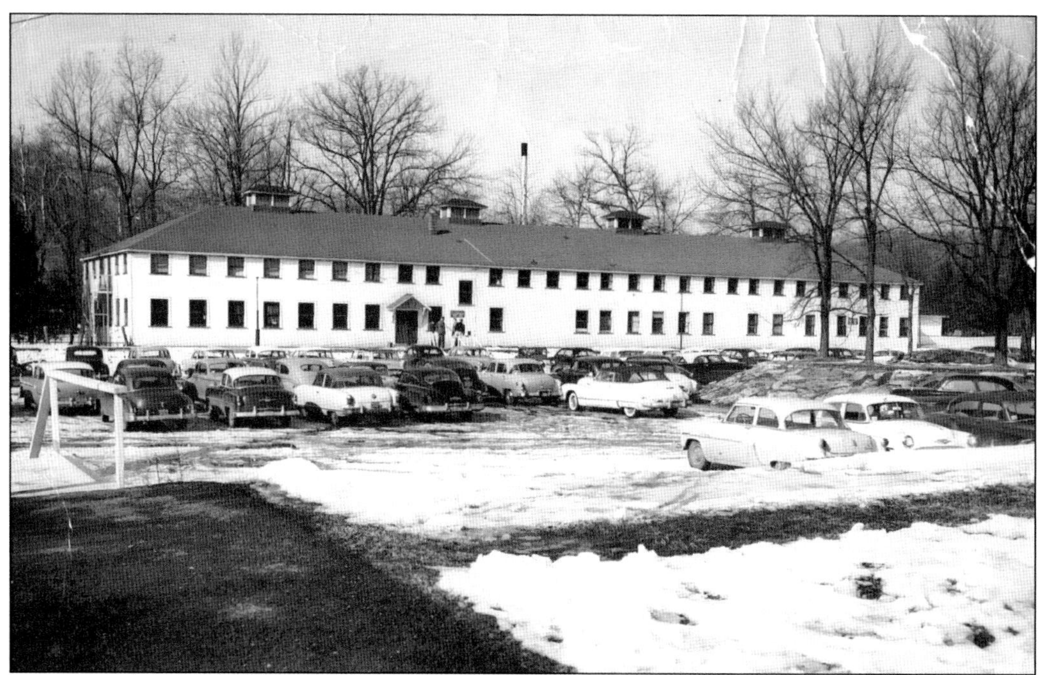

The bathhouse served as the campus's primary classroom and faculty office building during the heyday of Bathhouse U. The two-story building housed 32 classrooms.

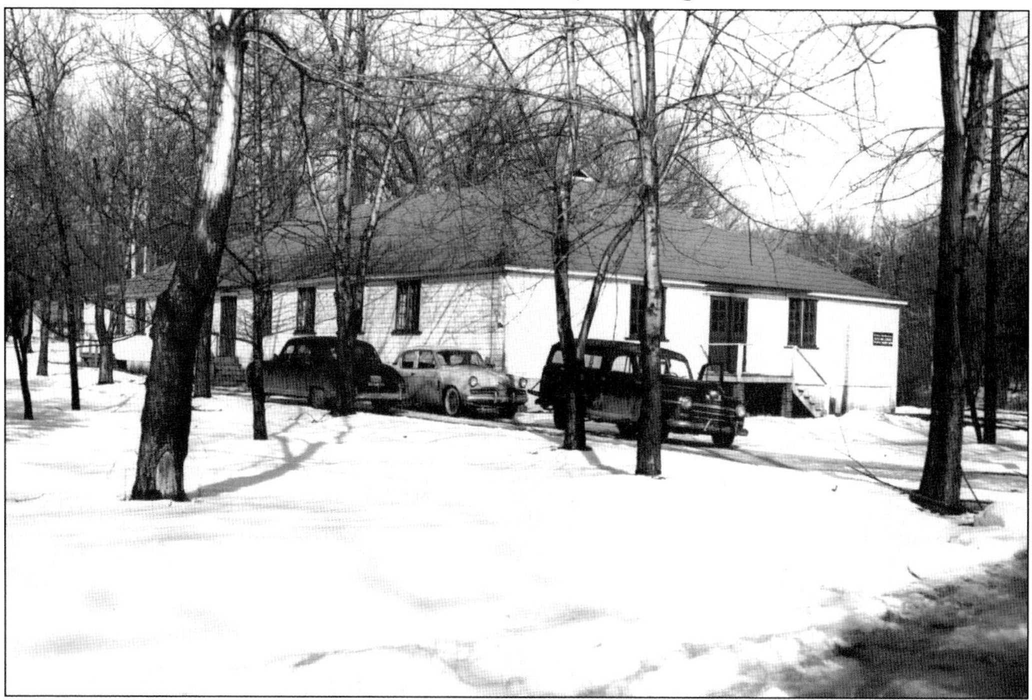

The Ivyside Building, also known as Ivy Hall, served as the Altoona Undergraduate Center's student union building from 1948 until 1964. The building featured a cafeteria, a bookstore, and a recreation area, complete with Ping-Pong tables. Ivy Hall was razed in January 1990 to make way for new facilities.

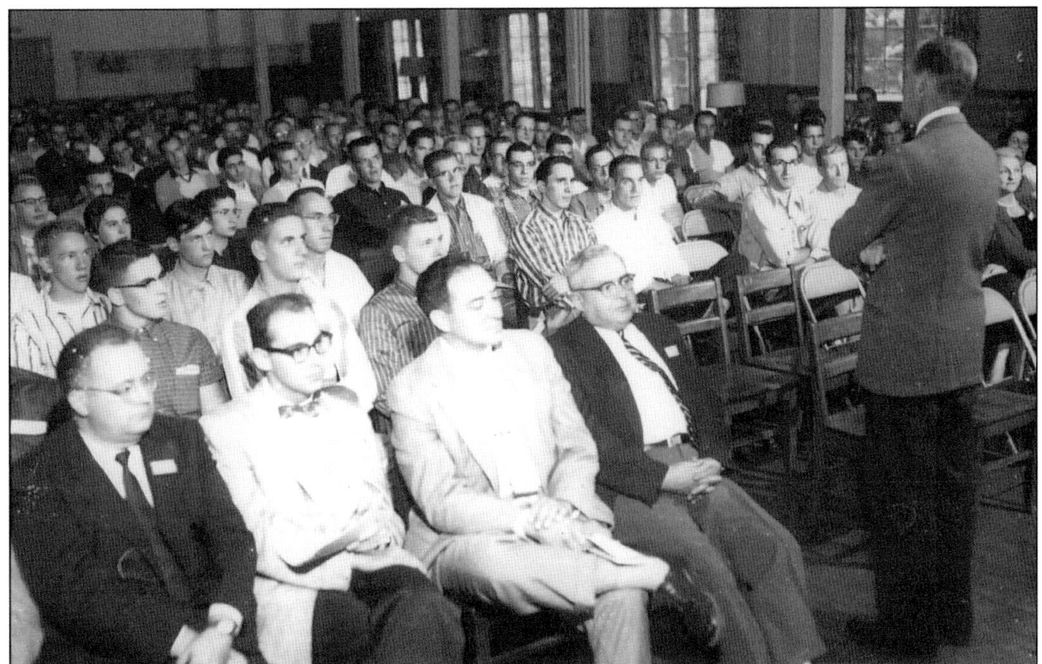

The Ivyside Building's former ballroom was an ideal venue for large lecture classes, assemblies, and theatrical productions.

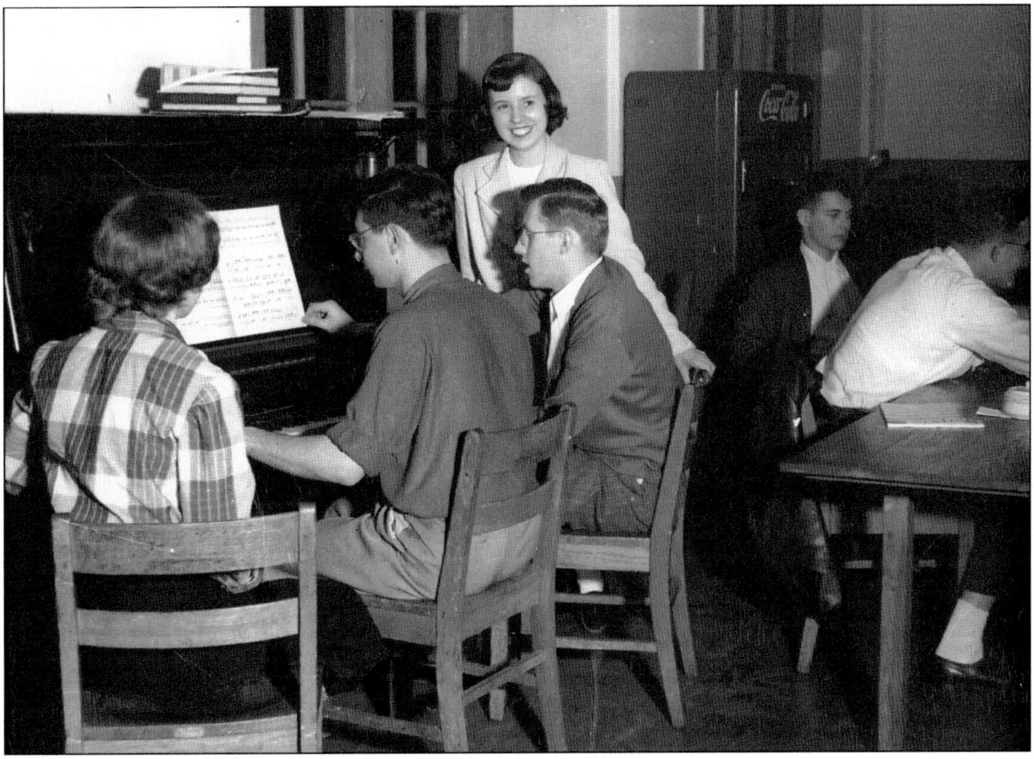

In addition to Ping-Pong tables and study spaces, the recreation area also featured a piano.

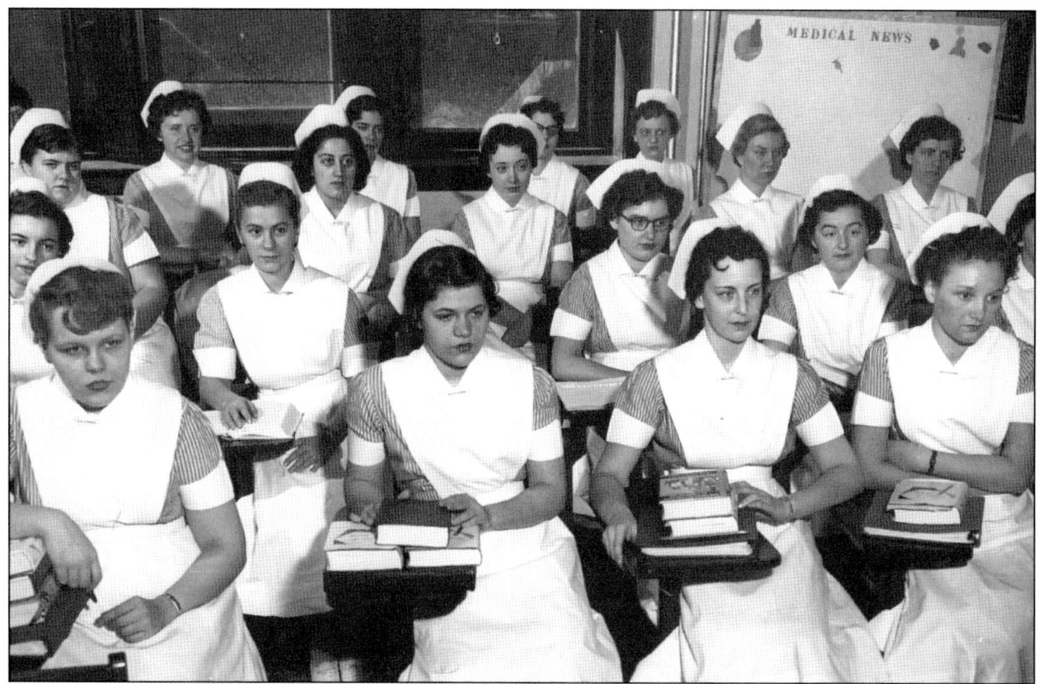

In this 1950s-era photograph, the Altoona Undergraduate Center's thriving nursing program, administered in cooperation with the Altoona Hospital, held classes in the bathhouse building.

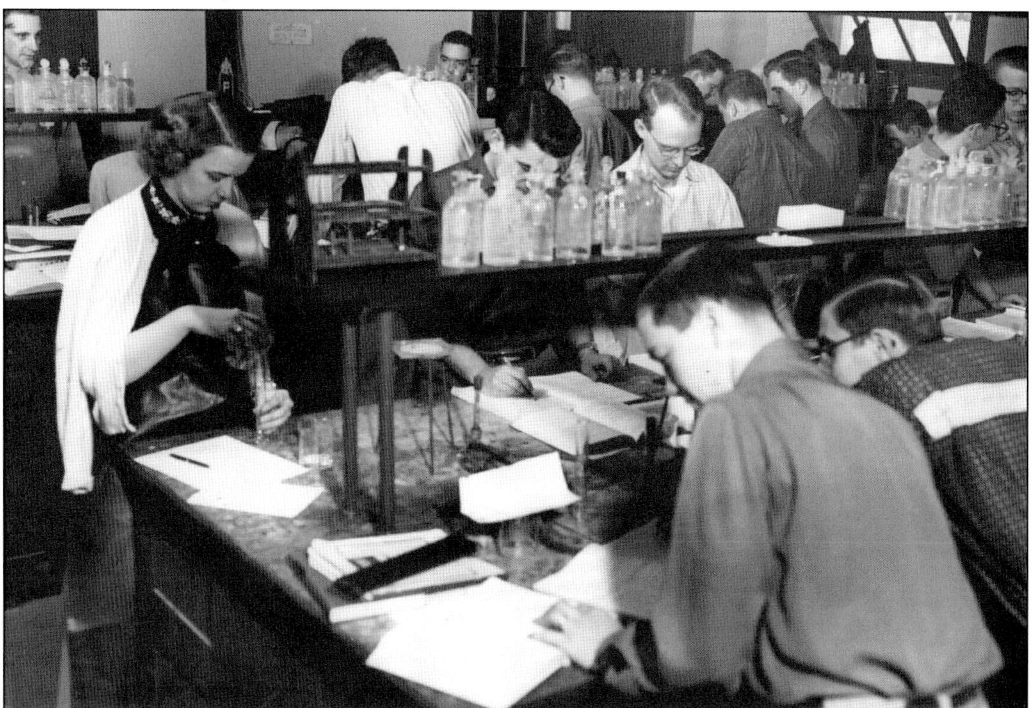

The Altoona Undergraduate Center's chemistry laboratory was located in the Elm Building.

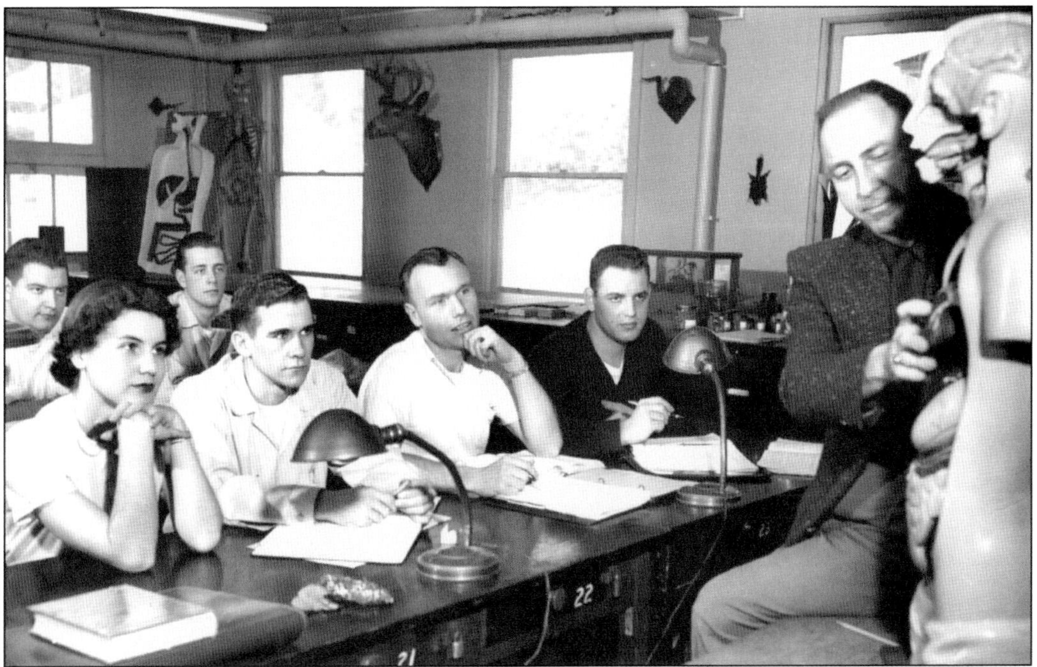

In this photograph, biology instructor Jack G. Zubrod conducts an anatomy class in the Pine Building.

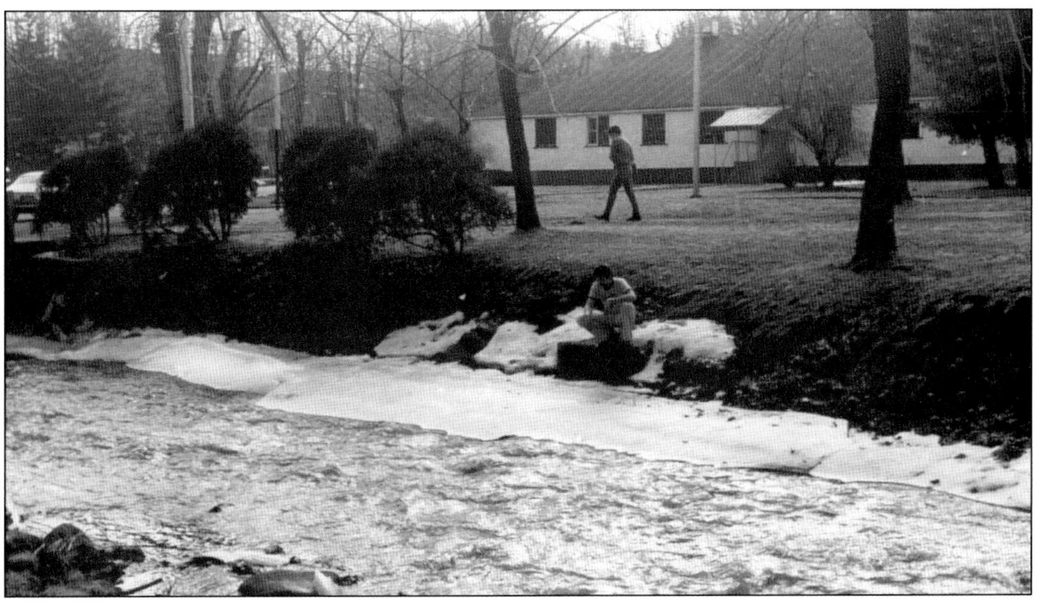

"In the heart of old Altoona, / 'Neath the smoky skies / Smeared against the arch of heaven / Stands old Ivyside." Composed by Arthur L. Barrett, Mary B. Barrett, and Hayden C. Oliver, "The Ivyside Alma Mater" served as the unofficial campus anthem during the early years of Bathhouse U. Oliver served as associate professor of music, working at the campus from 1948 until his retirement in 1969. The Barretts were English instructors at the campus from 1947 to 1952. Pictured above is the Ivyside Building in its academic heyday, with the Spring Run Creek in the foreground.

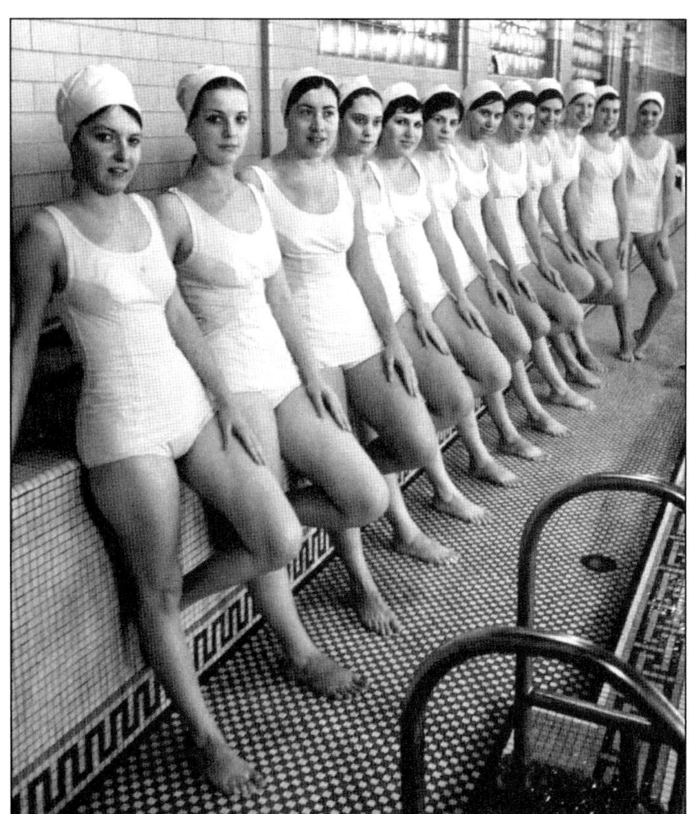

During the early years of the Altoona Undergraduate Center, the institution assembled a team of synchronized swimmers who performed elaborate water shows.

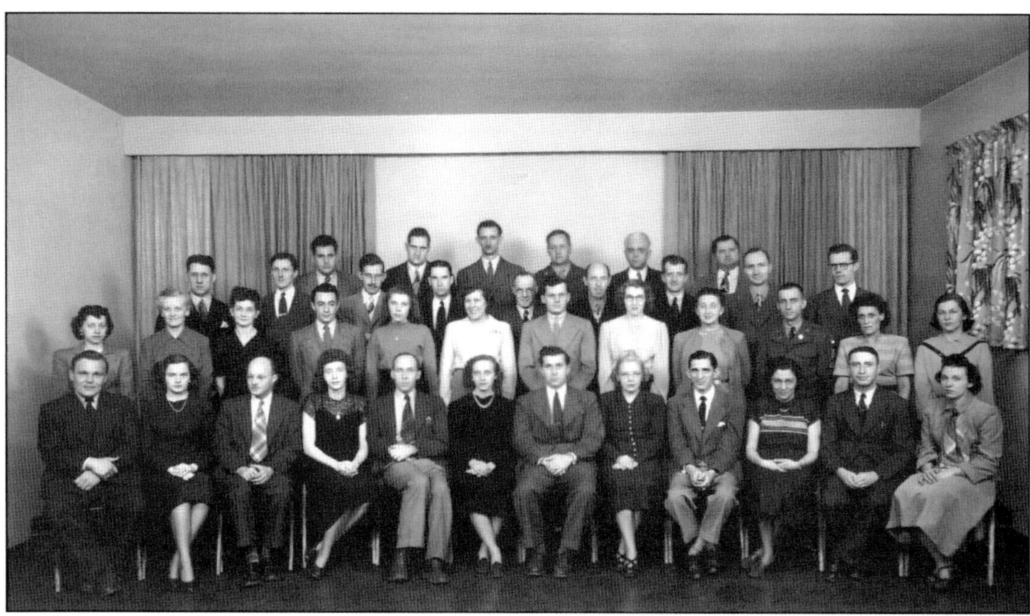

By the early 1950s, the Altoona Undergraduate Center's enterprising faculty quickly moved beyond the institution's business and engineering heritage, generating strong support for the arts and humanities throughout the 1940s and beyond. By the late 1940s, foreign language clubs supported the study of German, French, Spanish, and Russian.

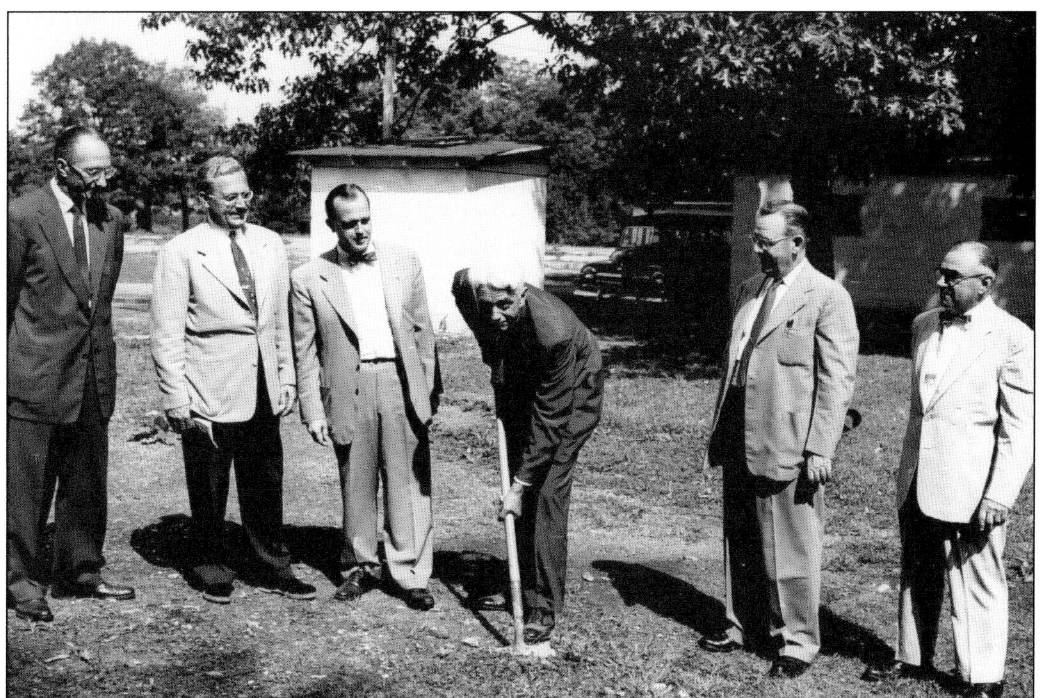

In this August 1954 photograph, Robert Eiche (shovel in hand) presides over the groundbreaking ceremony for the electrical engineering laboratory building.

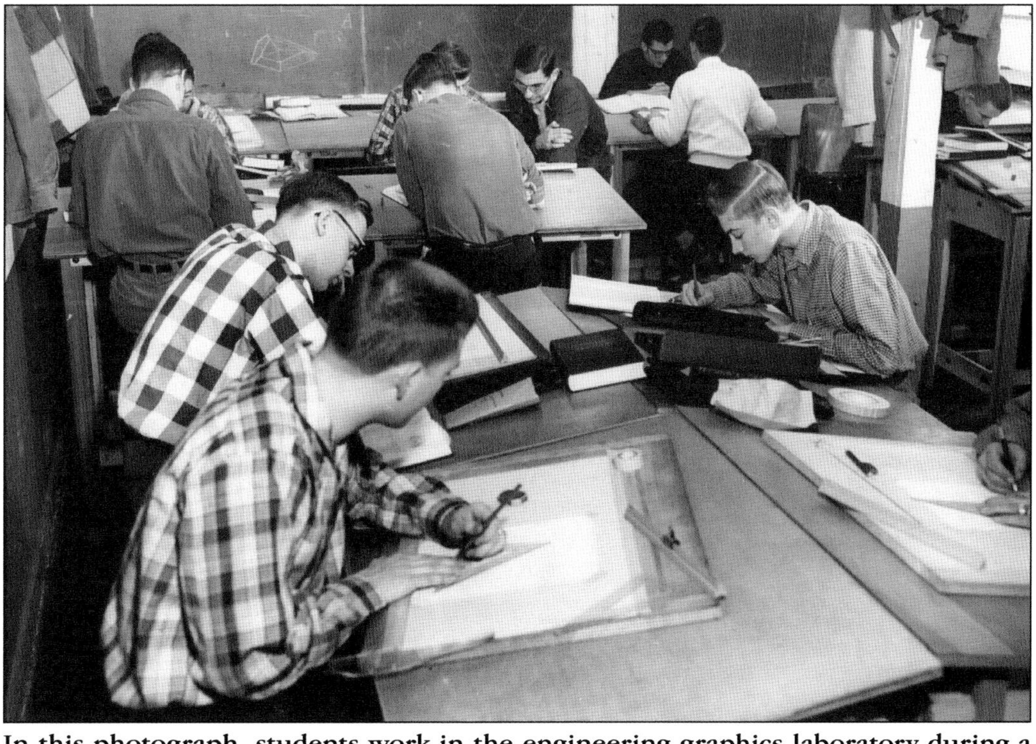

In this photograph, students work in the engineering graphics laboratory during a technical drawing course in the electrical engineering laboratory building.

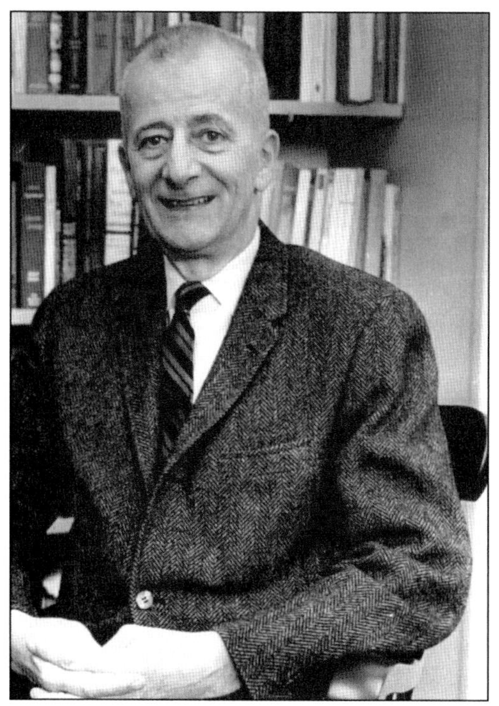

Steven A. Adler served in various capacities at Penn State Altoona across 26 years, most notably as dean of student affairs. He earned a degree in electrical engineering from Penn State in 1931. During his time at the campus, which began at the old Webster School building, Adler saw the student body grow from 100 to 1,000 students. Adler was a key member of the administrative vision that saw the campus achieve remarkable growth during the 1950s and 1960s.

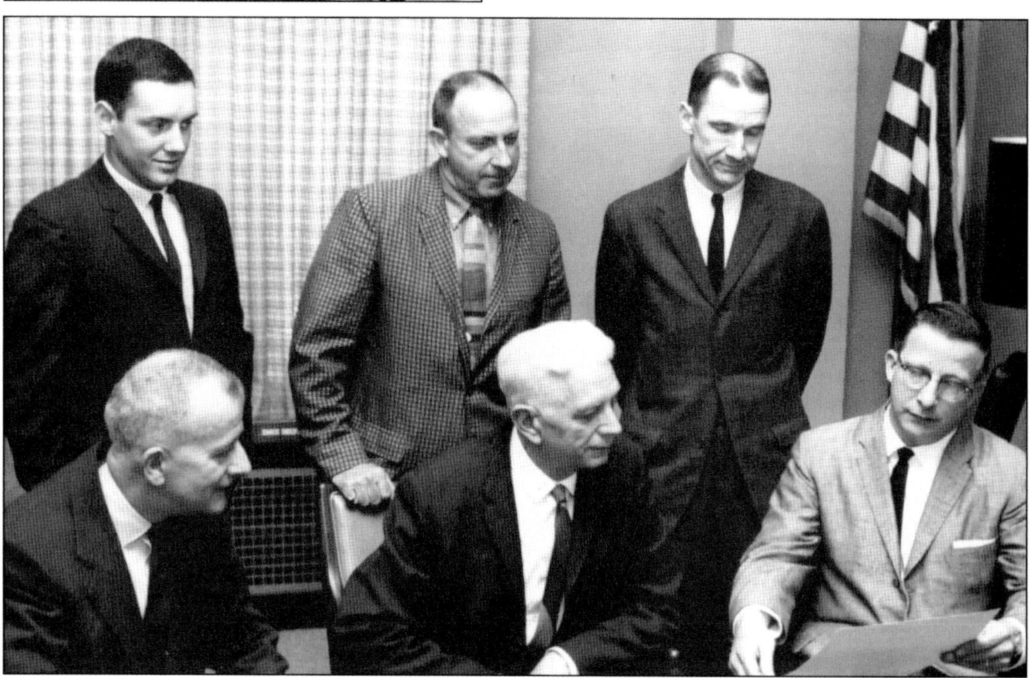

Under Robert Eiche's leadership, the Altoona Undergraduate Center purchased the former Ivyside Recreation Park, which allowed the institution to expand significantly its curriculum and services—not to mention its faculty, staff, student body, and facilities. Pictured are, from left to right, (first row) Adler; Eiche; and Altoona mayor William H. Prosser; (second row) an unidentified student; Jack G. Zubrod, associate director of academic affairs; and Robert L. Smith, director of business operations.

Over his long and distinguished career at Penn State Altoona, Zubrod served in a variety of capacities, including as a biology instructor, dean of instruction, and later associate director of academic affairs. His career spanned from 1957 until his retirement in 1977. Along with Eiche and Adler, he was a central player in the campus's development during the immediate decades after the Altoona Undergraduate Center relocated to the former grounds of the Ivyside Recreation Park. In this 1968 photograph are, from left to right, Joan Shiffler, campus registrar Ronald Petak, and Zubrod.

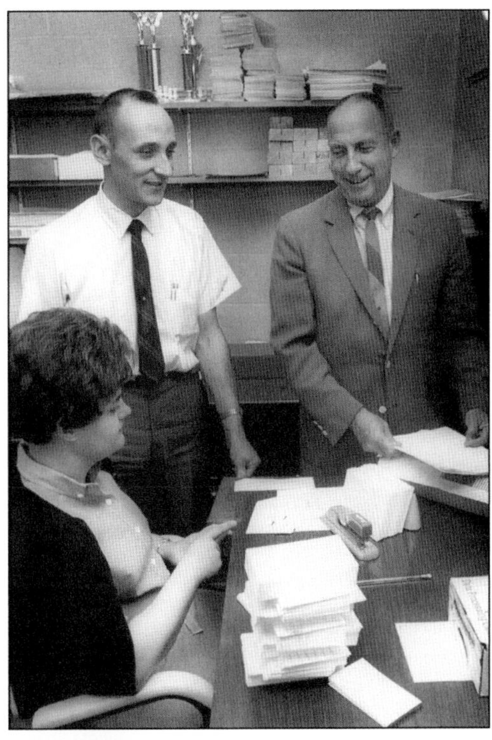

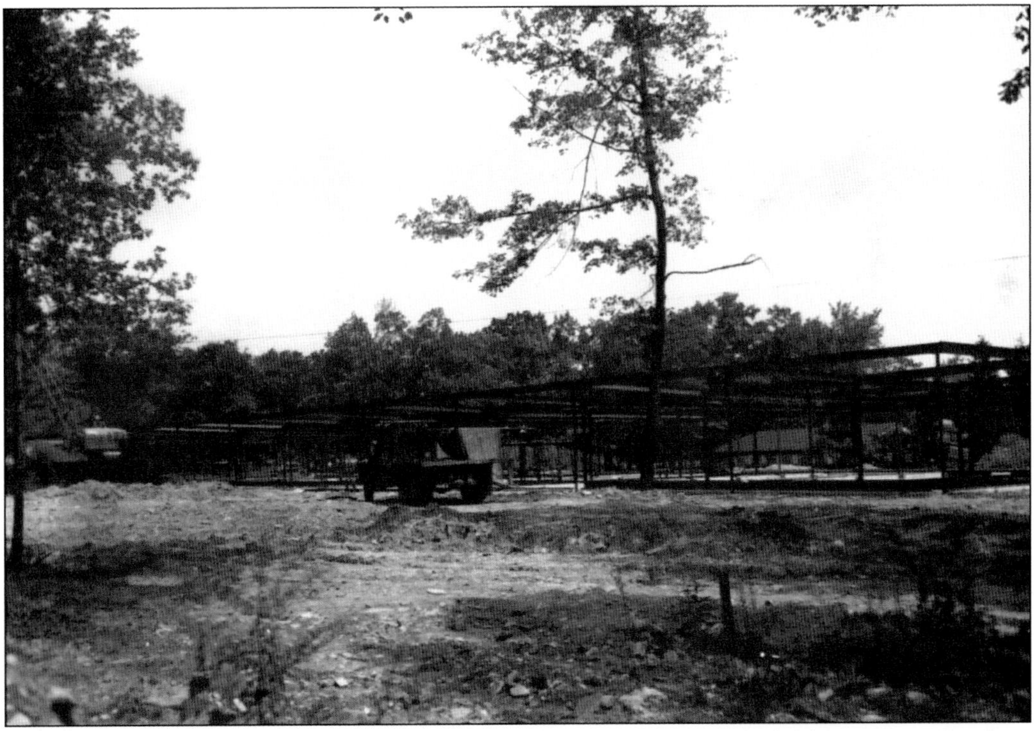

The citizens of Altoona, including some 3,000 donors, provided $400,000 in funding toward construction of the E. Raymond Smith Building, along with $150,000 allocated by the university.

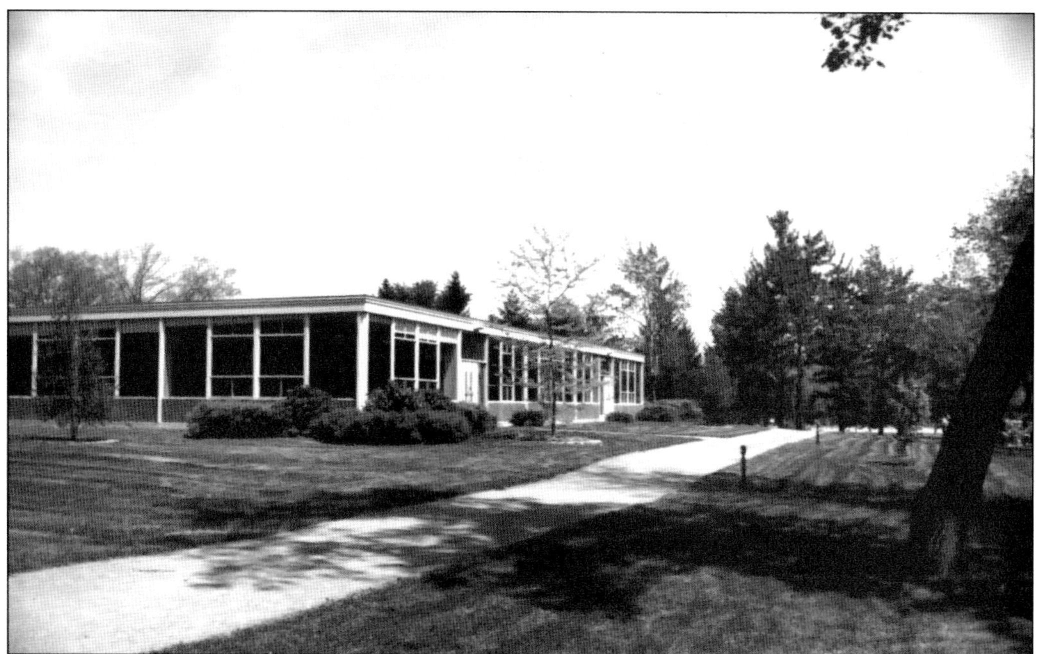

The E. Raymond Smith building opened on September 15, 1958, officially replacing Ivy Hall as the campus's central administration center. The Smith building was formally dedicated by Penn State president Eric A. Walker on October 5, 1958. In addition to administrative offices, the building originally included classroom and library facilities.

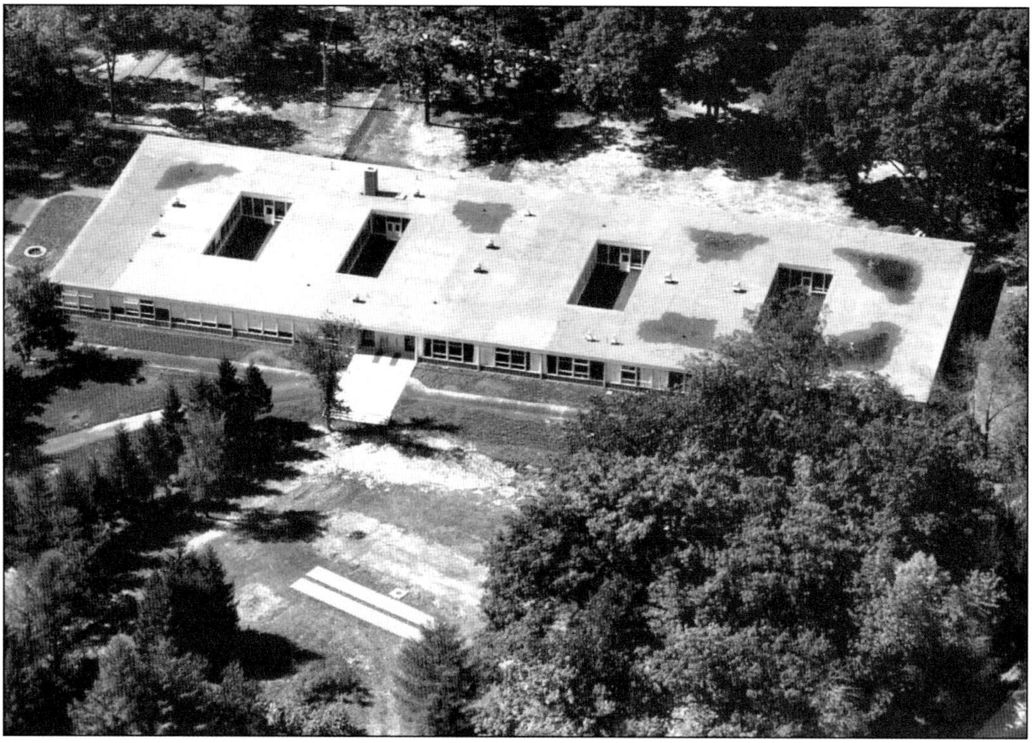

This aerial photograph highlights the building's distinctive quartet of atria.

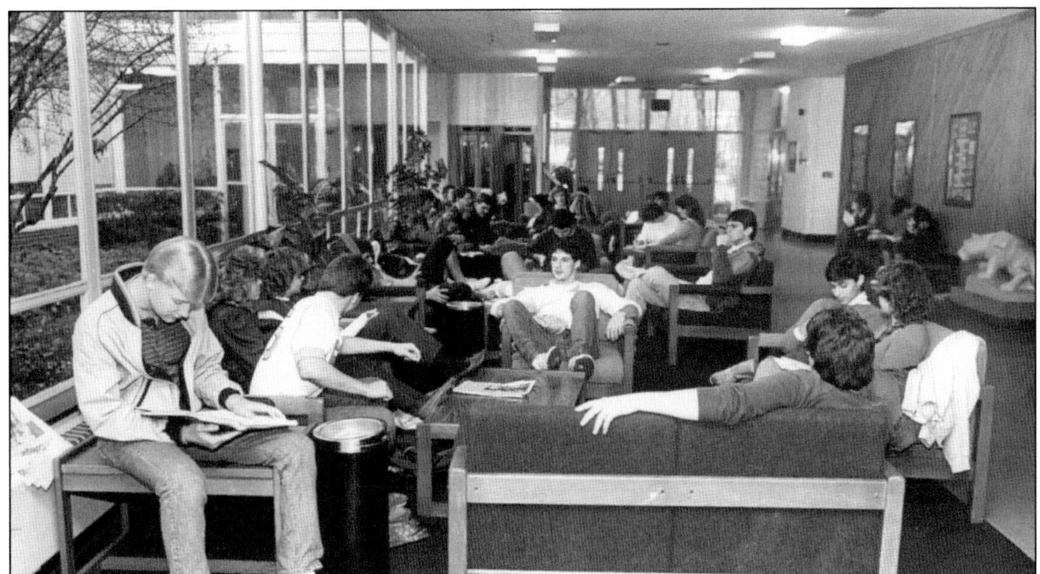

For some four decades, the central lobby in the Smith building functioned as a student gathering area, as well as a popular study spot. In this 1986 photograph, Penn State Altoona students socialize between classes.

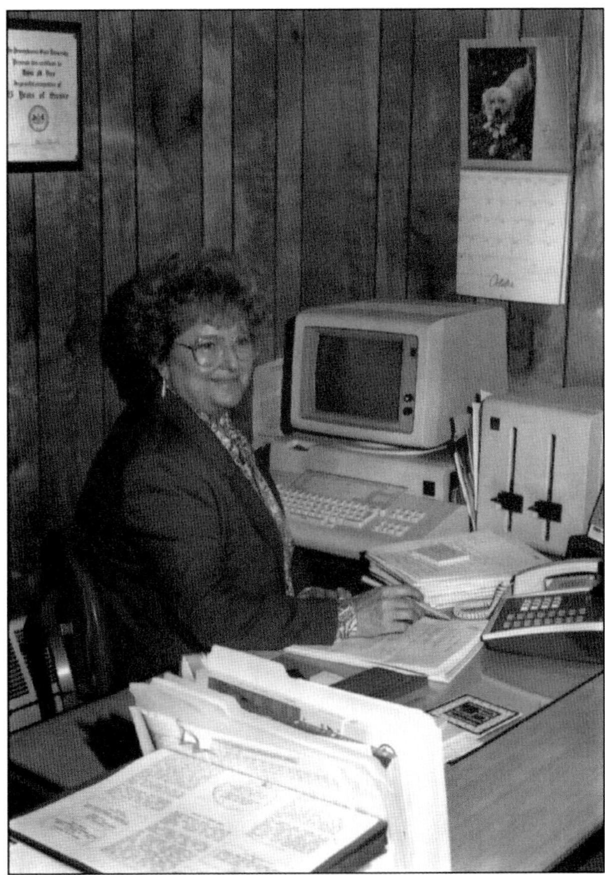

Anna May Very began working at the college in May 1958 in the former bathhouse building. As one of Penn State Altoona's chief administrative assistants, Very worked for Jack G. Zubrod for 19 years until his retirement; for the next 26 years, she served as the staff assistant for Kjell Meling, associate dean for academic affairs. Retiring after 48 years of service in 2006, Very turned in a remarkable career characterized by her intense professionalism and loyalty—a career that spanned from the world of typewriters and mimeographs to personal computers and fax machines.

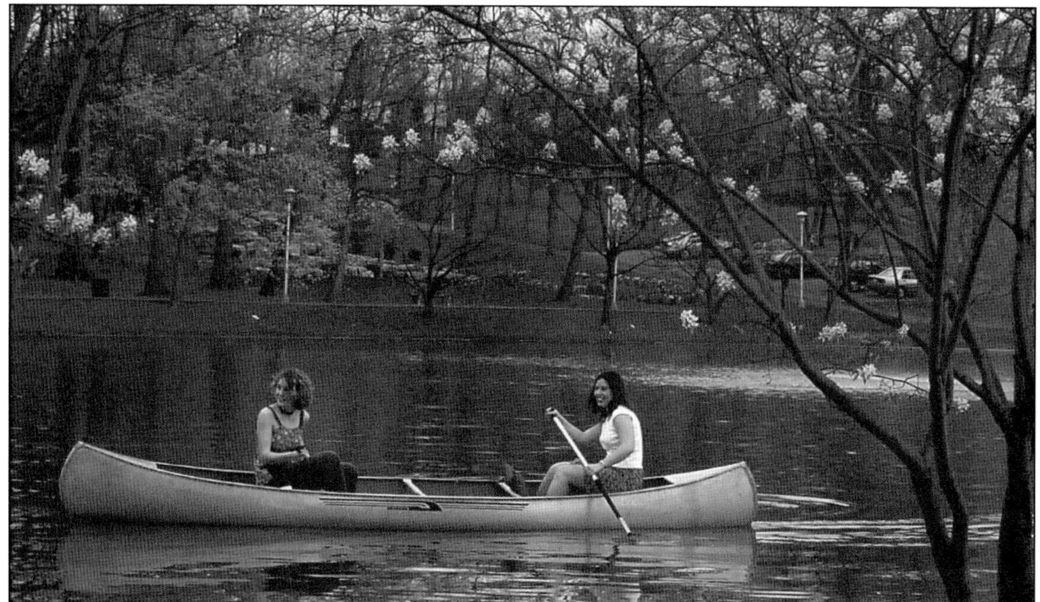

The reflecting pond is one of the campus's central aesthetic features. The pond was originally designed to be a warming pond and holding tank for the Ivyside Recreation Park's colossal swimming pool. In the 1960s and 1970s, the pond became the focal point of freshmen activities, including watermelon relay races, canoe races, and a mammoth game of tug-of-war that frequently ended with most of the participants floundering in the pond.

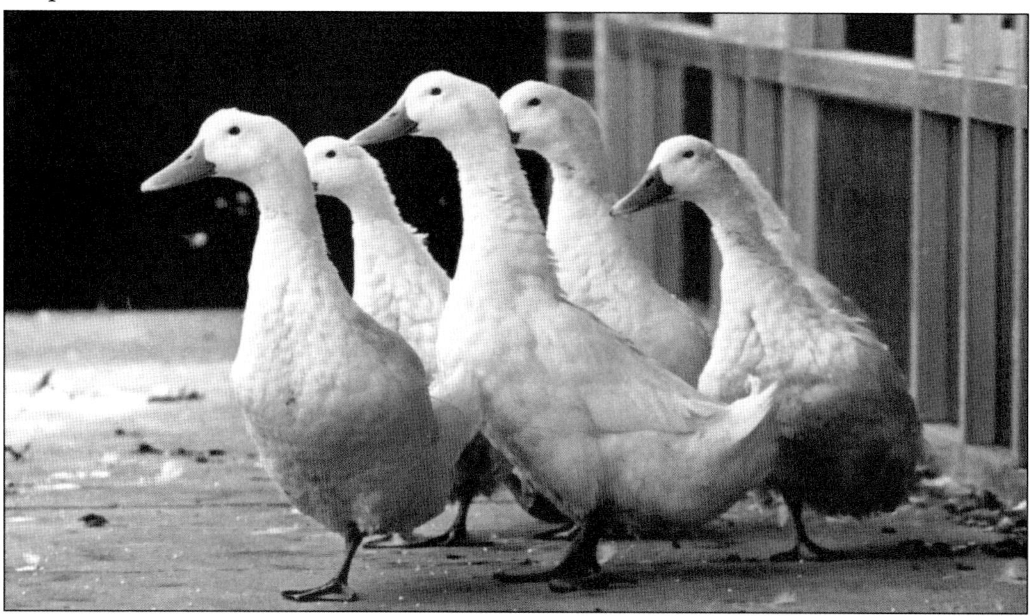

In addition to serving as the year-round home to the campus's population of mallards and Canadian geese, the pond features prominently in Pulitzer Prize–winning novelist and former Penn State Altoona faculty member Richard Russo's *Straight Man* (1997), the fictionalized account of the life and times of the "West Central Pennsylvania State University."

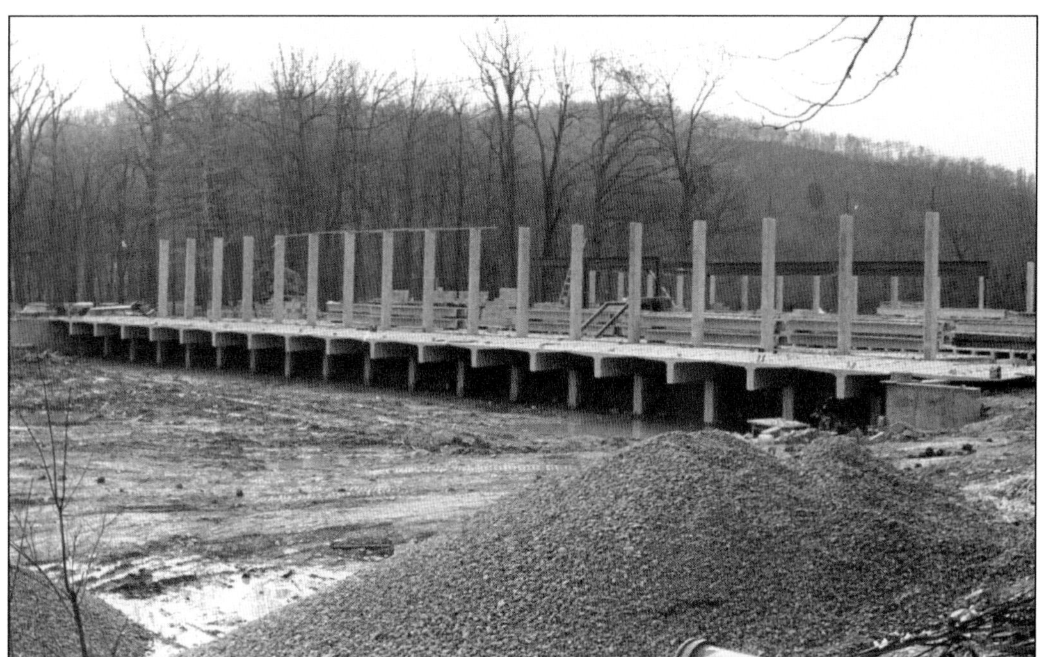

Originally known as the Altoona Campus Student Commons, the Harry E. Slep Student Center was funded, along with the East Hall dormitory, through $1.25 million in university-backed loans.

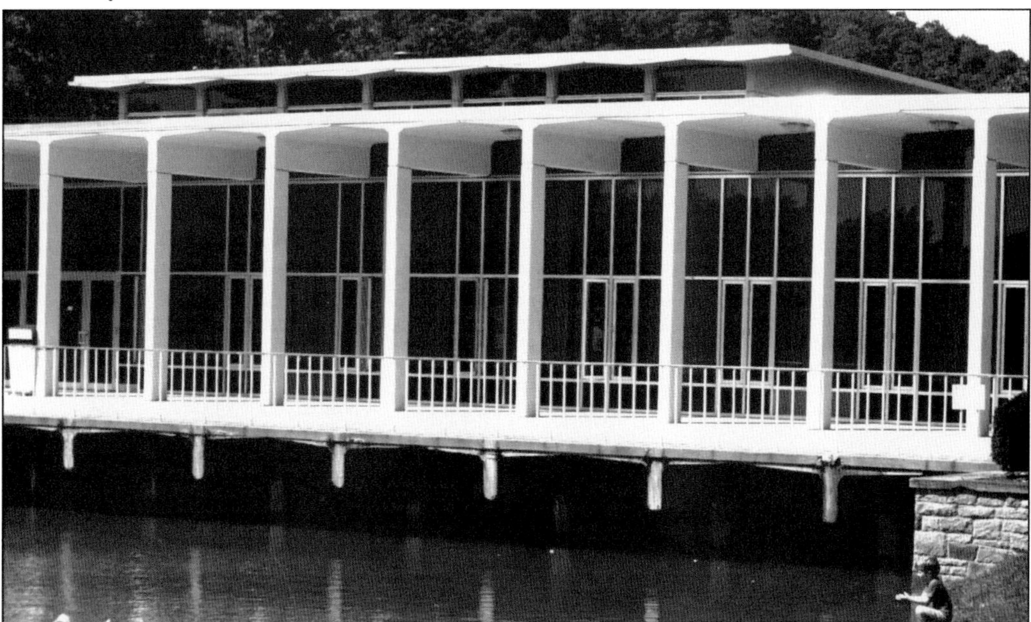

Completed in 1964, the Altoona Campus Student Commons—later rededicated as the Harry E. Slep Student Center—provided the Altoona campus with a student recreational and relaxation center. In addition to study and television lounges, the Harry E. Slep Student Center houses offices for a wide range of student organizations, as well as the Division of Student Affairs and Career Services. The center is named for Harry E. Slep, the visionary local businessman who founded the *Altoona Mirror*, the city newspaper.

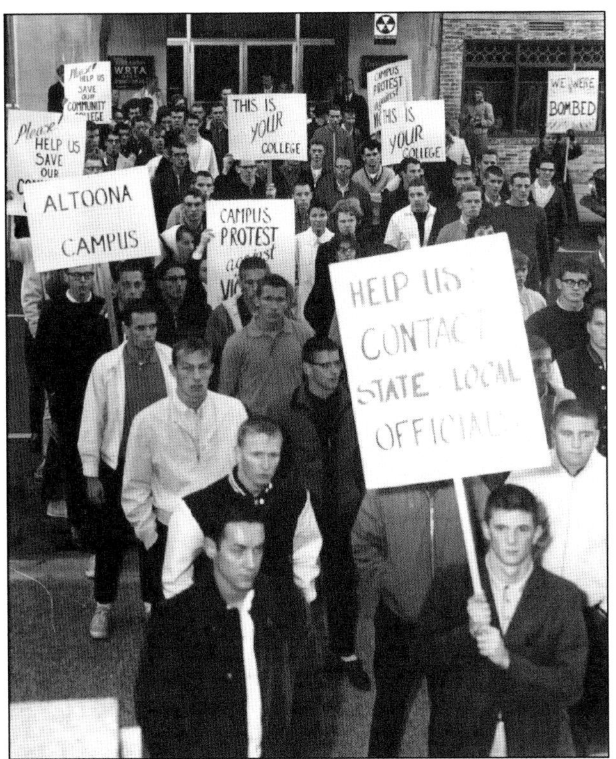

On November 10, 1963, the eastern wing of the nearly completed women's dormitory, now known as Oak Residence Hall, was bombed. University police estimated that a dozen sticks of dynamite were used to cause the explosion, which cracked and weakened the structure, ripping open eight-inch concrete blocks and blowing out some 30 windows. The result of a labor dispute between Pittsburgh carpenters unions and a Huntingdon contractor over the use of union versus nonunion employees, the bombing prompted students to march on downtown Altoona in protest.

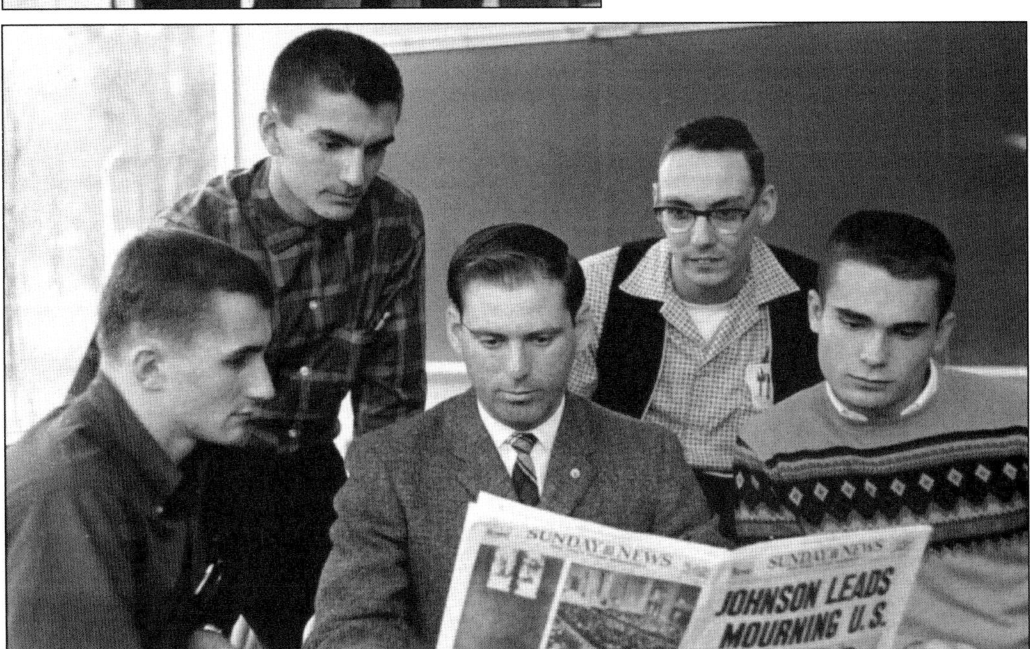

In this November 30, 1963, photograph, Penn State Altoona students reflect upon the recent assassination of Pres. John F. Kennedy. The students traveled to Washington, D.C., to share in the nation's grief and attend the vigil in the Capitol rotunda. Pictured are, from left to right, Thomas Sigrest, Bernard Geishauser, history instructor Jack Larner, Harold Traux, and Allen McGlathery.

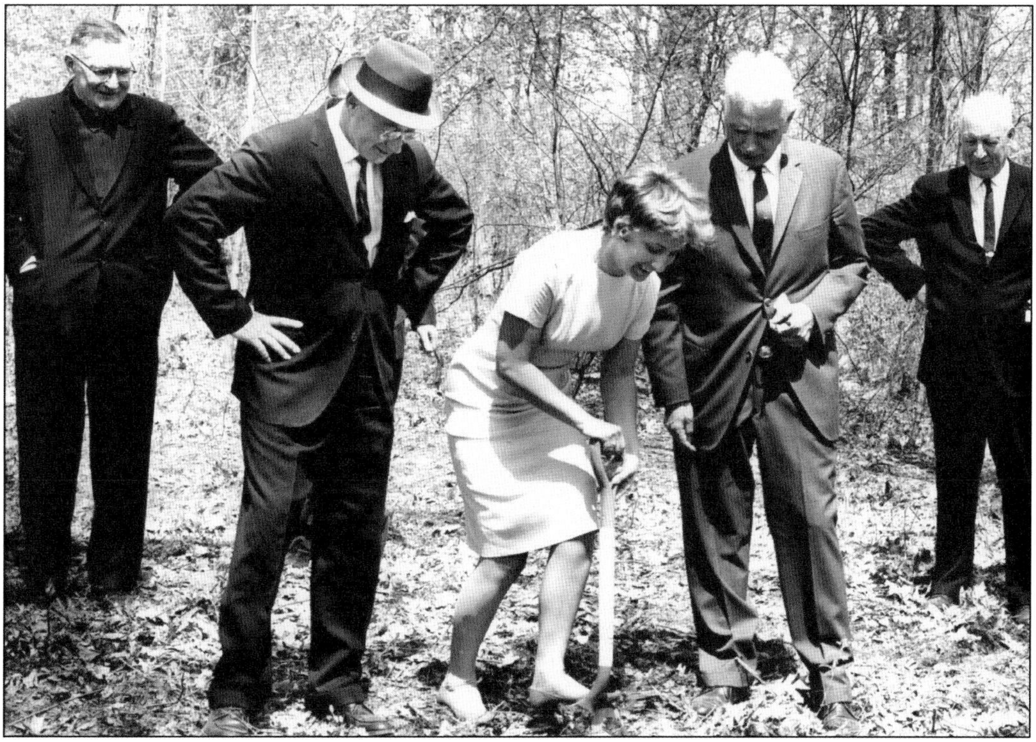

Penn State University president Eric A. Walker (second from the left) and campus director Robert E. Eiche (second from the right) observe as student Betty Bish (center) breaks ground for East Hall on May 8, 1963.

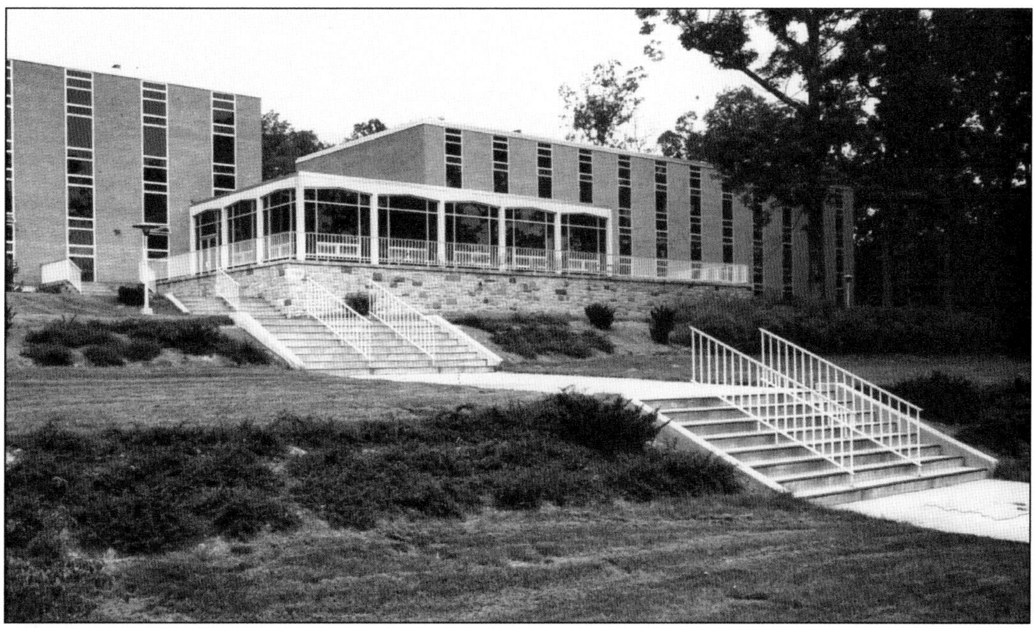

First occupied during the fall 1964 semester, Oak Residence Hall was originally known as East Hall. The dormitory houses some 226 students in traditional-style rooms. Today the hall's residents are arranged coeducationally by wing.

25th Anniversary

OF THE

ALTOONA CAMPUS

THE PENNSYLVANIA STATE UNIVERSITY

1939-1964

ANNIVERSARY CIVIC DINNER
Monday, May 11, 1964
JAFFA MOSQUE

Penn State Altoona celebrated its 25th anniversary with a gala May 1964 dinner at the Jaffa Mosque. In addition to greetings from advisory board chairman J. E. "Ted" Holtzinger and Altoona mayor William H. Prosser, the evening included a keynote address from Penn State University president Eric A. Walker. As President Walker remarked in his address, "The citizens of Altoona must certainly be congratulated on having taken so active a part in creating a thriving and growing campus that graces Altoona today."

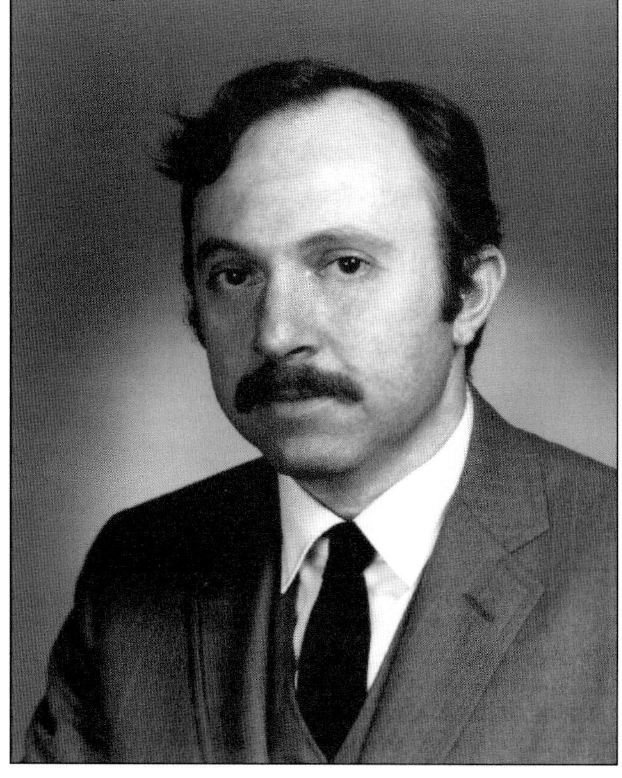

Thomas J. Russo joined the faculty in 1964, having earned his doctorate in organic chemistry from Penn State University. Russo was the first faculty member to earn a prestigious National Science Foundation grant. Having retired in 2002, Russo served as commencement speaker for the summer 2003 graduation. "There may be times when you need to be flexible, open, and prepared to change your opinion," Russo remarked. "But at other times you will need to hold firm beliefs or defend a deep faith. In this world, there are lunatics who would harm you for your beliefs—or even more frightening, if that's possible, for your freedom to believe."

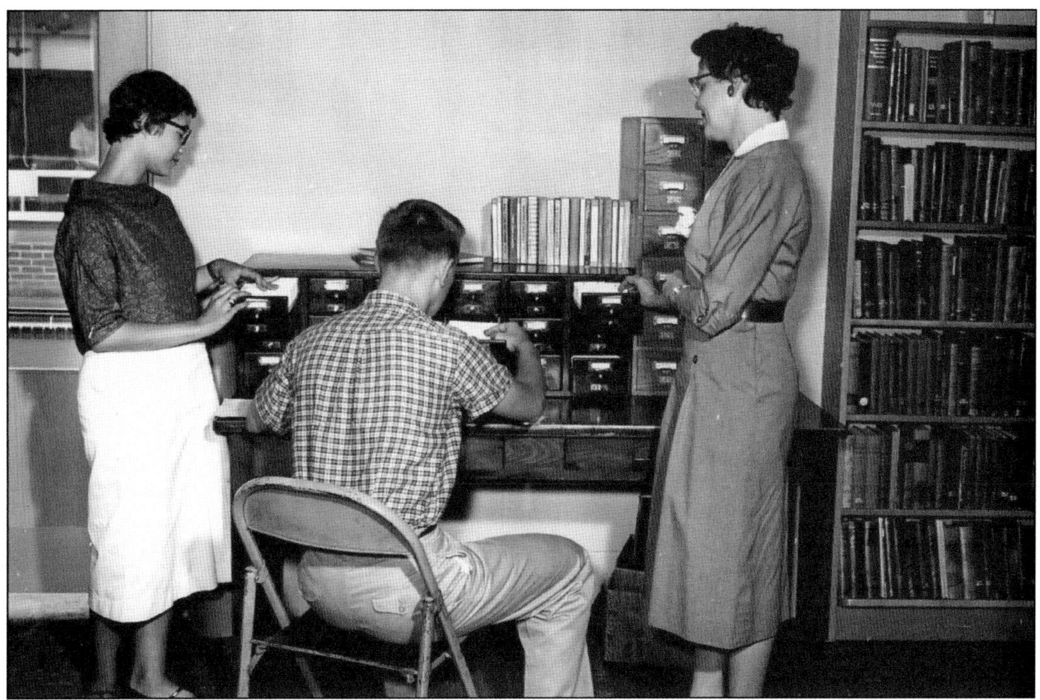

For more than a decade, the campus library holdings were housed in the Smith building. In 1969, the collection was relocated to the present-day Eiche Library.

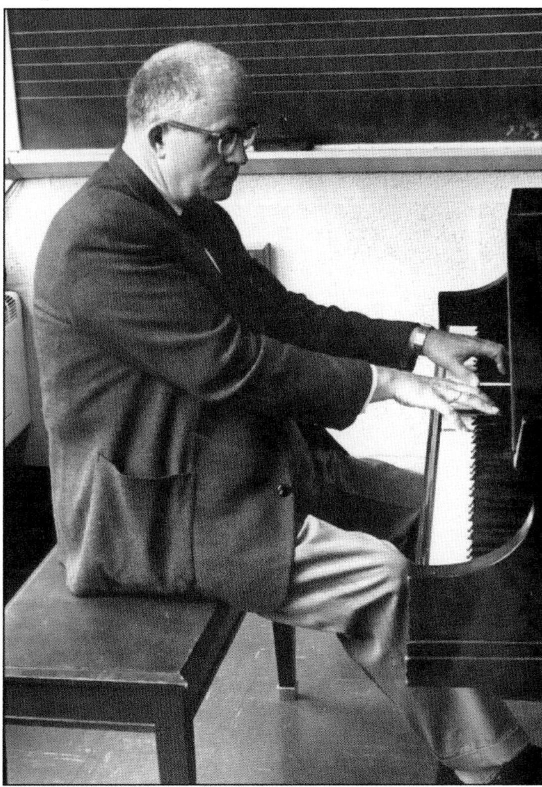

Named in honor of former Penn State president Milton S. Eisenhower, the Milton S. Eisenhower Award for Distinguished Teaching is presented annually to two faculty members from across the university who have an extensive record of outstanding teaching and who provide teaching support or mentoring to other faculty. From 1958 to 1991, the award was known as the Lindback Award. Penn State Altoona has garnered five Eisenhower award winners, including Hayden C. Oliver (pictured right), associate professor of music (1965); Louis D. Goodfellow, professor of psychology (1967); Athleen J. Stere, associate professor of biology (1980); Donald E. Fahnline, associate professor of physics (1986); and Roger Zellner, associate professor of visual arts (1994).

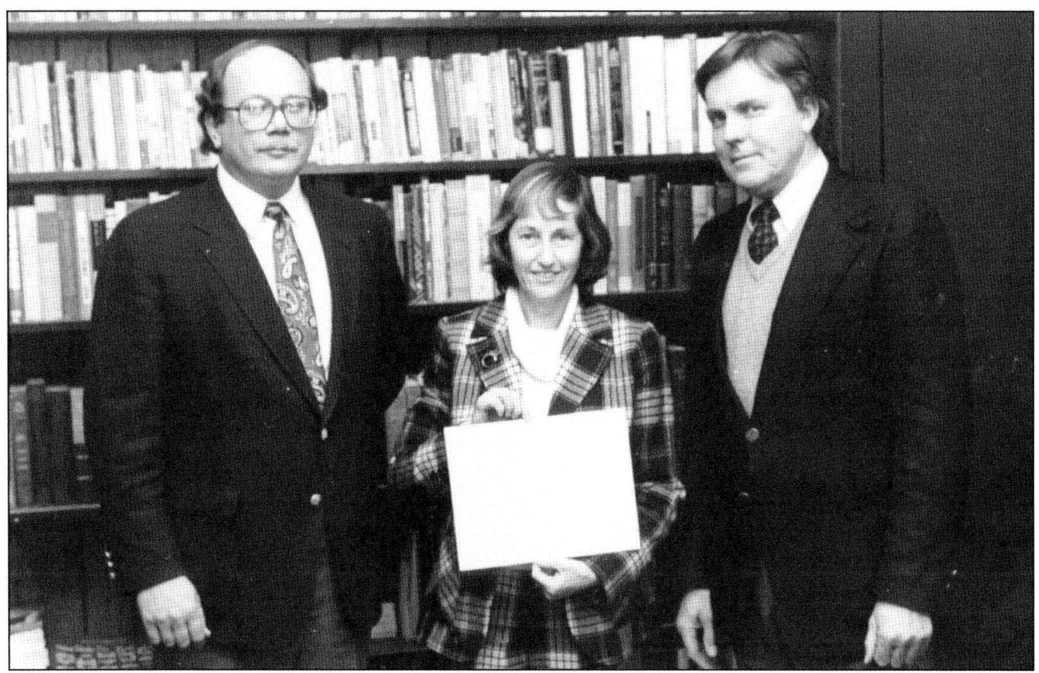

In this photograph, Athleen J. Stere, associate professor of biology, receives the Lindback Award for Distinguished Teaching. From left to right are Kjell Meling, director of academic affairs; Stere; and Carson W. Veach, campus director.

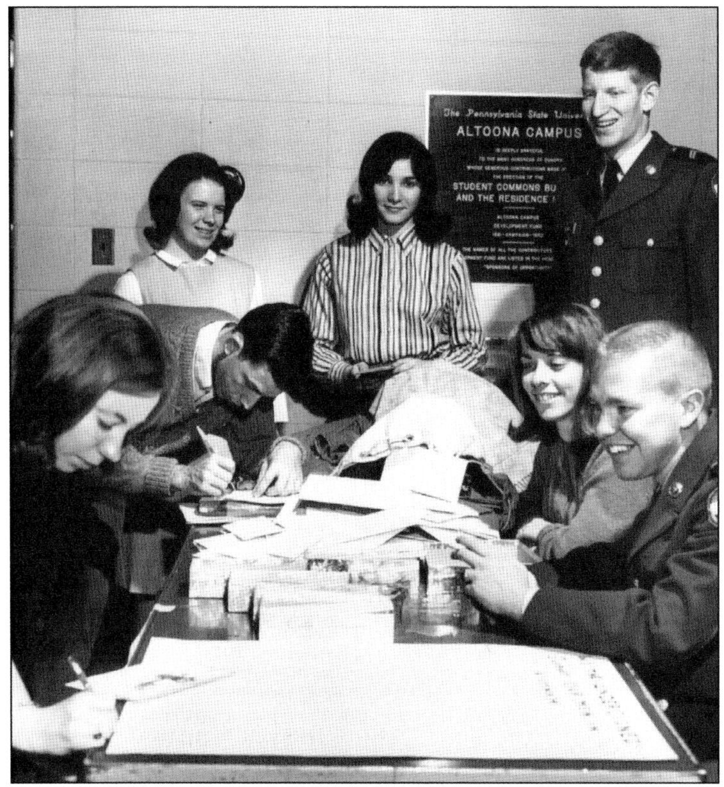

In this November 1965 photograph, students sign cards as part of Operation Patriot for the American troops serving in Vietnam. The initiative was prompted by an editorial in the *Altoona Collegian* in which the newspaper's staff urged readers to support Operation Patriot, the "Altoona Campus project designed to bolster the morale of the men in Vietnam." From left to right, clockwise, are Elmira Conlon, Tom Tedeschi, Michelle Kuhn, Joy Santopietro, Stuart Silver, Sharon McGregor, and Gerry Hamilton.

During the heyday of Penn State Altoona's homecoming festivities, the 1966 homecoming queen's court included, from left to right, Jane Eisenhower, Kay Nystrom, homecoming queen Shirley Hiltner, Anita Lustig, and Susan Messinger.

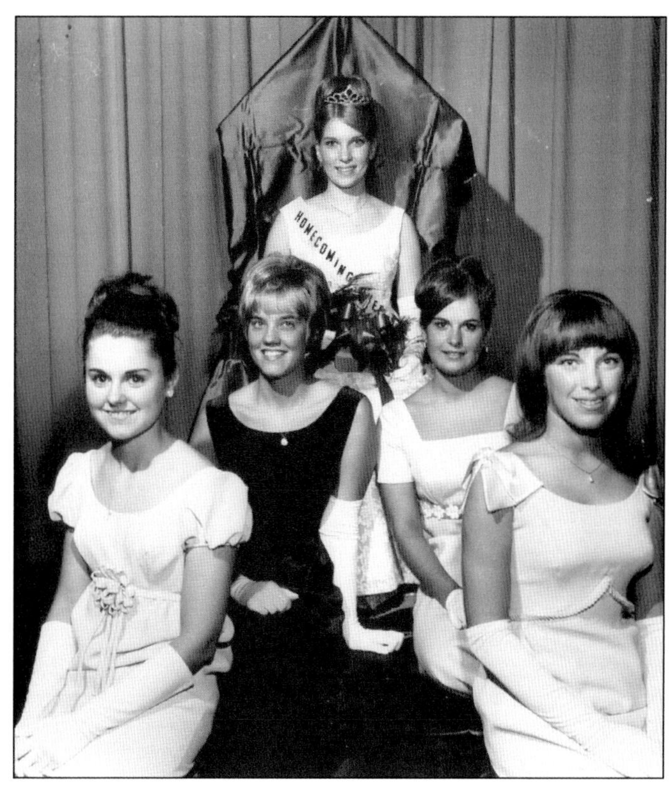

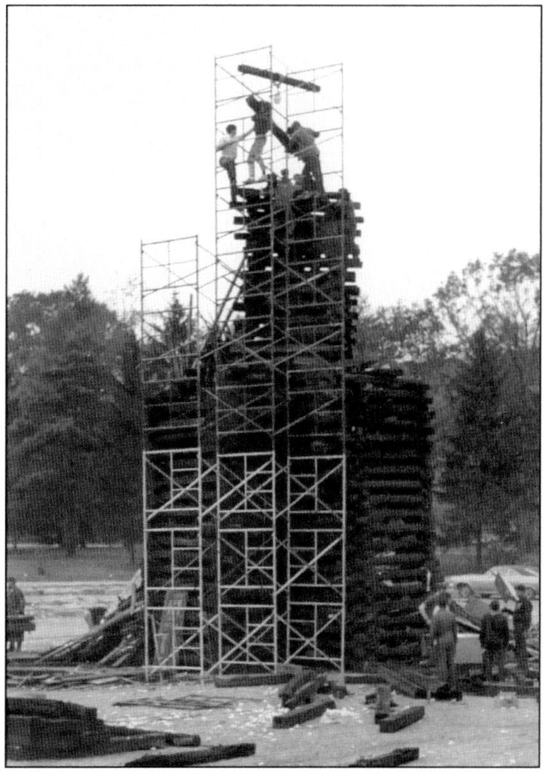

During the 1960s and early 1970s, the annual freshman bonfire was a central feature of Penn State Altoona's homecoming festivities. The bonfire was built in the former Ivyside Park swimming pool.

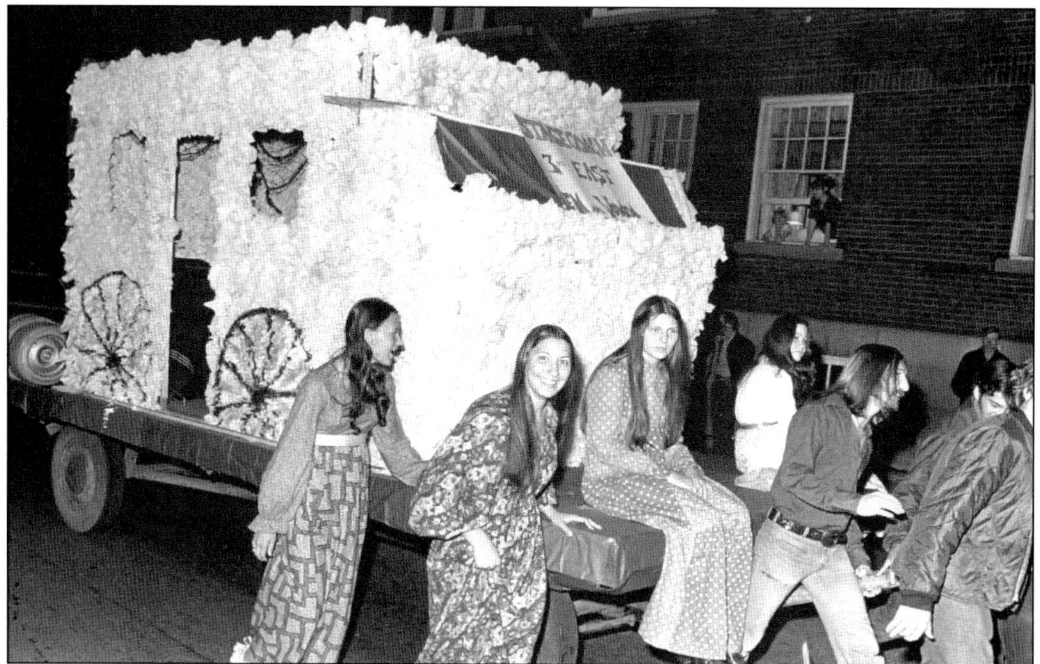

In later years, homecoming activities included a parade across Altoona. In 1970, the parade began and concluded at the Jaffa Mosque, including some 60 floats overall. The 1970 homecoming theme was "Youth around the World," with the winning float, Switzerland, being assembled by a group of enthusiastic dormitory students.

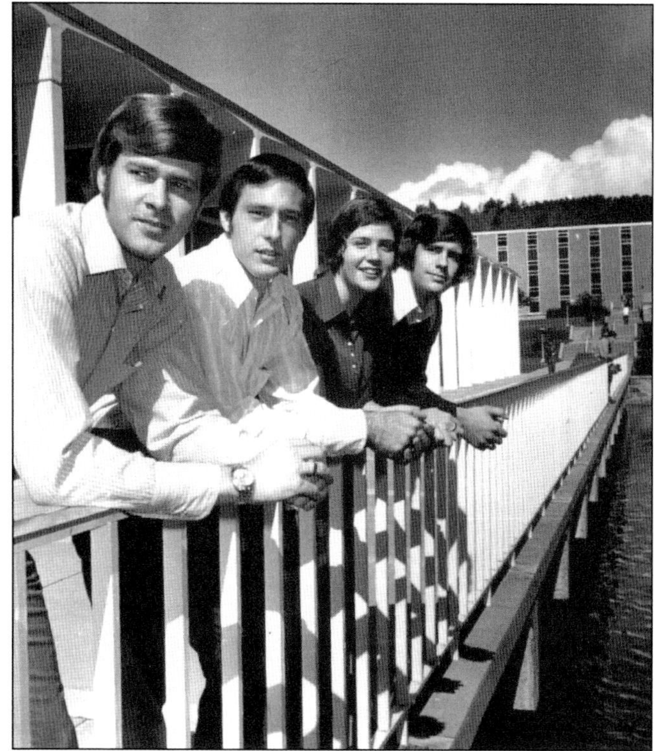

Homecoming festivities were organized by the general student chairmen. In 1971, this steering committee included, from left to right, in front of the Harry E. Slep Student Center, Gary O'Neal, Woody Lavinia, Patty Dumm, and Scott Woodring.

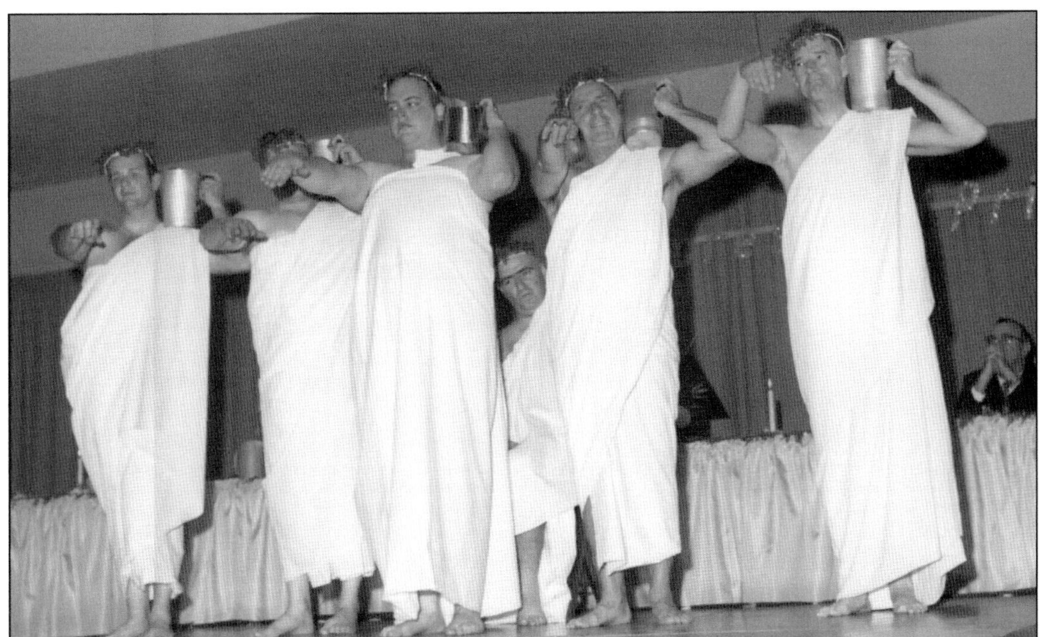

An integral part of the annual homecoming activities involved the "Stage Review" tradition in which students, faulty, staff, and alumni performed skits and selections from Broadway musicals. From left to right are C. David Kimmel, an unidentified student, Ray Nycum, Ron Hoover, Jack G. Zubrod, and Bob Smith.

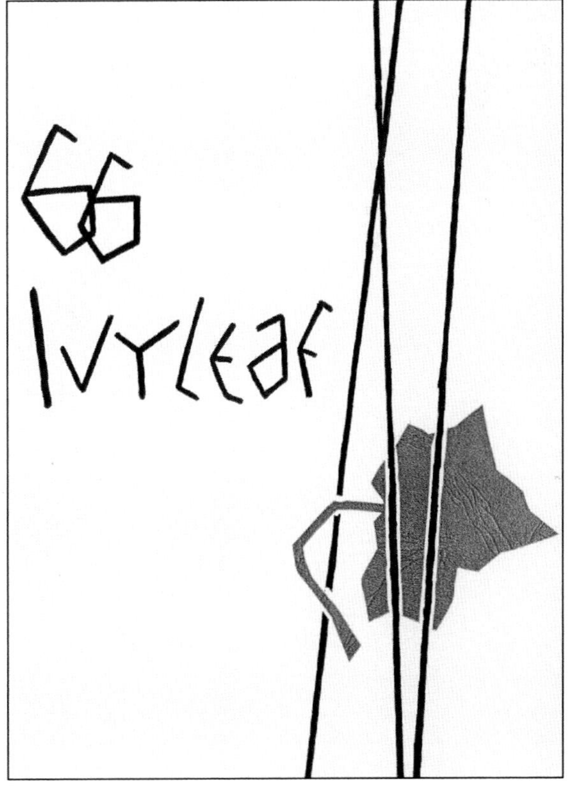

After selling some 250 subscriptions, *The Ivy Leaf* yearbook was given formal authorization in April 1966 to begin publication by the Penn State Altoona Student Government Association. Under the initial editorship of Pam Lackard and Dori Depp, the yearbook commemorated student, faculty, and staff activities. *The Ivy Leaf* remained in production for the next six years before going defunct because of lack of interest after the 1972 issue. In 2002, the college published an online yearbook entitled *Tempus*, and in 2009, the student government association revived the yearbook as an annual tradition at Penn State Altoona.

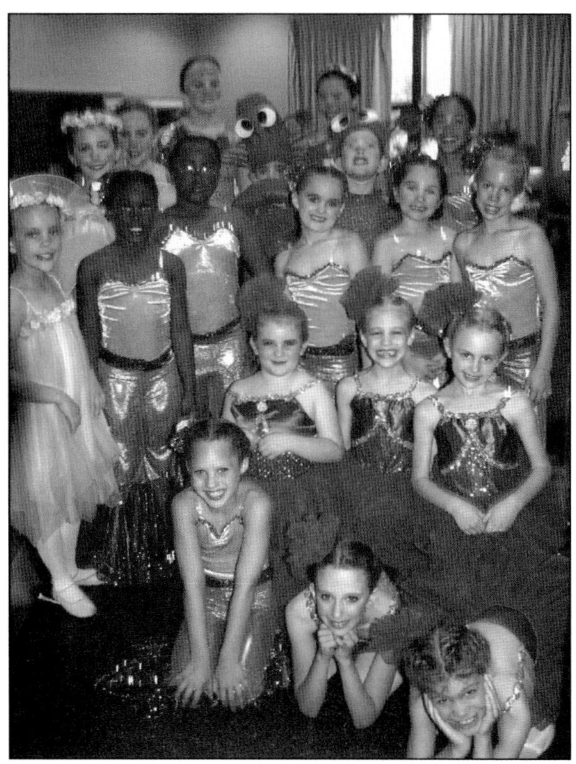

The original Blair County Arts Festival was held on May 21, 1966, and was known as the Spring Arts Festival. The celebration included such events as a hootenanny, an ROTC review and drill demonstration, a photography exhibit, a campus band concert, a student-faculty softball game, and a student-faculty variety show. Taking on a carnival atmosphere, the arts festival now hosts hundreds of artists, craftspeople, and vendors from across the Allegheny Mountain region, as well as a series of juried art exhibitions and performances.

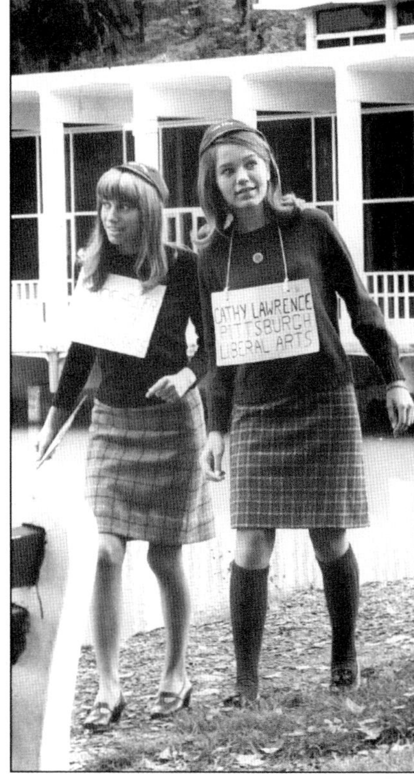

Throughout the 1960s and 1970s, students participated in freshmen initiation events. The activities centered around hazing traditions such as freshmen doing push-ups in piles of shaving cream, wearing name tags, singing Penn State songs on command, cleaning campus sidewalks with toothbrushes, and pushing grapes along the ground with their noses. Pictured in this 1967 photograph are name tag–wearing freshmen Nancie Heller (left) and Cathy Lawrence (right).

Freshmen who violated the name tag tradition were required to parade around the campus with giant sandwich boards fashioned to their bodies. Pictured in this 1967 photograph are students Linda Beck and Larry Lashert.

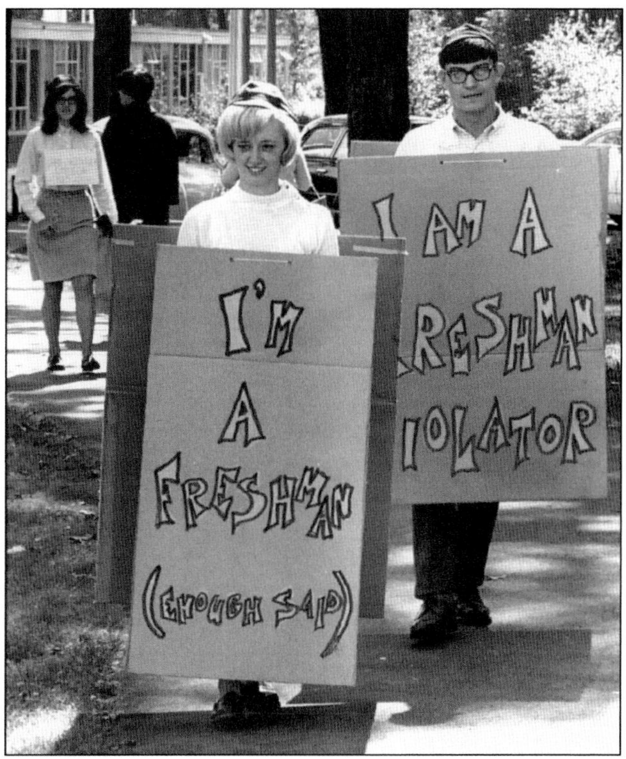

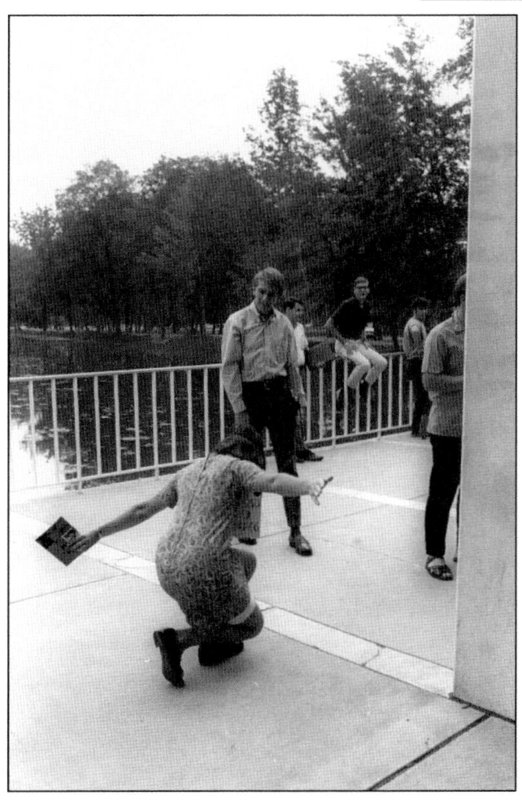

Freshmen women—or "frosh" women, as they were known around campus—were required to curtsey for upperclassmen upon the command of "curtsey, frosh." As with their male counterparts, frosh women were also required to know, and recite upon command, the names of the director of academic affairs, the campus director, and the university president.

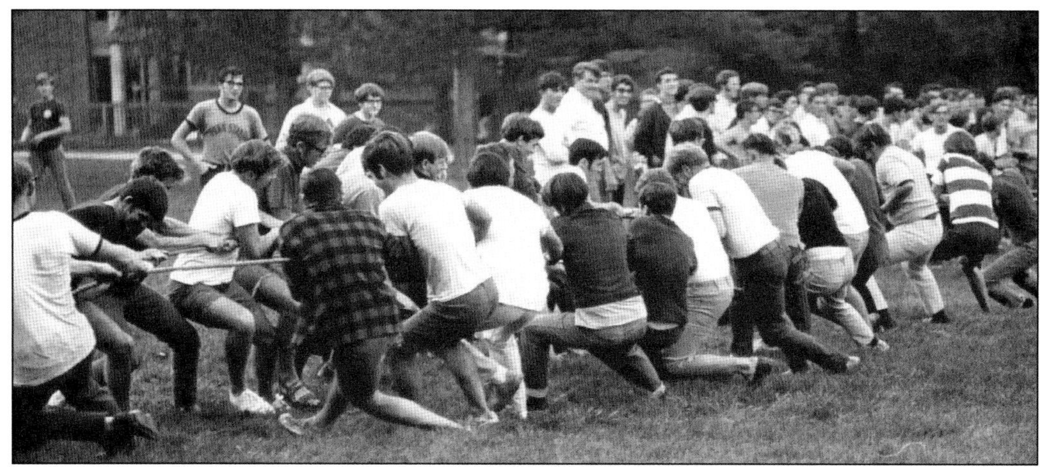

Penn State Altoona's freshmen initiation exercises concluded with a customary tug-of-war match between the incoming freshmen and the sophomores. The match typically ended when the contestants stumbled into the nearby reflecting pond.

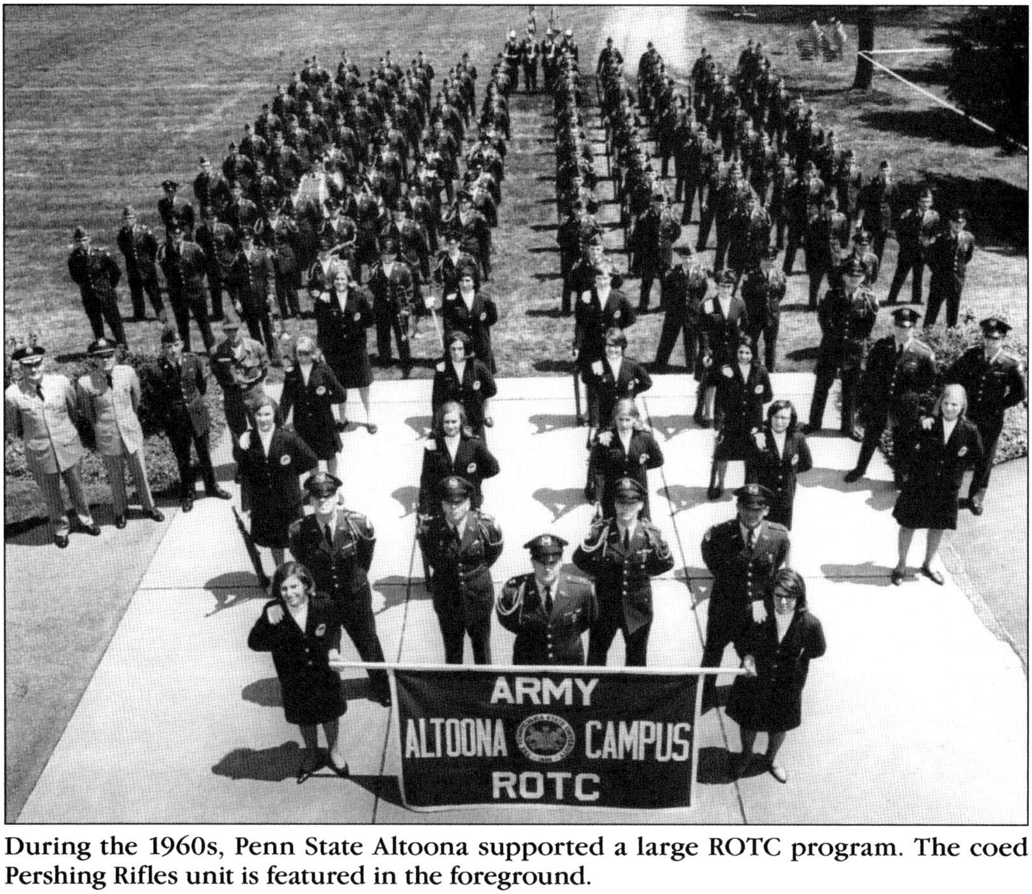

During the 1960s, Penn State Altoona supported a large ROTC program. The coed Pershing Rifles unit is featured in the foreground.

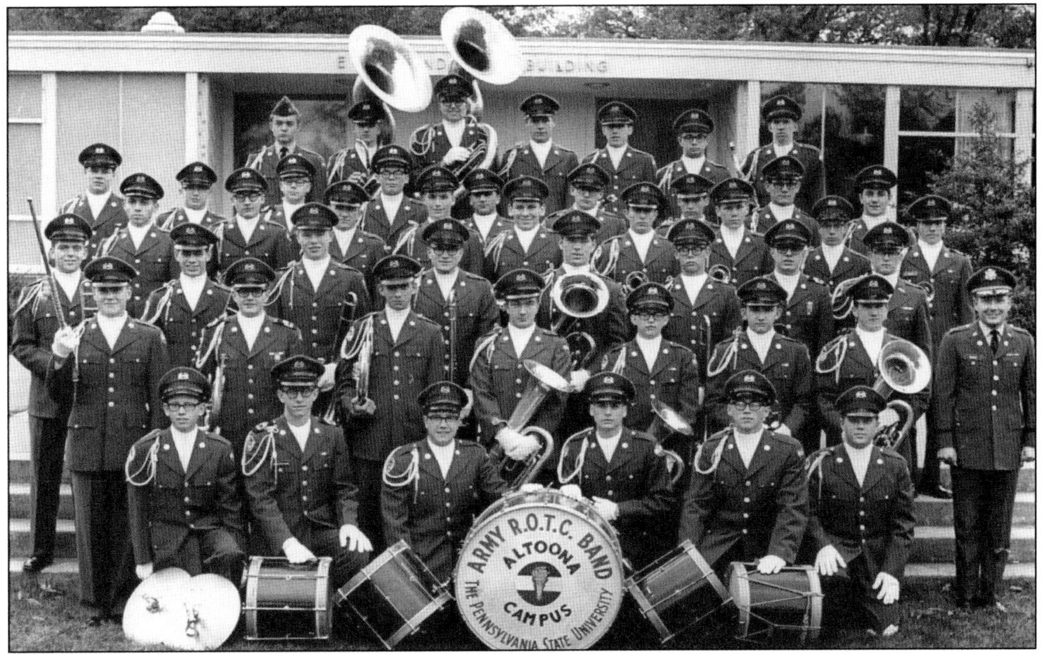

In this 1967 photograph, the campus's military band is pictured in front of the Smith building.

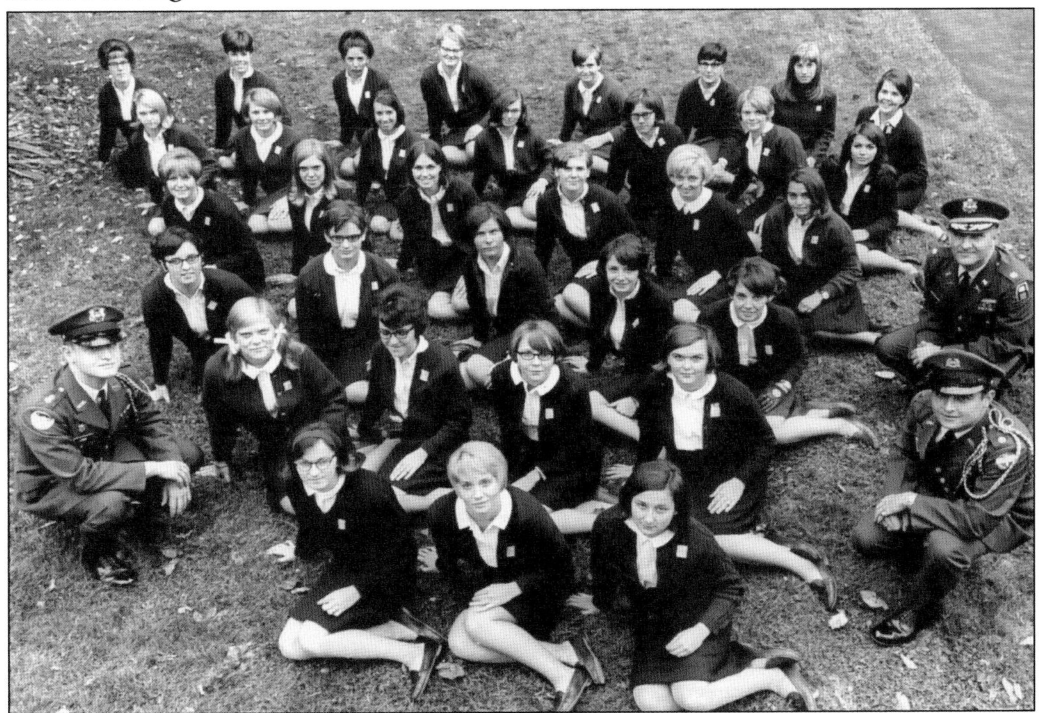

The coed unit of the ROTC's Pershing Rifles known as Capers poses in this 1967 photograph. In April 1967, the group placed third in a national show competition at the University of Maryland. In April 1970, Capers placed fifth in Washington, D.C.'s annual Cherry Blossom Festival.

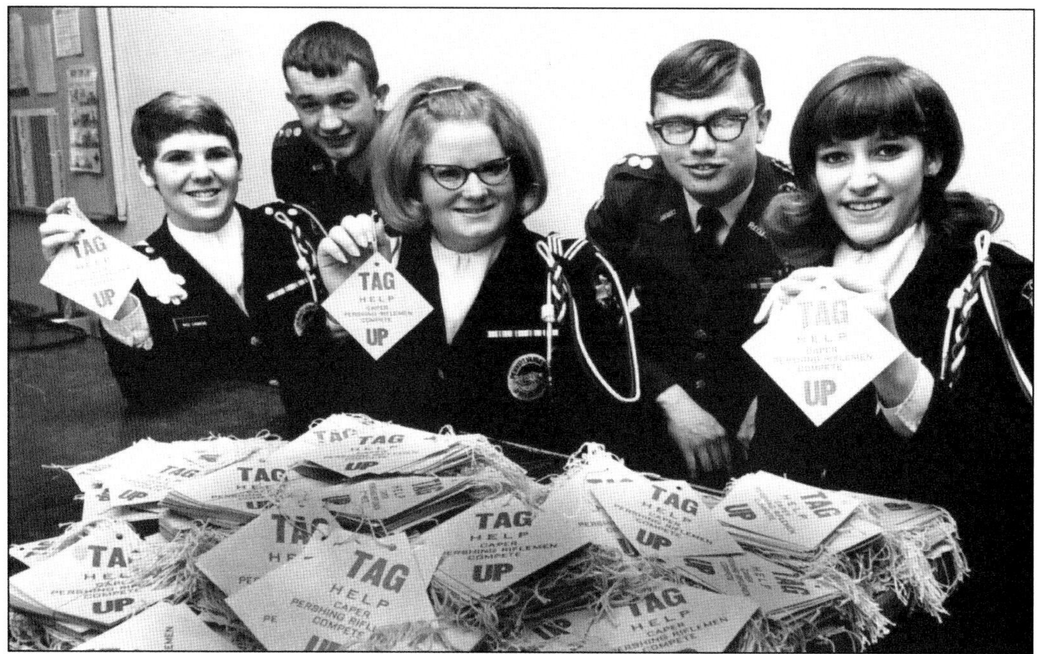

In this 1969 photograph, Capers members participate in their annual "Tag-Up" day in which they raise funds on campus in order to support the expenses associated with their competitions.

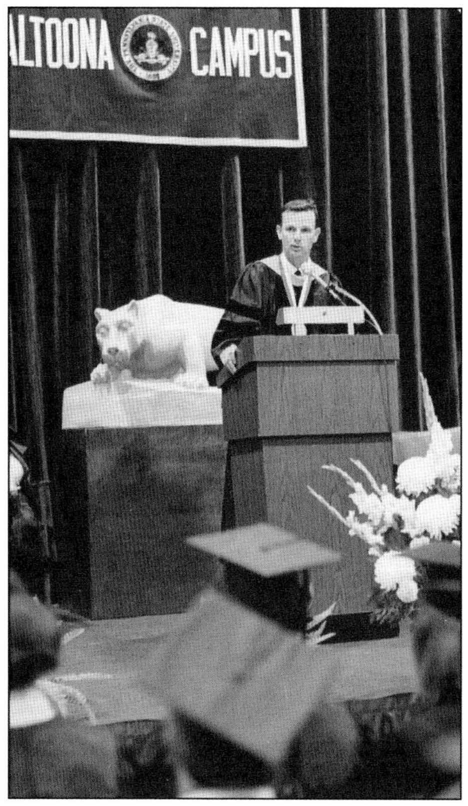

John L. Leathers served as campus director from 1968 to 1975, when he was promoted to the position of administrative director of Penn State University's commonwealth campus system. Having earned his doctorate in higher education at Penn State, his career began in 1957 at Muskingum College in New Concord, Ohio, where he served as dean of men and assistant professor of education and psychology.

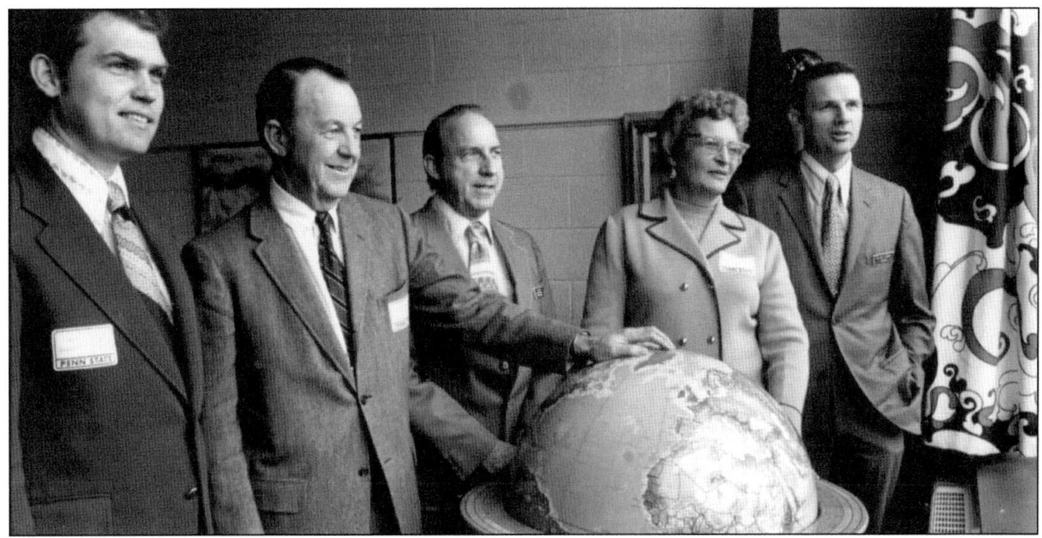

In this photograph, Leathers (far right) is joined by Robert Quinn, the dean of the commonwealth campuses (far left); Jack G. Zubrod, associate director of academic affairs (center); and Martha Mae Schlow, instructor in speech. After Leathers's stint as director at Penn State Altoona, he served in a wide variety of interim capacities for the university. In 2001, he retired from the university as vice president emeritus of the commonwealth education system after 33 years of service.

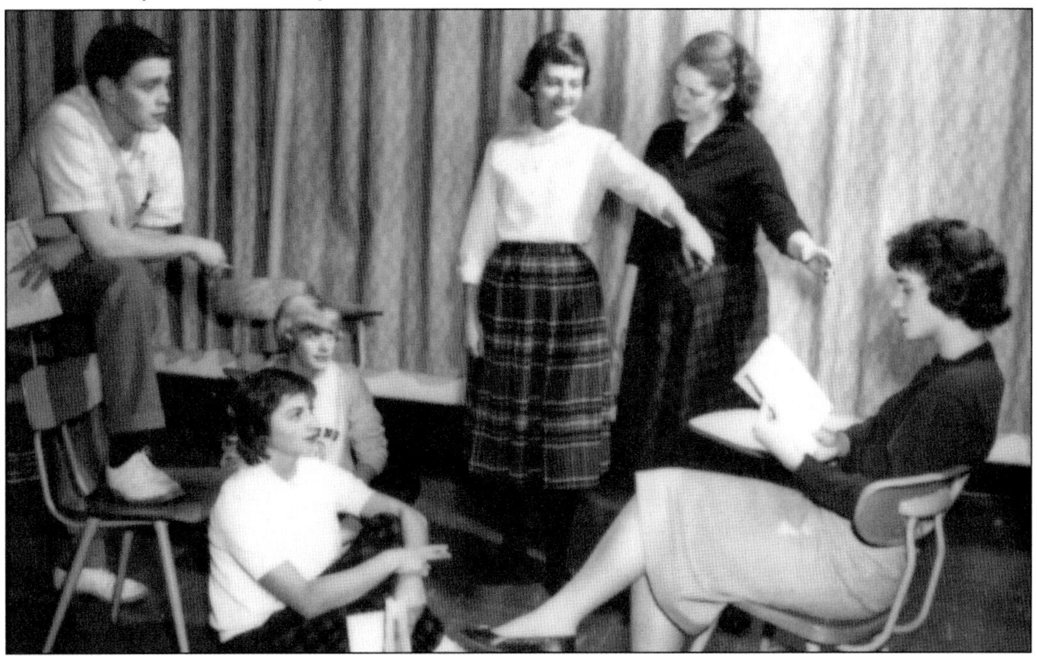

During its heyday, the Ivyside Players served as the student body's official acting troupe. Under the direction of faculty member Joyce Kipp, the group offered regular performances, including a series of one-act plays, in the Harry E. Slep Student Center commons lounge. In the early 1940s, the campus's first theatrical troupe fashioned itself as the Little Theatre (pictured above), holding a series of performances of Emlyn Williams's *Night Must Fall* in the Keith Junior High School auditorium in October 1941.

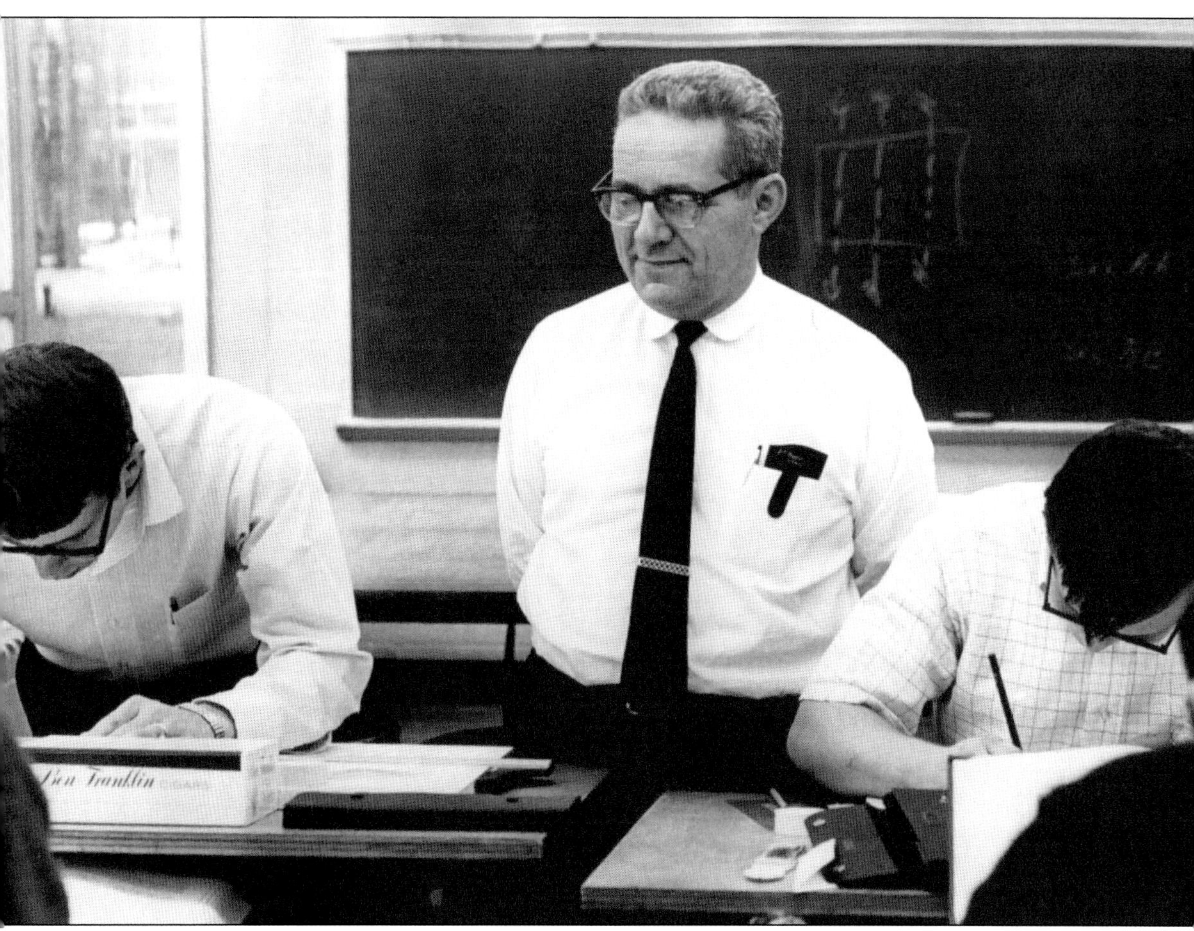

Prof. Ernest Dejaiffe (pictured above) was promoted in 1967 to professor of general engineering. He holds the distinction of being Penn State Altoona's first full professor, as well as the second full professor overall among the nonuniversity park campuses. In subsequent years, Penn State Altoona has promoted 17 additional faculty members to this esteemed academic rank, including Louis D. Goodfellow (psychology, 1968); Lawrence J. Pilione (physics, 1988); Nicholas M. Miskovsky (physics, 1994); Lori J. Bechtel (biobehavioral health, 1997); James A. Winsor (biology, 1997); William Balch (psychology, 1999); Indrani Basak (statistics, 1999); John E. Lennox (microbiology, 1999); Michael W. Wolfe (history, 1999); Mary D. Menachery (chemistry, 2001); Ian Marshall (English and environmental studies, 2000); Dinty W. Moore (English and integrative arts, 2000); Michael Gannon (biology, 2005); Hossein Movahedi-Lankarani (mathematics, 2005); Kenneth Womack (English, 2006); Sandra Harbert Petrulionis (English and American studies, 2007); and Brian Black (history and environmental studies, 2009).

Three

Ivyside Renaissance

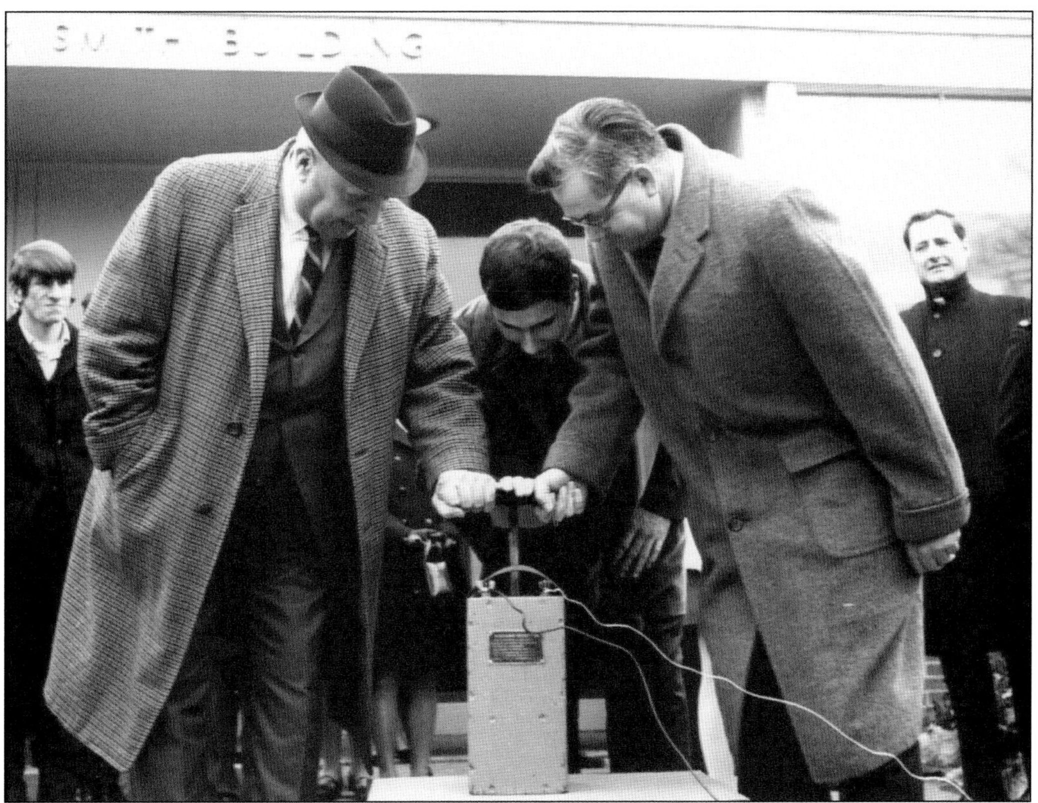

A new era in the history of Penn State Altoona was inaugurated on January 17, 1969, when Penn State University president Eric A. Walker held a unique groundbreaking ceremony in front of the Smith building for the new science complex and the library learning center. Set up by members of the physics faculty, a light laser was used to activate a sensitized element that in turn caused the simultaneous detonation of explosives at each of the groundbreaking sites.

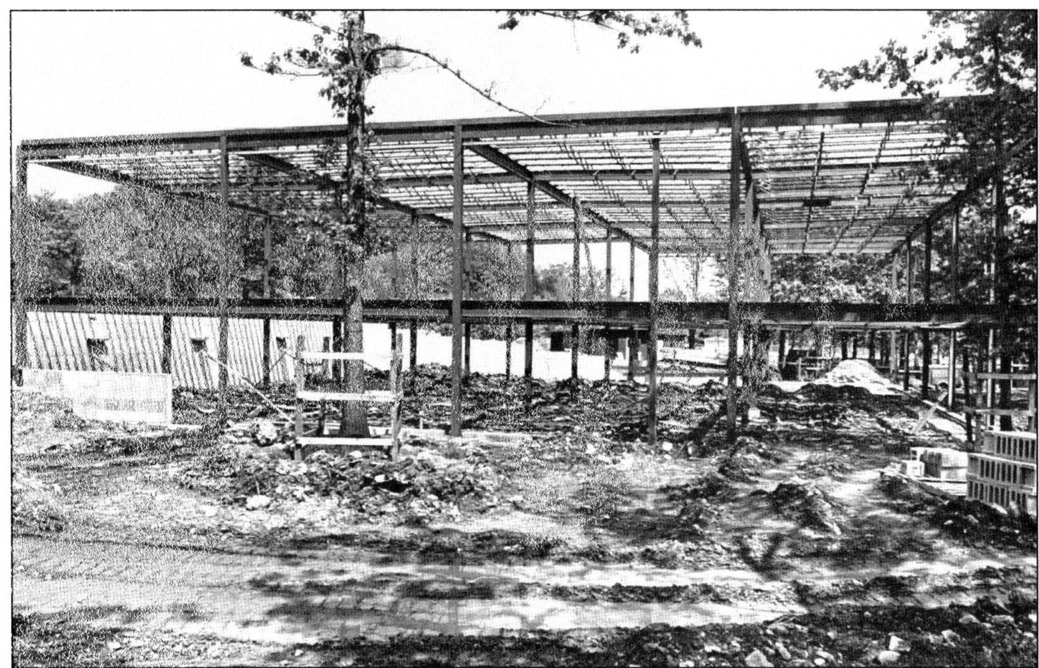

To fund the library and science complex's construction, more than 4,000 local donors pledged $1.1 million in capital gifts, which the university supplemented with internal loans.

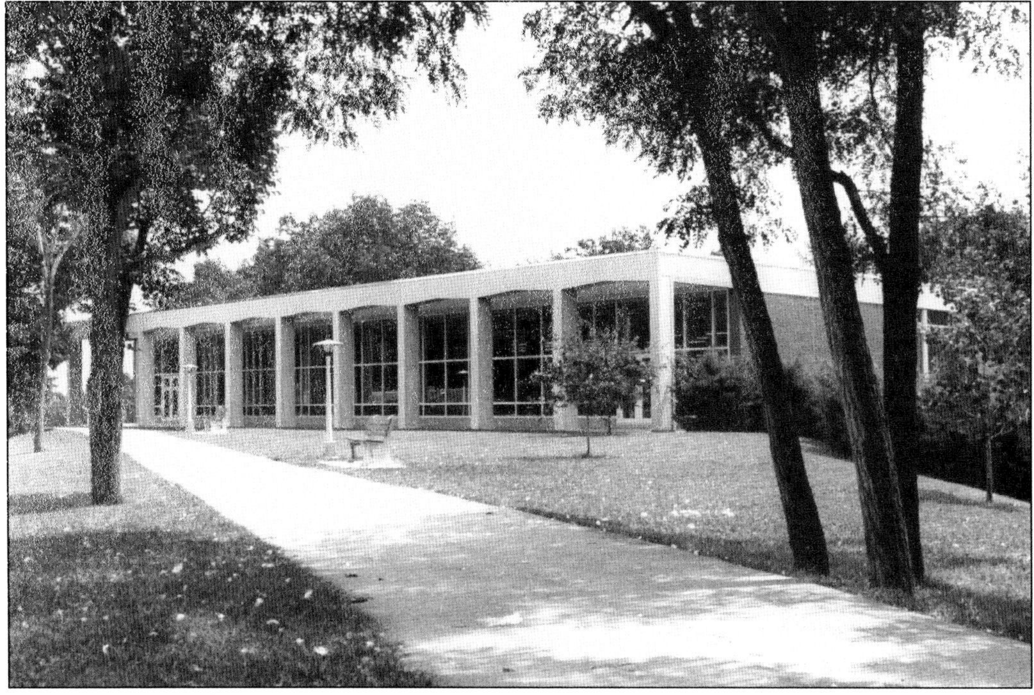

Completed in 1969, the Robert E. Eiche Library houses a collection that contains some 90,000 books and over 300 magazines and newspapers. The library is named in honor of Robert E. Eiche, Penn State Altoona's inaugural director.

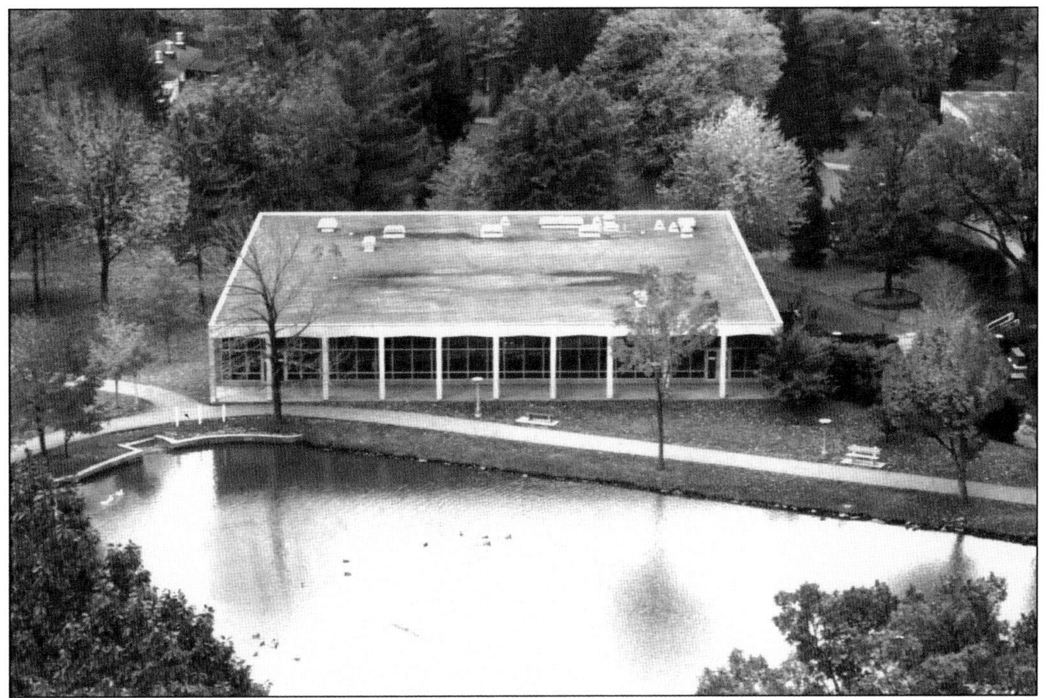

In this 1969 photograph of the Robert E. Eiche Library, the reflecting pond sits in the foreground. A 2006 renovation increased the library's study spaces considerably, including adjoining new facilities for the college's learning resources center and the addition of the Timothy L. Wherry and Lori J. Bechtel-Wherry Study, which is named for their philanthropy.

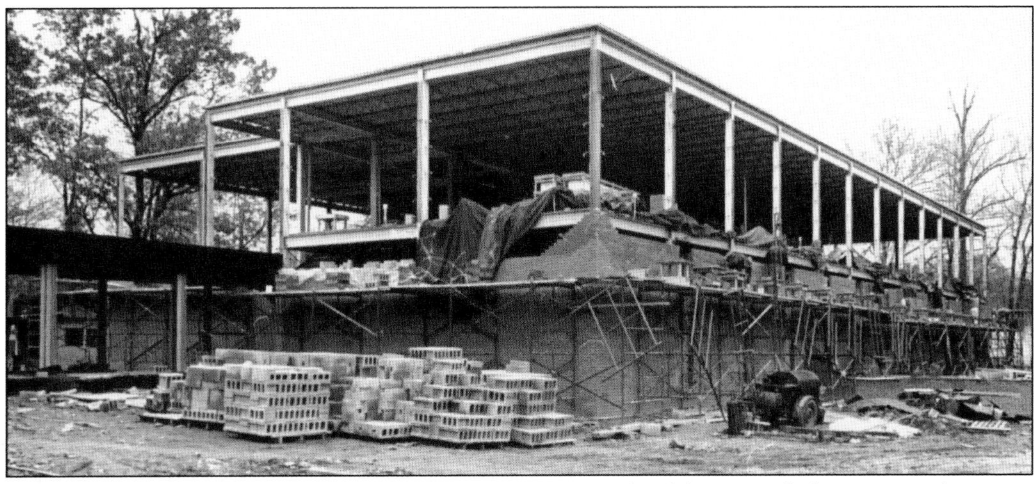

Together, the Robert E. Eiche Library, the science building, and the J. E. Holtzinger building accrued construction costs of $6.4 million.

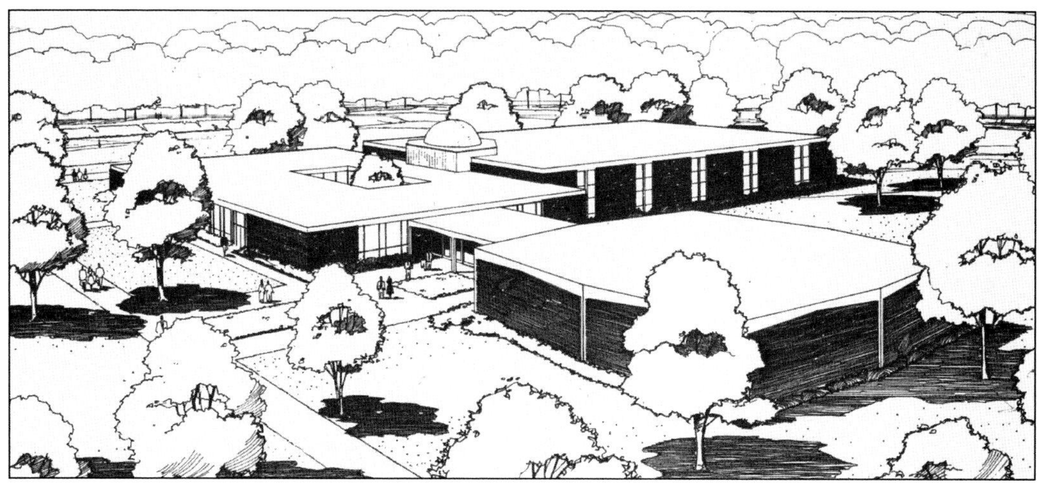

Completed in 1969, the science building features three chemistry laboratories (including one organic and two inorganic laboratories) as well as a 120-seat lecture hall. The facility is connected to the J. E. Holtzinger building.

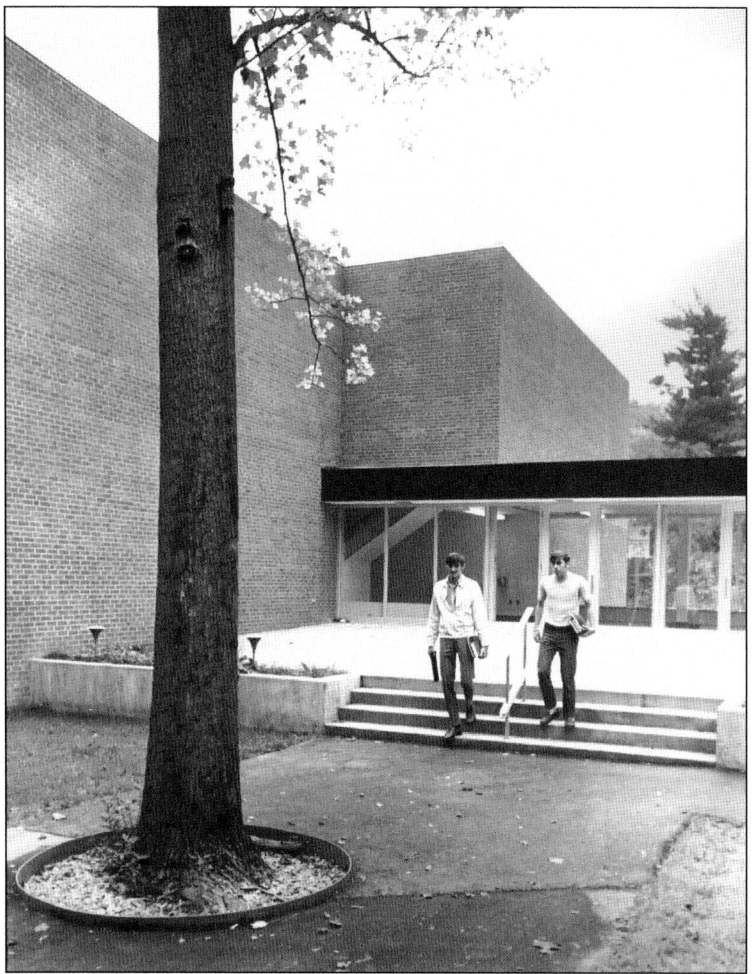

Named in honor of one of the principal forces behind the founding of the college, the two-story J. E. Holtzinger building features three engineering graphics laboratories, two physics laboratories, two biology laboratories, and a greenhouse. In 1996, the Ralph and Helen Force Advanced Technology Center was constructed on the eastern end of the building.

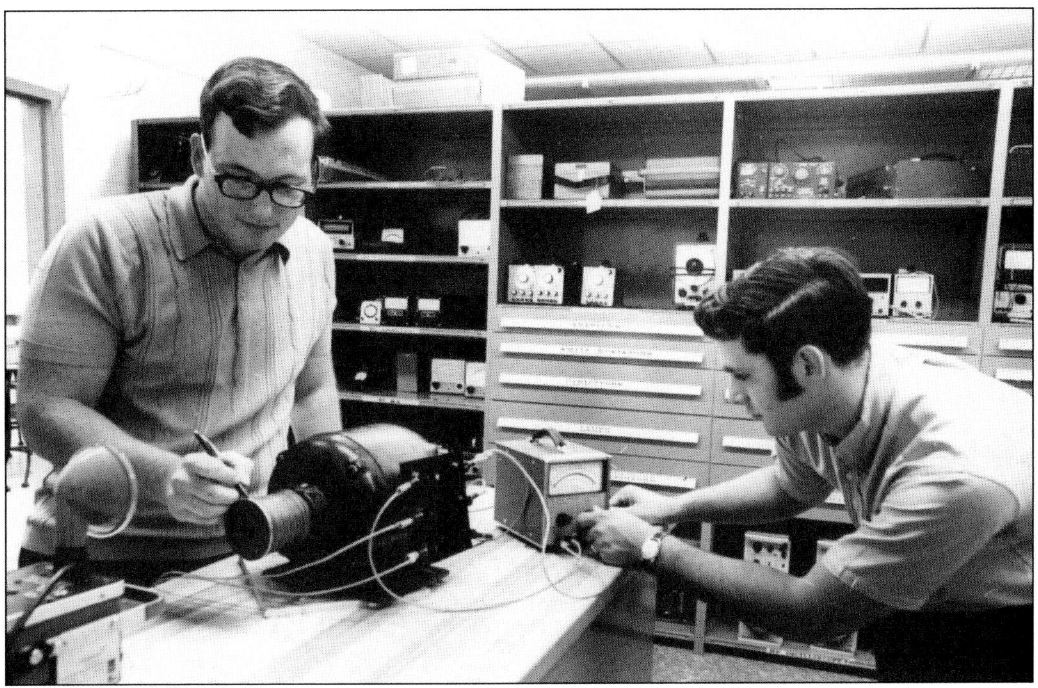

In this August 1970 photograph, students work in an electronics laboratory in the J. E. Holtzinger building.

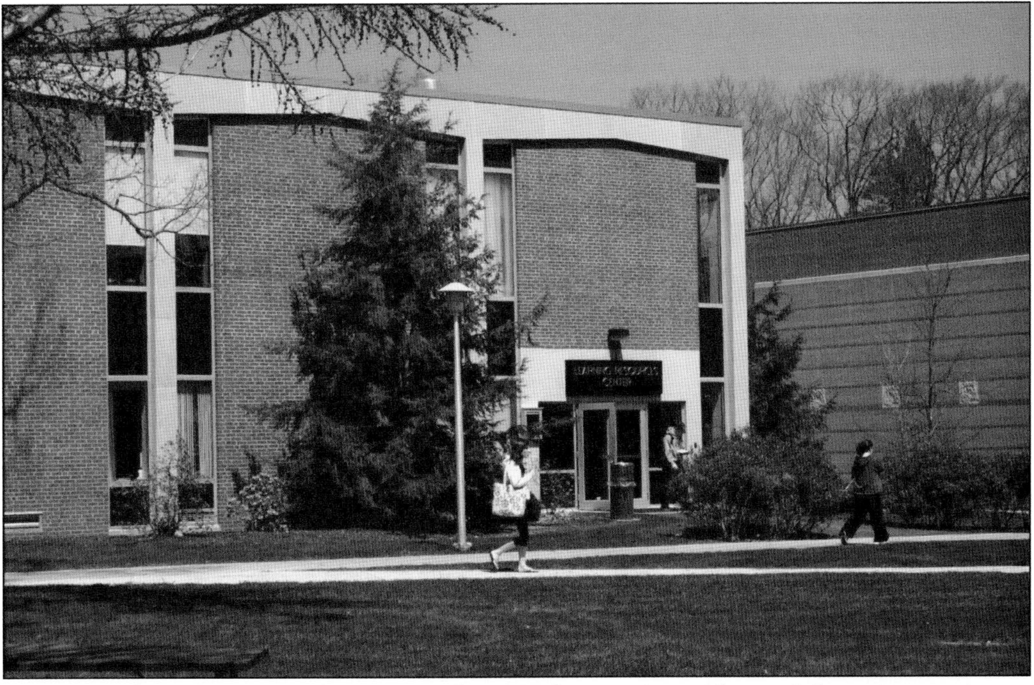

Built in 1969 and extensively renovated in 2006, Penn State Altoona's learning resources center provides students with a host of tutoring and study resources. Under the direction of Paula Ford, the learning resources center also serves as the home for the college's internship and study abroad offices.

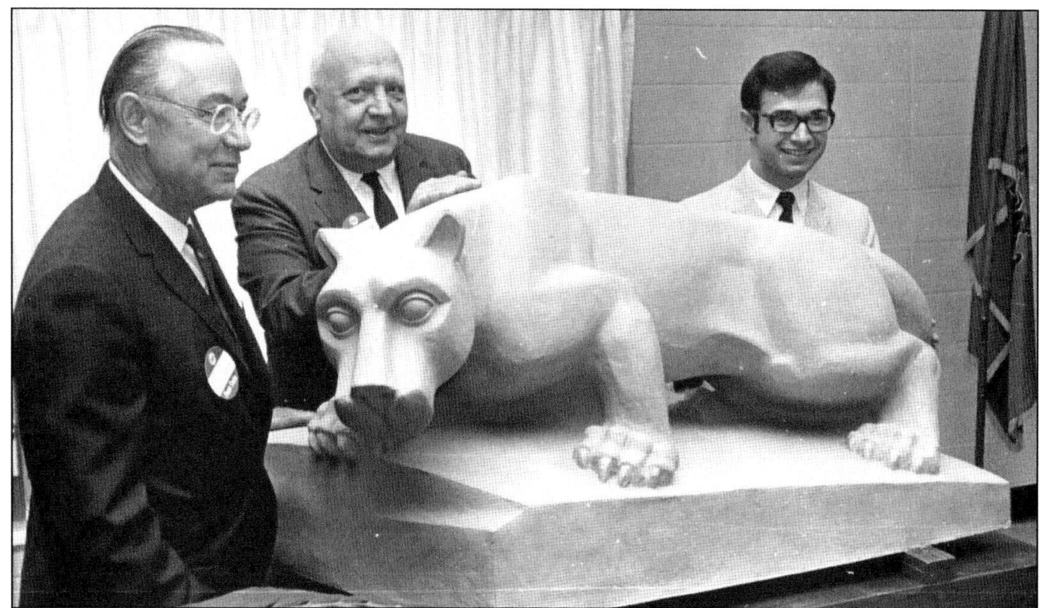

In April 1969, Penn State Altoona became the first commonwealth campus to receive a replica of the Nittany Lion Shrine. The dedication was held in the alumni lounge of the student commons. From left to right are Eric A. Walker, Penn State University president; J. E. "Ted" Holtzinger, advisory board chairman; and Penn State Altoona Student Government Association president Gary Discavage.

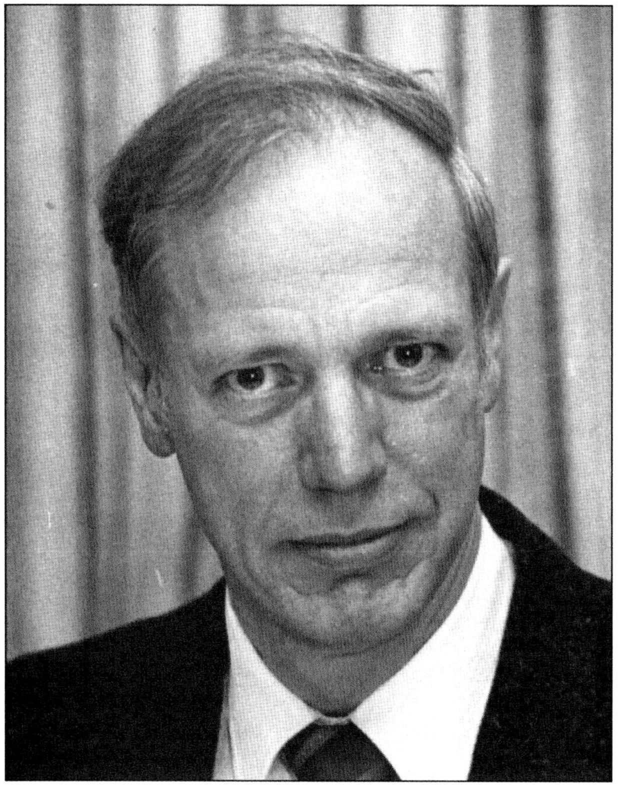

Joining the faculty in 1969, Donald E. Fahnline was one of the campus's most steadfast citizens. Over the years, he served in a variety of capacities, doing yeomen's service for the Altoona College faculty senate as well as on behalf of the university faculty senate. Having earned the rank of associate professor of physics during his tenure, he taught for two years in Africa before completing his doctorate at Penn State University. Fahnline retired in 2006.

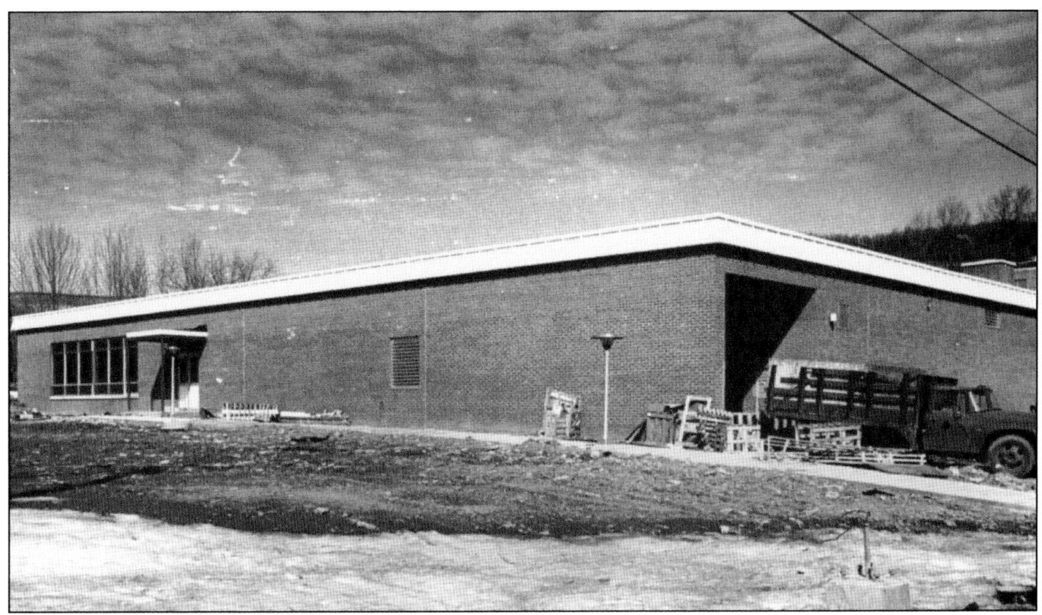

The campus dining facility, the Hickory Court Café and food services building, was bankrolled using university-backed loans accrued during the construction of the Robert E. Eiche Library, the science building, and the J. E. Holtzinger Building.

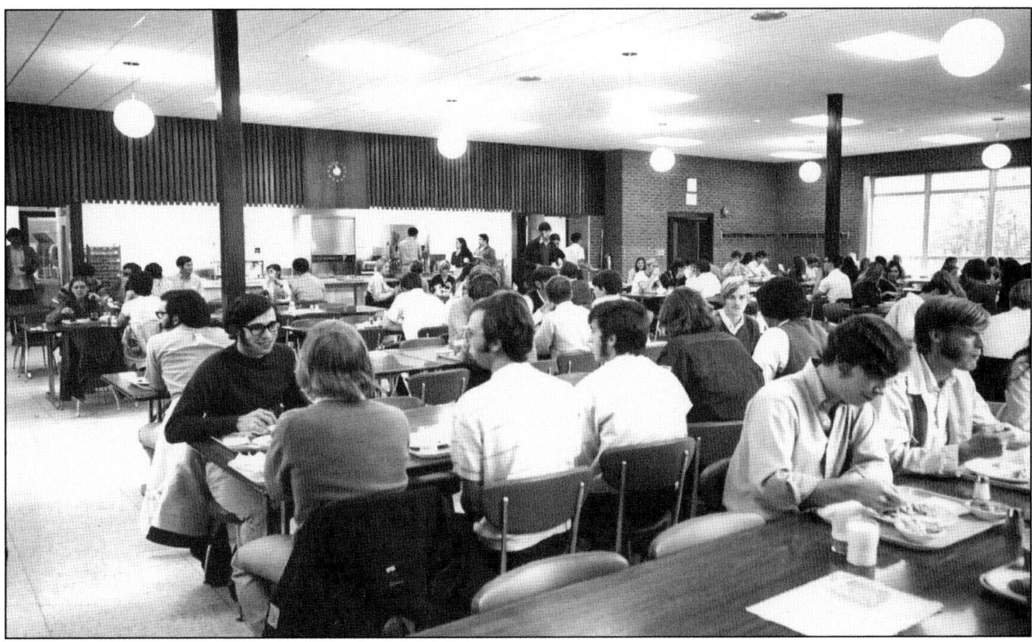

In 1970, the Hickory Court Café opened on campus, affording Penn State Altoona its first stand-alone dining hall.

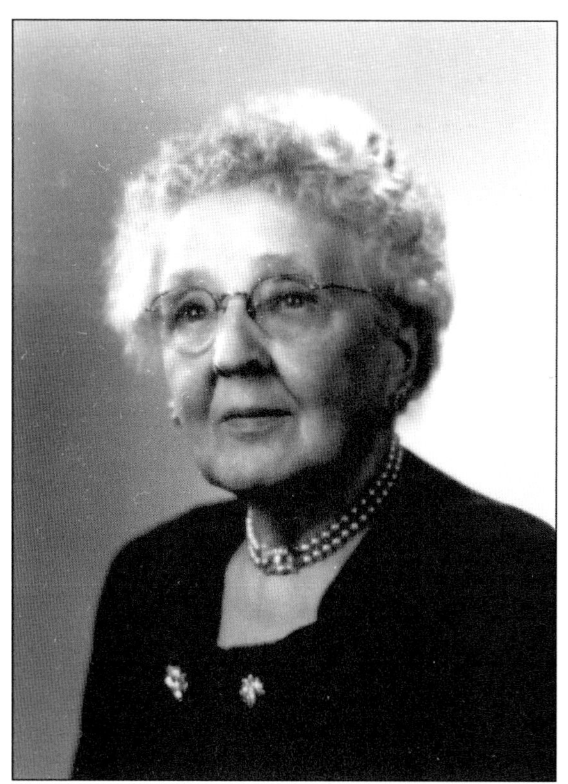

Altoona native Edith Davis Eve graduated from the Philadelphia School of Design, later attending a kindergarten training academy in Michigan. In 1908, she married Oswell B. Eve, and the couple moved to Augusta, Georgia, where she taught kindergarten for three decades. After her retirement in 1939, Eve returned to her hometown, where she developed a fondness for the Altoona campus. The Edith Davis Eve Memorial Chapel offers a legacy regarding her dedication to education and her desire to transform her community through learning.

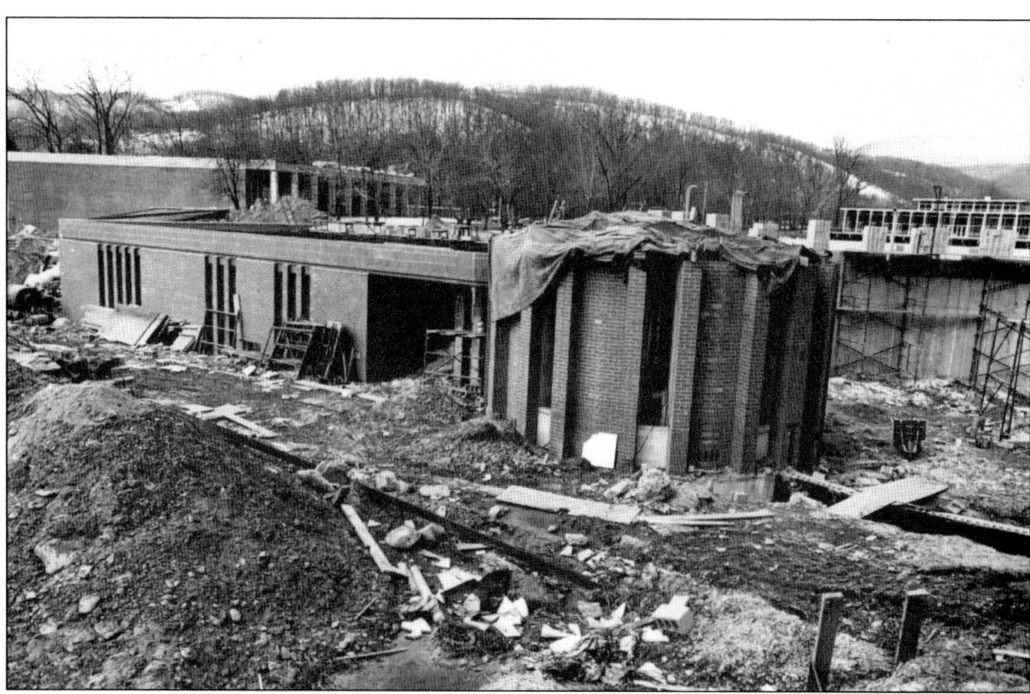

The Edith Davis Eve Memorial Chapel was funded with a $125,000 matching gift from Edith Davis Eve that the advisory board received for the construction of an all-faiths chapel.

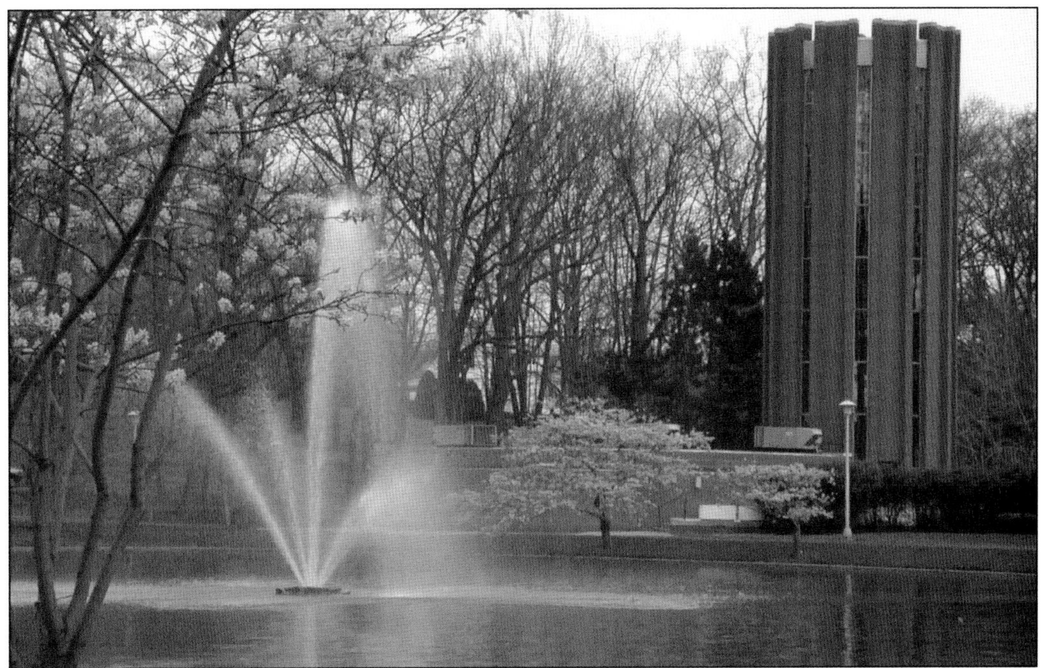

Completed in 1970, Penn State Altoona's all-faiths chapel is managed and operated by the office of student life. In addition to a sanctuary and an all-faiths altar, the chapel features an organ, piano, and choir loft. The Meling Fountain, commemorating the life and work of Associate Dean Kjell Meling, sits in the foreground.

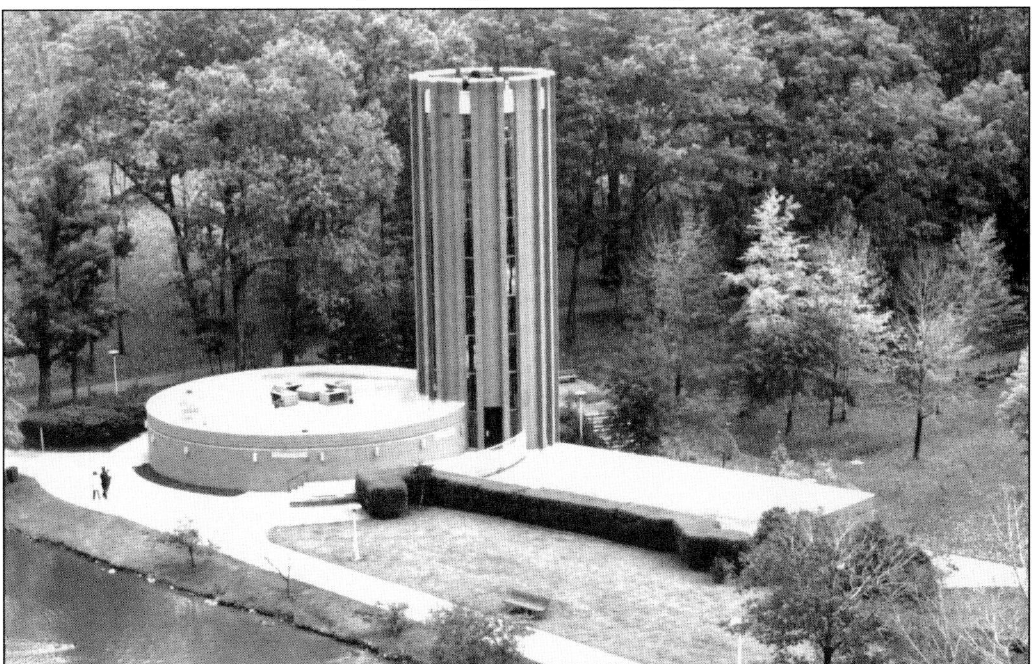

The chapel's 65-foot tower was begun during the building's final stages of construction. The tower, complete with stained-glass windows, contains a 50-bell carillon, whose musical accompaniment has become an integral aspect of campus daily life.

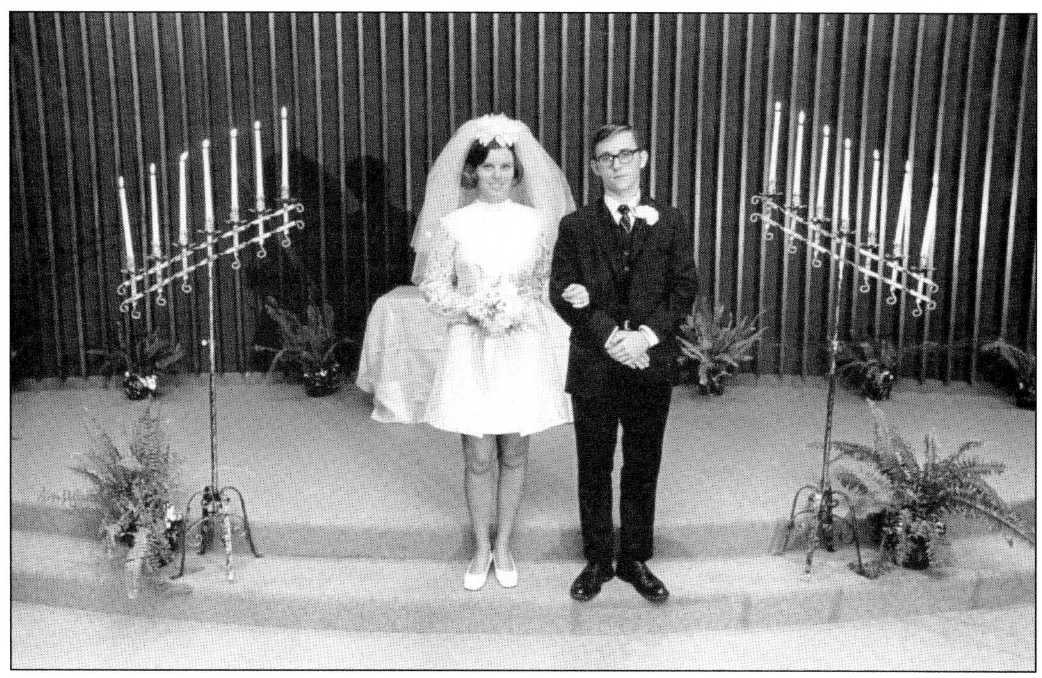

The inaugural wedding ceremony was held in the chapel in December 1970, when Robert D. Helsel and Betty R. Brown were married. In the ensuing years, the chapel has become a popular wedding site among the local citizenry.

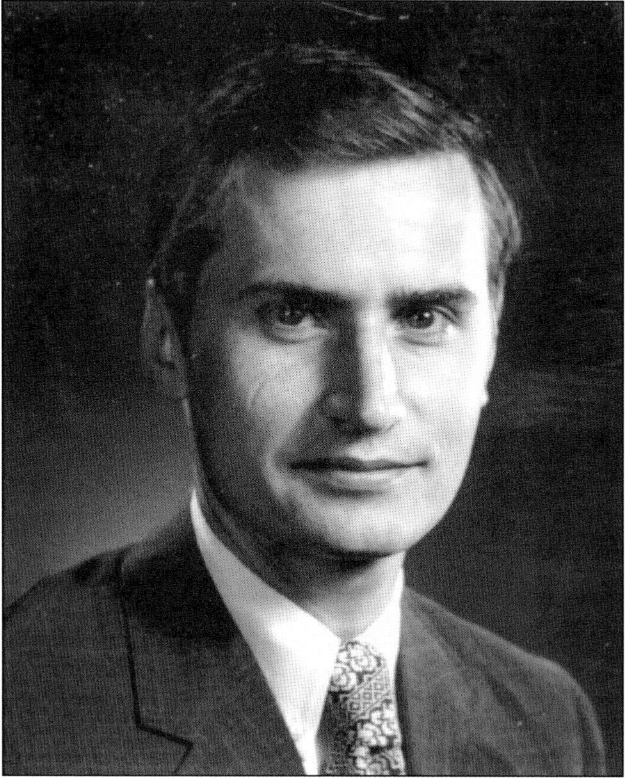

A 1970 doctoral graduate of Penn State University, Nicholas M. Miskovsky is an expert in solid-state physics. He has published numerous articles in his discipline over the years, while also earning grants from the prestigious National Science Foundation, among other agencies. Having joined the Penn State Altoona faculty in 1970, Miskovsky earned the rank of professor of physics in 1994. Beginning in 2000, Miskovsky served as head of the Division of Mathematics and Natural Sciences for nine years, a period in which the division achieved remarkable growth in terms of generating research dollars, as well as adding new faculty and degree programs. Miskovsky retired in 2009 after 39 years of distinguished service.

From 1970 until his retirement in December 2008, William D. "Denny" Stewart served as assistant dean of student affairs before settling into a distinguished career as senior director of business operations. Under Stewart's leadership, the college brought numerous facilities and renovation projects to fruition. In June 2008, the college dedicated the Stewart Athletic Field in honor of Denny and his wife Dianne Stewart's philanthropy.

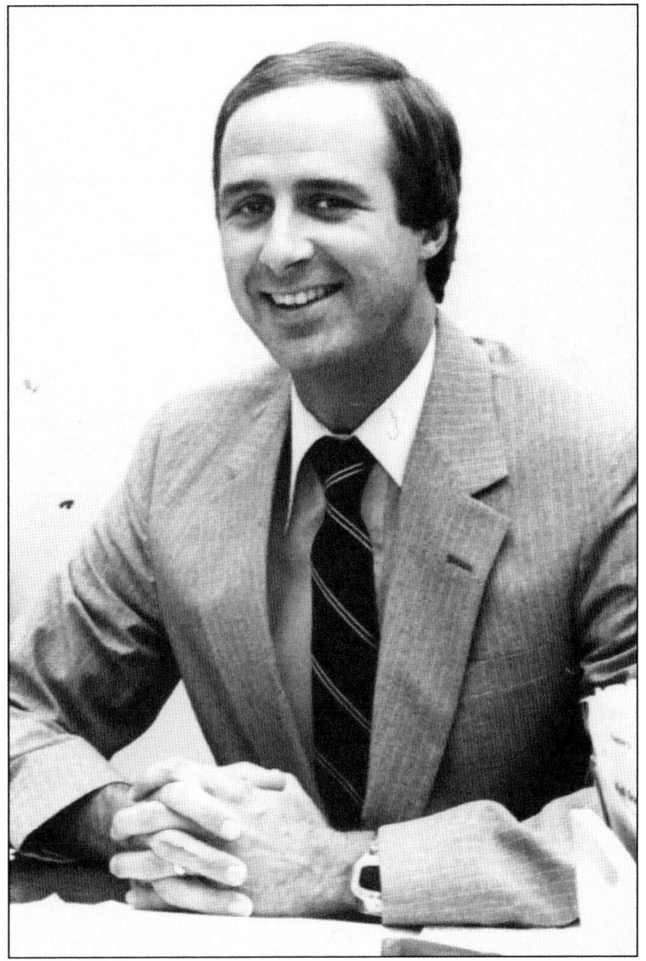

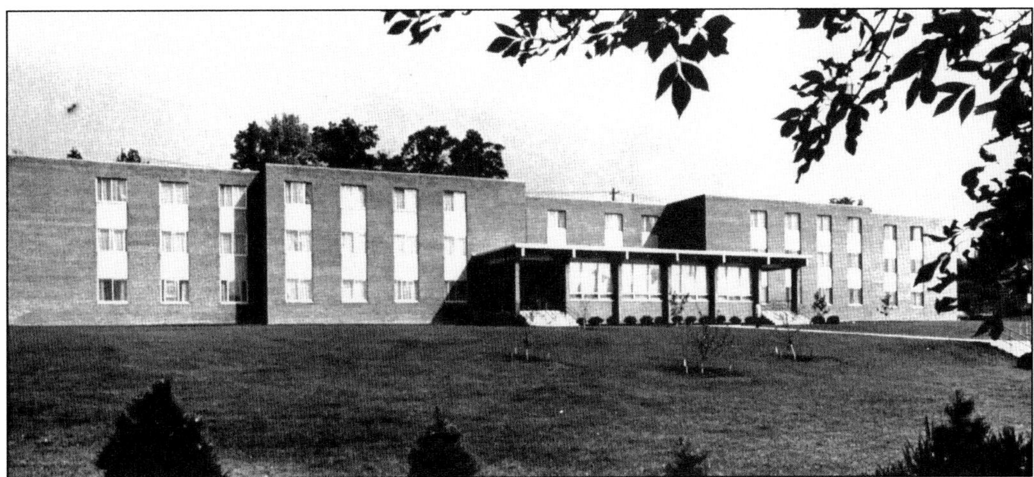

First occupied during the fall 1970 semester, Maple Residence Hall was originally known as West Hall. The dormitory houses some 214 students in traditional-style rooms. As with Oak Residence Hall, Maple's residents are arranged coeducationally by wing.

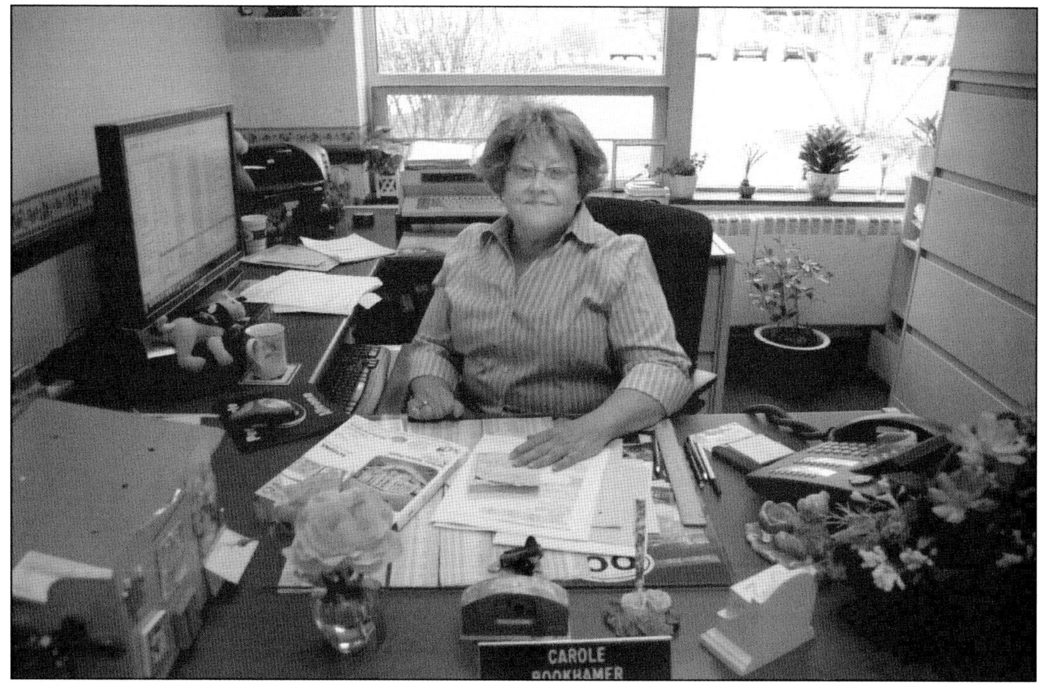

Hired by campus business manager Bob Smith in 1970, Carole A. Bookhamer has been a mainstay at Penn State Altoona for nearly four decades. She has worked the college's switchboard and, for the past 20 years, has been an esteemed faculty administrative assistant. In 2000, Bookhamer was awarded the Ted J. Long Staff Excellence Award. In 2006, she earned an associate's degree in letters, arts, and sciences.

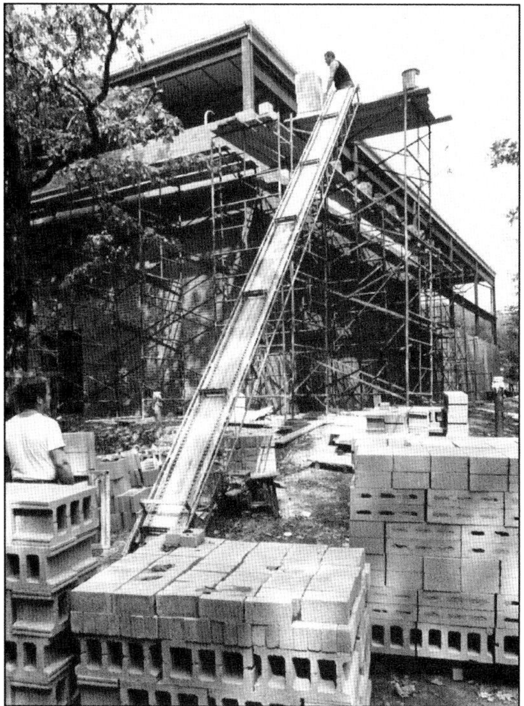

Completed in 1970, the Steven A. Adler Athletic Complex features a large gymnasium with a 700-seat grandstand. In addition to faculty and coaches' offices, the building houses facilities for intramurals and recreational sports, the office of intercollegiate athletics, and Army ROTC.

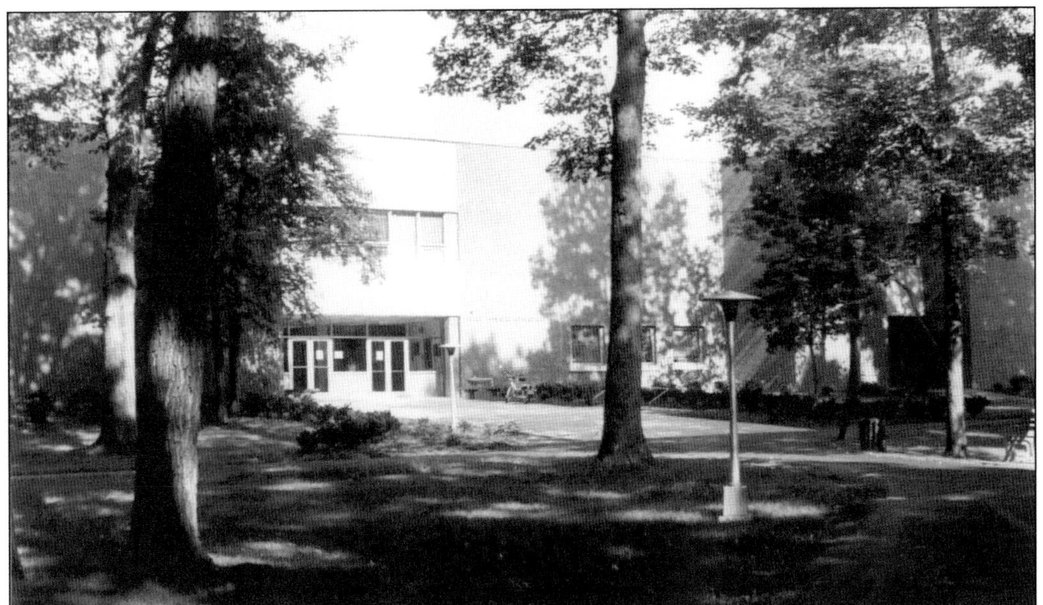

An extensive renovation, completed in 1977, supplemented the indoor facilities at the complex, which include an National Collegiate Athletics Association (NCAA) competitive indoor swimming pool, racquetball courts, a fitness loft, and locker rooms. The outdoor athletic facilities include tennis courts, basketball courts, sand volleyball courts, a baseball field, and an all-purpose athletic field.

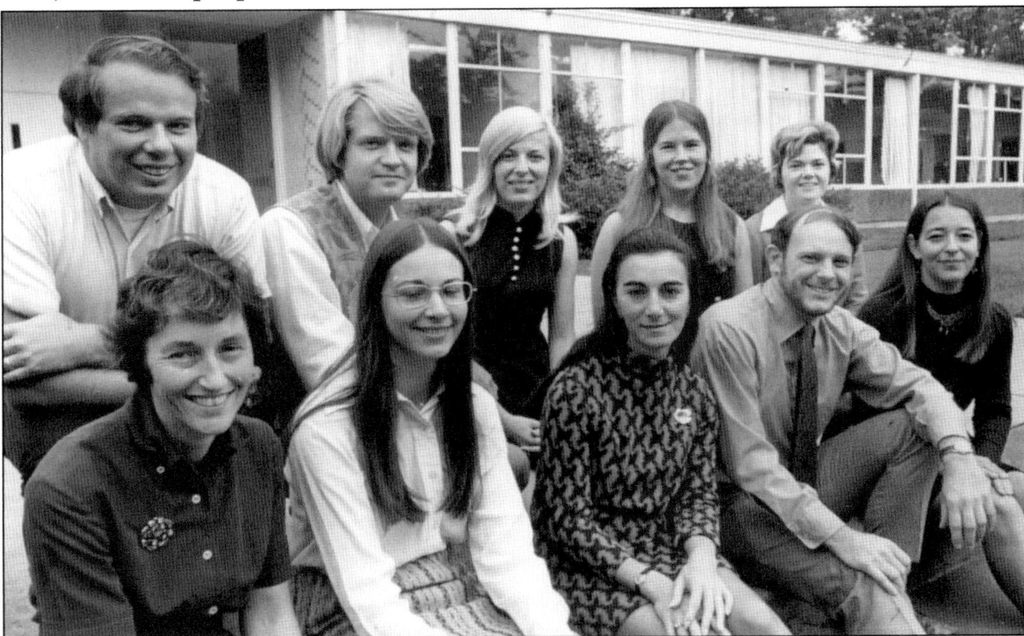

In this fall 1971 photograph, new faculty members pose in front of the Smith building: from left to right, (first row) Athleen J. Stere (biology), Valerie Stratton (psychology), Concetta Miller (psychology), John Lennox (microbiology), and Judy Katz (English); (second row) Robert Larkin (environmental sciences), Roger Zellner (visual arts), Cynthia Mable (statistics), Claudia Geyer (kinesiology), and an unidentified instructor.

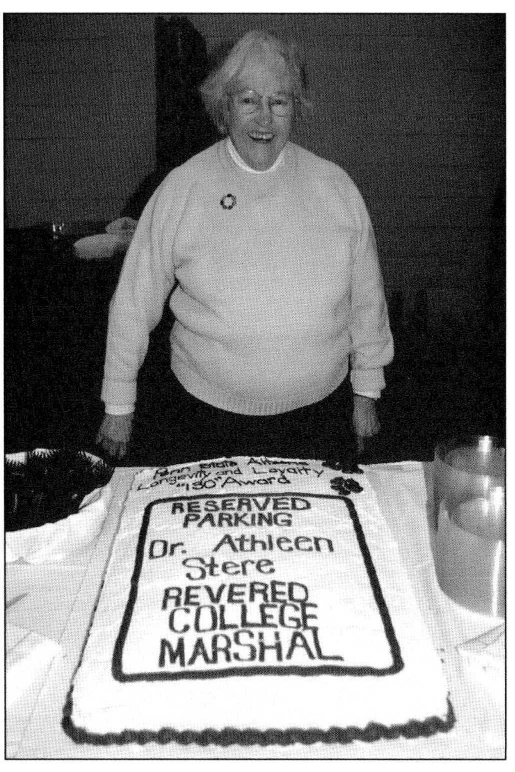

Penn State Altoona's revered college marshal Athleen J. Stere was the first woman to hold a teaching fellowship at Harvard University. Having completed her doctorate at Penn State, Stere joined the university in 1963 and accepted an appointment in 1971 at Penn State Altoona, eventually rising to the rank of associate professor of biology. Stere's contributions are honored annually with the Athleen J. Stere Teaching Award. In 2006, her colleagues endowed a $50,000 Trustee Matching Scholarship in her name. In 2009, she earned the Longevity and Loyalty Award, which afforded her a reserved parking space for life.

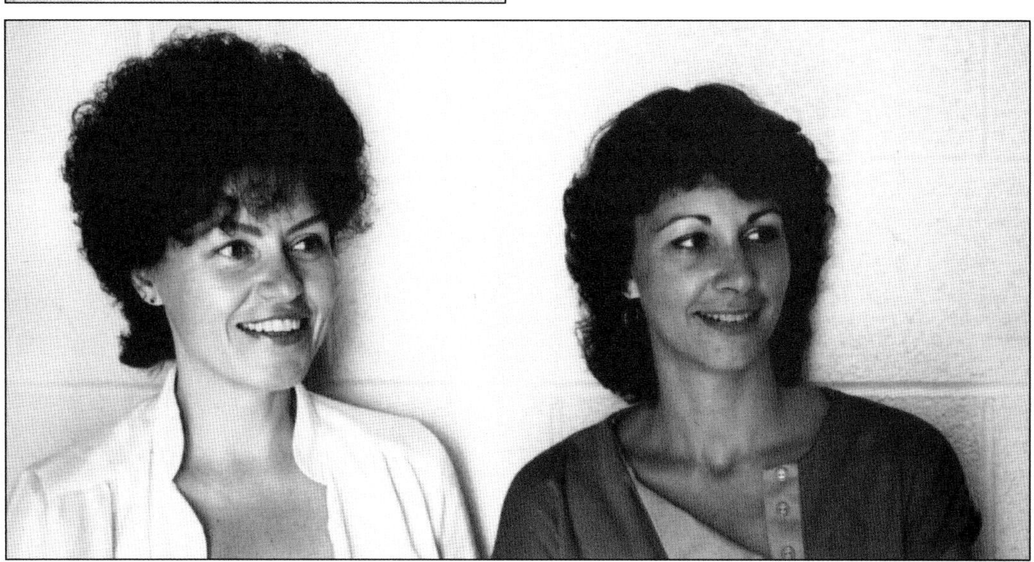

A 37-year veteran professor and administrator, Valerie Stratton (pictured above, right) joined the faculty in 1971, eventually achieving the rank of associate professor of psychology. With Annette N. Zalanowski (pictured above, left), associate professor of music, Stratton published numerous articles devoted to investigating the impact of music on human emotions and moods. Stratton served as the inaugural coordinator of the psychology program, chair of the faculty senate, and head of the Division of Education, Human Development, and Social Sciences. Retiring in 2008, Stratton established the Valerie Newby Stratton Trustee Scholarship.

A vital early player in establishing a women's studies curriculum at Penn State Altoona, Jo C. Searles earned her doctorate from Penn State University in 1971, joining the faculty during the fall 1974 semester. Having risen to the rank of associate professor of English and women's studies, Searles retired from Penn State Altoona in 1993. The following year, Searles was honored with the Marion von Rosenstiel Service Award from the Pennsylvania College English Association.

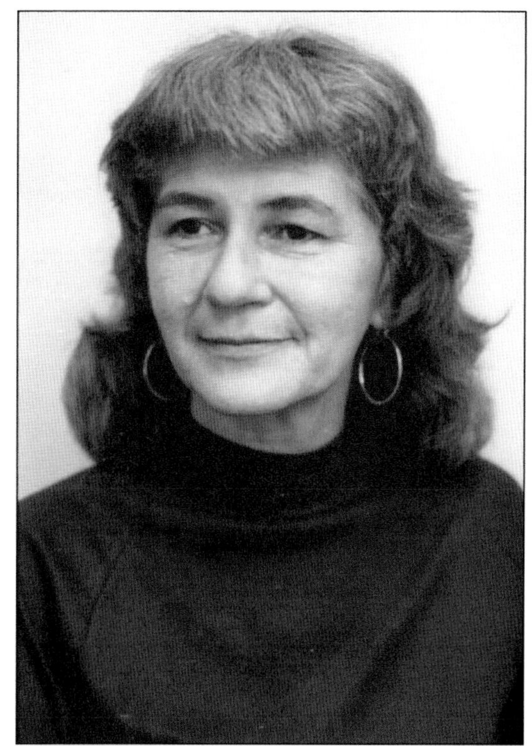

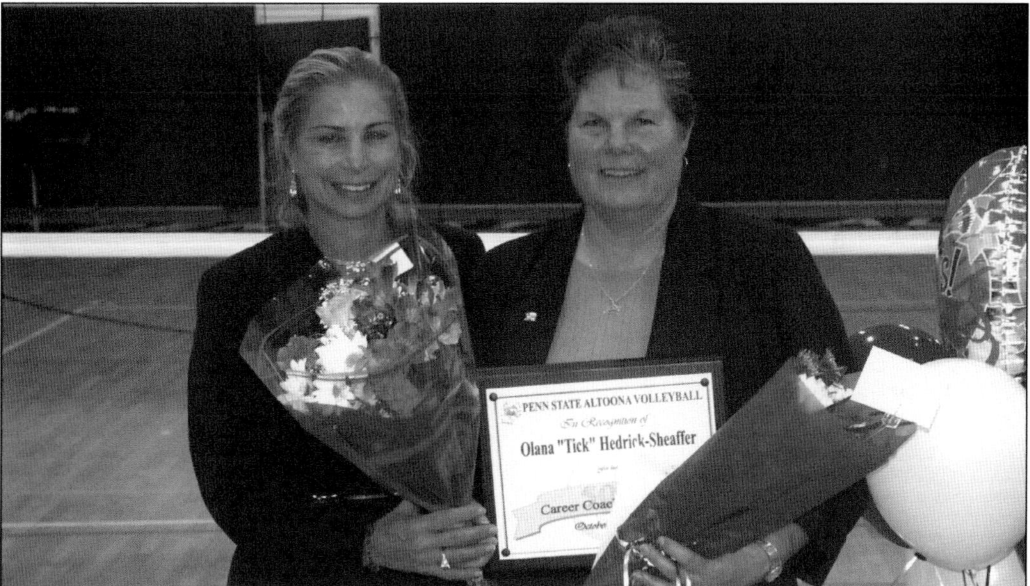

Olana "Tick" Hedrick-Sheaffer distinguished herself as one of the college's most enthusiastic citizens. During her volleyball coaching career, which began in 1973, Hedrick-Sheaffer earned eight State Junior College Championships, 13 Commonwealth Campus titles, and eight Western Pennsylvania Conference titles. Hedrick-Sheaffer earned Coach of the Year honors 11 times and posted 497 victories with a .748 winning percentage. Having retired in 2003, she created an endowed enhancement fund to benefit women's athletics. Pictured are Hedrick-Sheaffer (right) and athletic director Fredina M. Ingold (left).

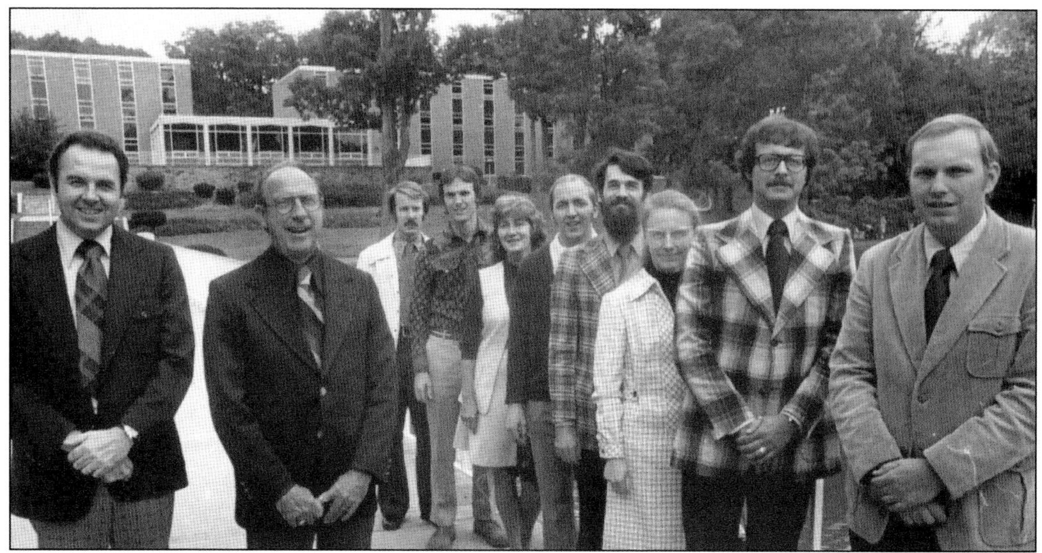

In this fall 1974 photograph, new faculty members pose in front of Oak Residence Hall. Pictured are, from left to right, Dennis Murray, assistant director of academic affairs; Jack G. Zubrod, director of academic affairs; Steven W. Stace (music); Frank T. Koe (engineering); Jo C. Searles (English); Garry L. Burkle (meteorology); David M. Myer (physics); Ruth Hollinger (physics); Fred Bates (sociology); and Carl A. Hultman (chemistry).

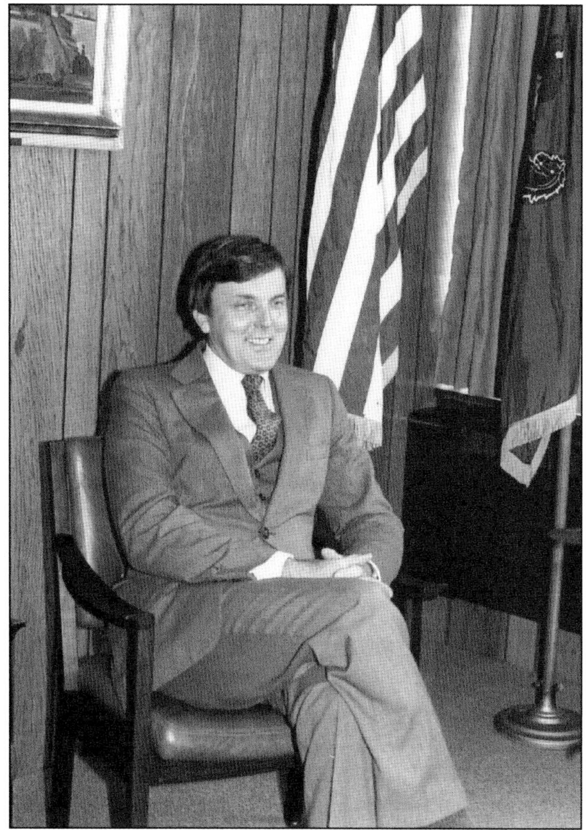

Carson Veach served as campus director from 1975 to 1983. A native of Poughkeepsie, New York, Veach was a Woodrow Wilson Fellow at Harvard before earning his doctorate at Indiana University. After leaving Penn State Altoona, Veach served as dean of the graduate school and continuing education at Bridgewater State College and later as vice president and provost for academic affairs at Chicago State University. Veach retired from academic life in 2004.

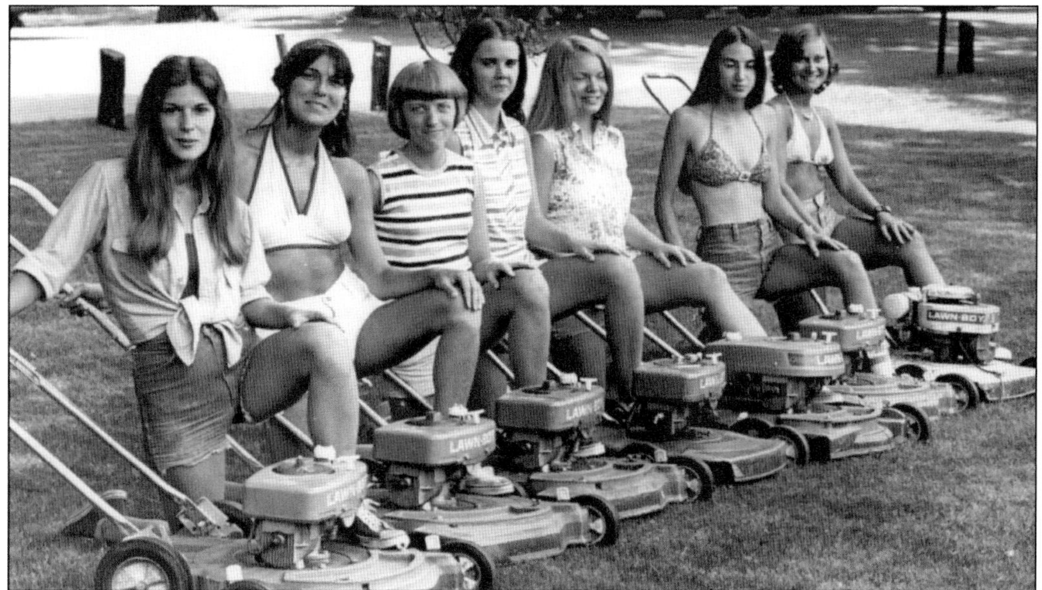

During the summer of 1975, the Tender Lawn Care Corps worked under the direction of Bill Stahl's maintenance and operations department at the campus, which included some 94 acres in the 1970s. The female grounds crew was part of a summer work-study program that involved 50 college students and was administered by the office of student affairs. Pictured are, from left to right, Elaine Boal of Tyrone, Mona Gullo, Monica Zeak, Peggy Smith, Patricia Breslin, and Joanne Gill (all of Altoona), and Jackie Kennedy of Martinsburg.

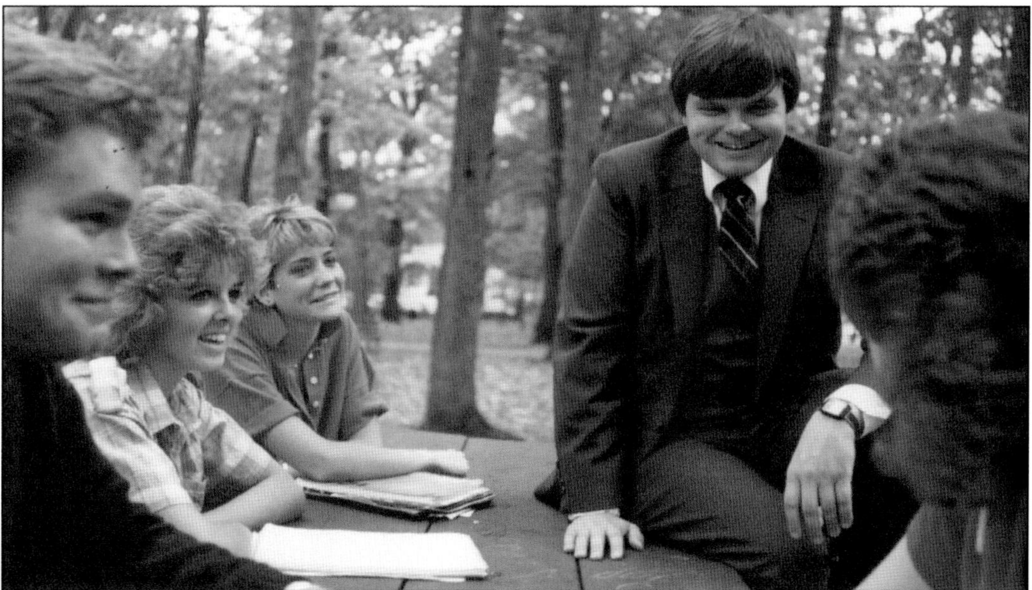

William G. Engelbret served as the college's inaugural head of the Division of Business and Engineering. Having earned his doctorate in accounting from Penn State University, Engelbret originally joined the campus in 1977. One of the college's most dedicated citizens and popular teachers, Engelbret is a five-time recipient of Penn State Altoona's Student Government Association Annual Faculty Award for outstanding teaching.

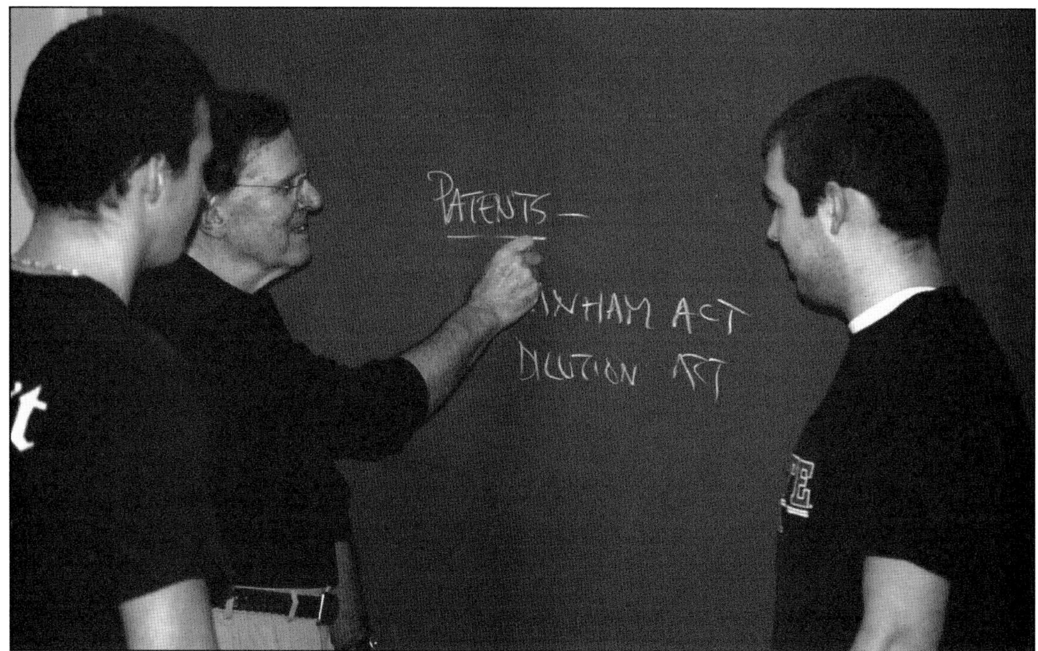

A local attorney, Benjamin I. Levine holds the distinction of being the Penn State Altoona adjunct faculty member with the most years of service. In 1962, Levine earned his juris doctor from the Dickinson School of Law and was admitted to the Pennsylvania Bar the following year. Levine is a partner with the Hollidaysburg law firm Evey, Black, Dorezas, Magee, Levine, Rosensteel, and Mauk. Having joined the Penn State Altoona faculty on a part-time basis in 1975, Levine teaches courses in business law for the college.

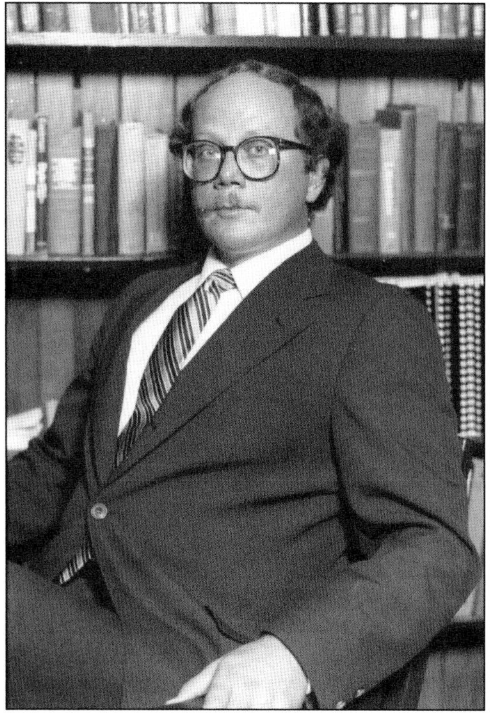

Kjell Meling joined Penn State Altoona as director of academic affairs in 1978. From 1991 to 1994, he served as interim campus executive officer before becoming the college's first associate dean for academic affairs. Known for his rapier wit, Meling developed a strong and capable faculty of scholars and artists. He is often credited with establishing the academic firmament for the college's elevation into four-year degree-granting status in 1997. In 2006, his widow Diane created the endowment for the Kjell Meling Award for Distinction in the Arts and Humanities.

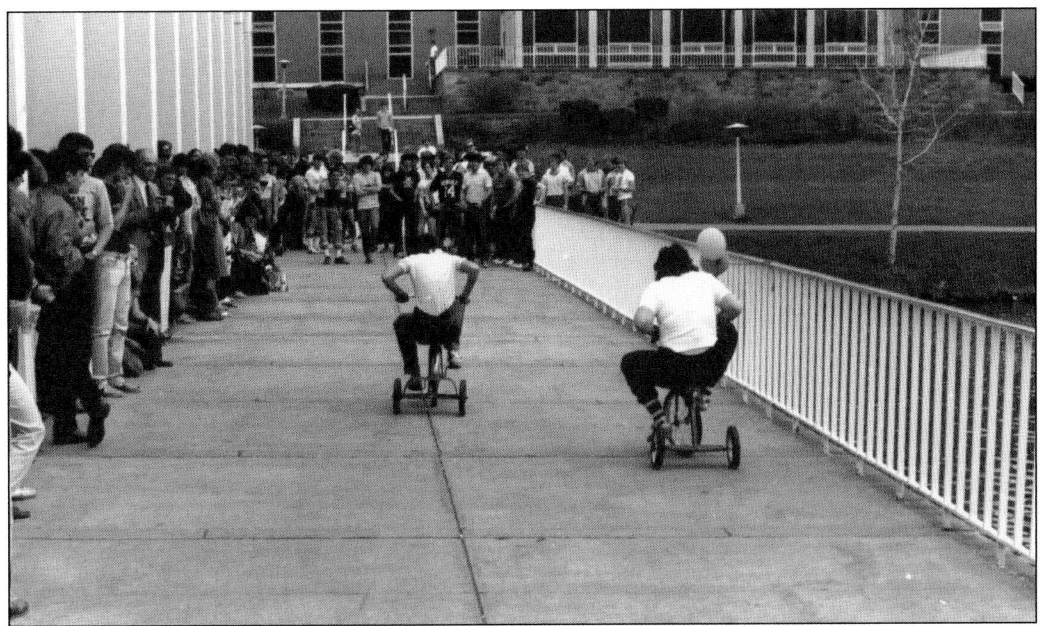

Over the years, students established Campus Spring Week as an annual Penn State Altoona tradition. In this 1978 photograph, students compete in a tricycle race in front of the Harry E. Slep Student Center.

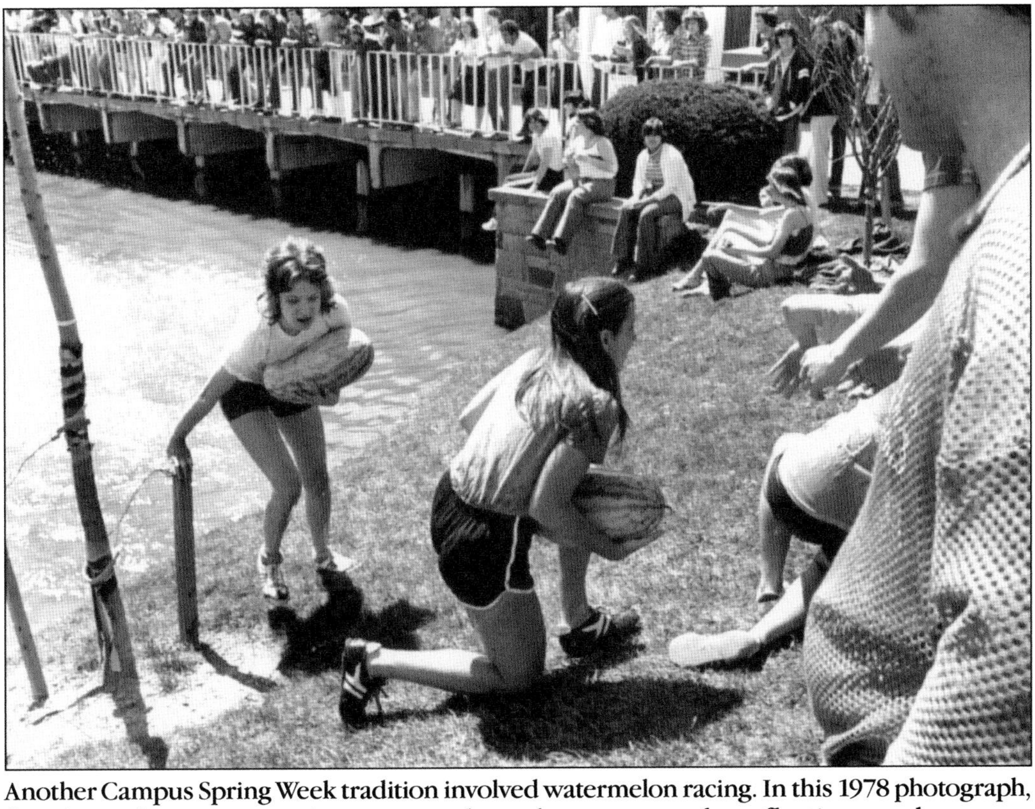

Another Campus Spring Week tradition involved watermelon racing. In this 1978 photograph, female students compete in a watermelon relay race near the reflecting pond.

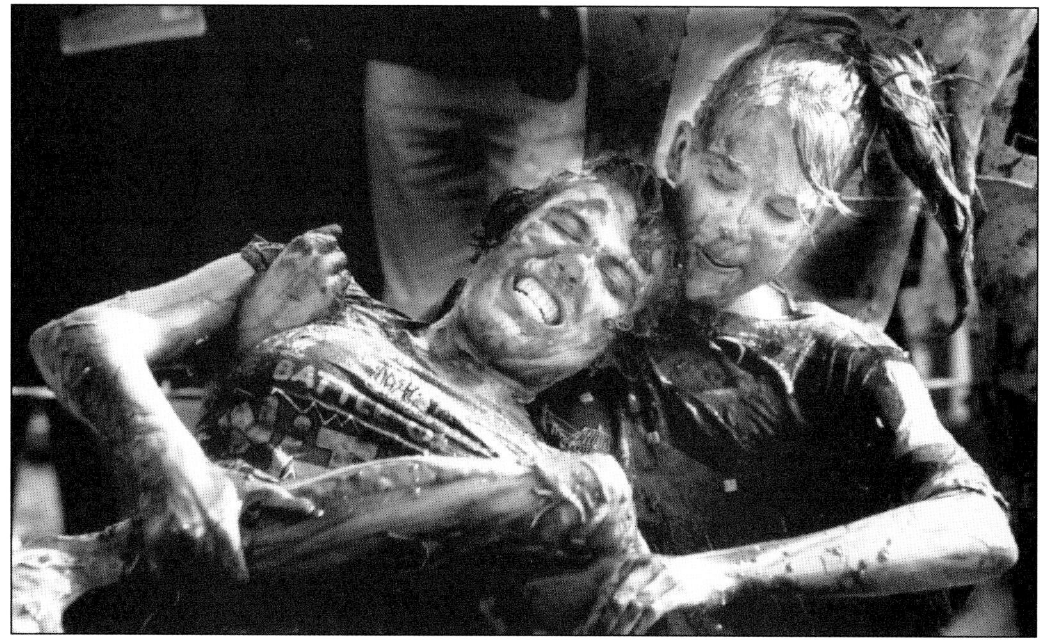

Students also participated in "muck wrestling" as part of Campus Spring Week in which combatants fight it out among such substances as Jell-O, chocolate pudding, and spaghetti noodles. In this 1991 photograph, Amy Cotner (left) and Tara Fosbre (right) try their hand in the muck.

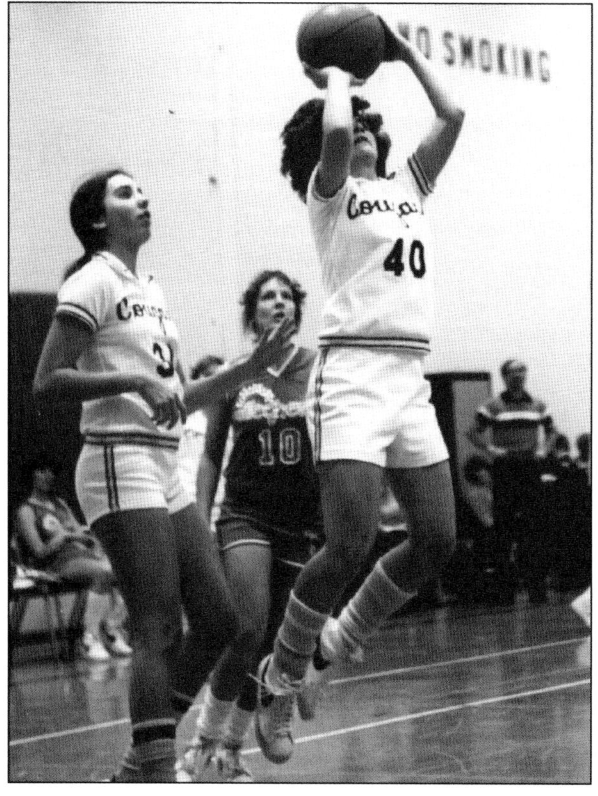

In this 1980 photograph, Altoona women's basketball players Anne Vidunas (left) and Beth Bassett (right) go on the offensive.

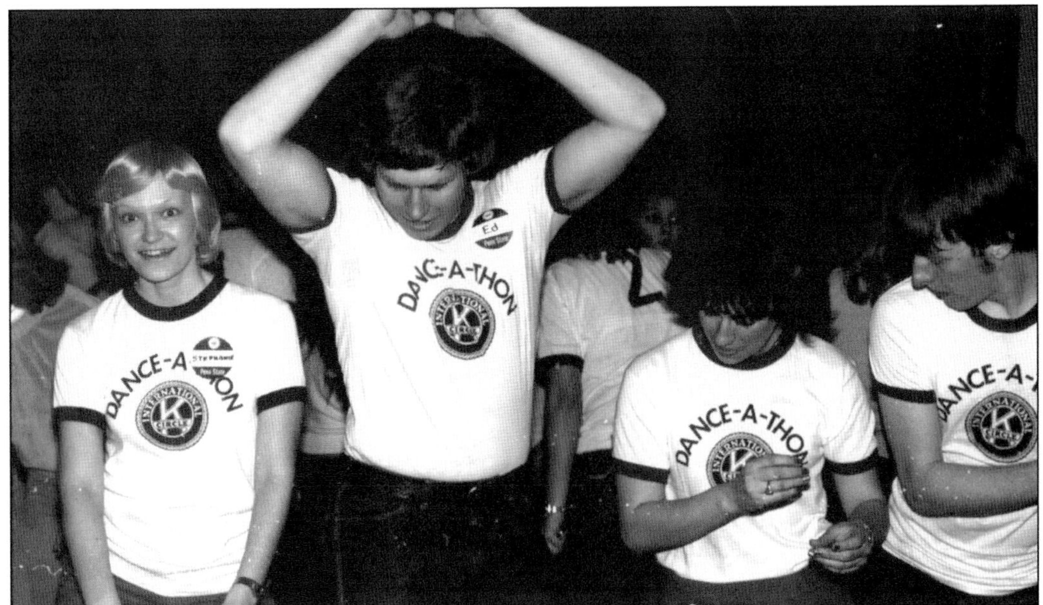

A precursor to the university's popular "Thon" annual fund-raising effort, the Circle K Dance-a-Thon was a central charity event on campus. Sponsored by the Altoona chapter of Kiwanis International, the dance-a-thon involved a 24-hour dance-off in the Harry E. Slep Student Center. In this 1980 photograph, students gyrate in support of a worthy cause.

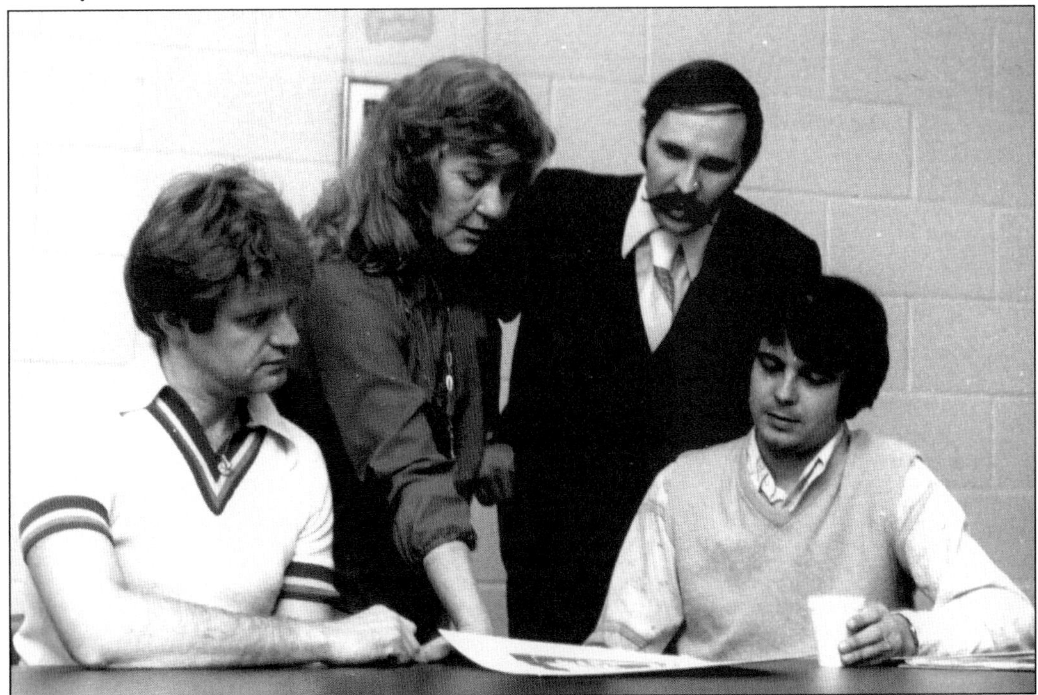

In this April 1980 photograph, faculty members work to establish a women in art juried exhibition series on campus. Pictured are, from left to right, Roger Zellner (visual arts), Jo C. Searles (English), Alan Mikula (instructional services), and Bill Balch (psychology).

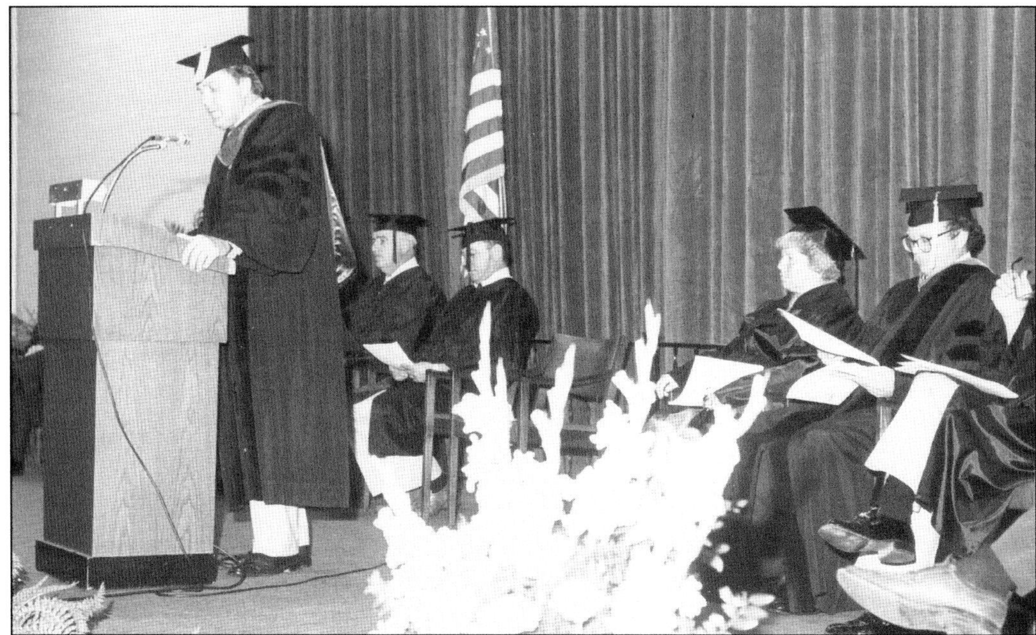

For some 30 years, Penn State Altoona commencement exercises were held almost exclusively in the gymnasium of the Steven A. Adler Athletic Complex. In this photograph, Carson Veach presides over the spring 1980 commencement. Behind him are, from left to right, Ronald Hoover, assistant professor of English; William Skillen; commencement speaker Cynthia Parsons; and Kjell Meling, director of academic affairs and nomenclator.

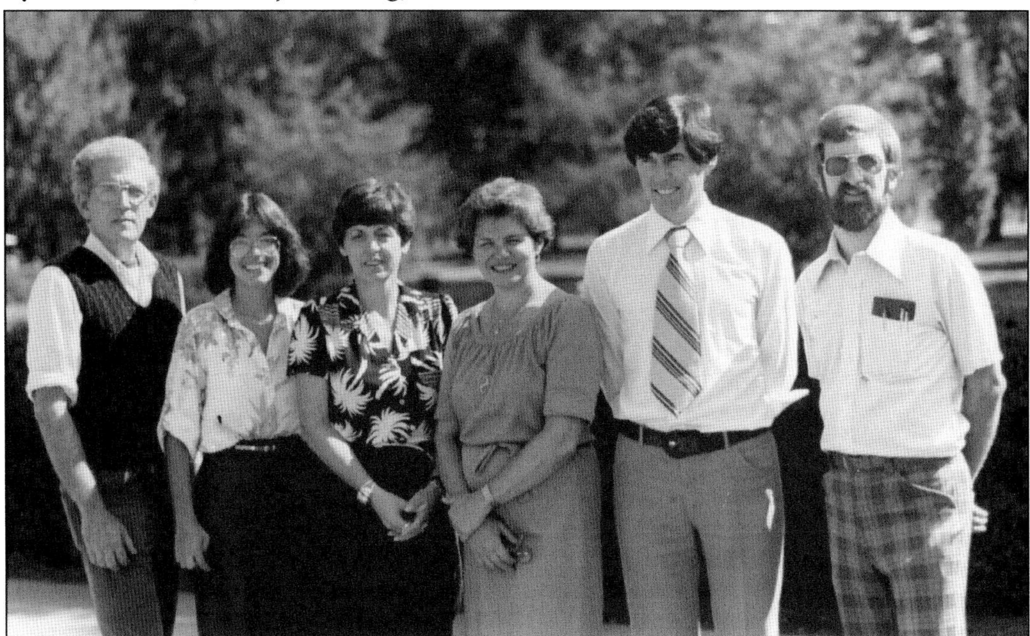

In this fall 1980 photograph, new faculty members include, from left to right, Julian Shuchter (English), Karen M. McGahan (mathematics), Liane M. Sillett (English), Marilyn Goldberg (English), Adrian Seabridge (surface mining), and Malcolm L. Van Blerkom (mathematics education).

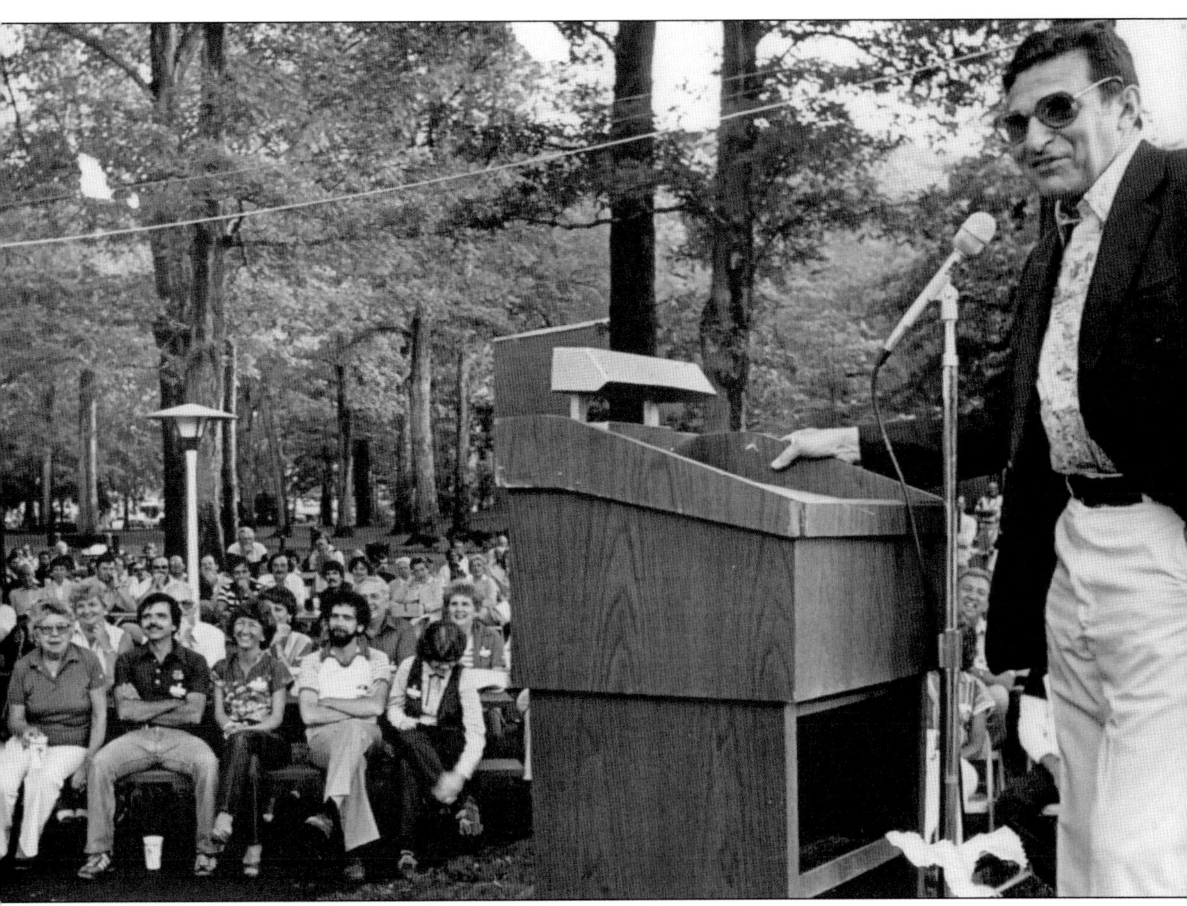

In this June 1981 photograph, legendary Penn State football coach Joe Paterno enjoys a summer picnic with the Blair County Penn State Alumni Club on the grounds of the campus.

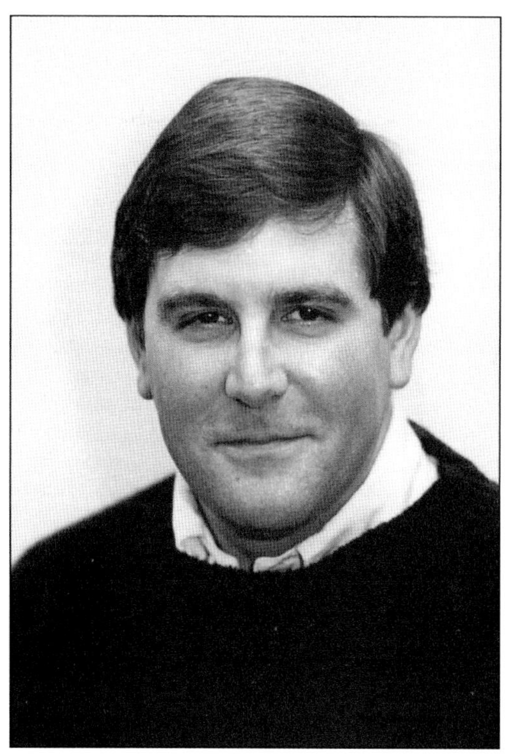

James A. Winsor served as the college's inaugural head of the Division of Mathematics and Natural Sciences. Having earned the rank of professor of biology, Winsor completed his doctorate in botany from the University of Michigan in 1981. In 1989 and 1993, he was twice honored with the student government association's outstanding faculty/advisor award.

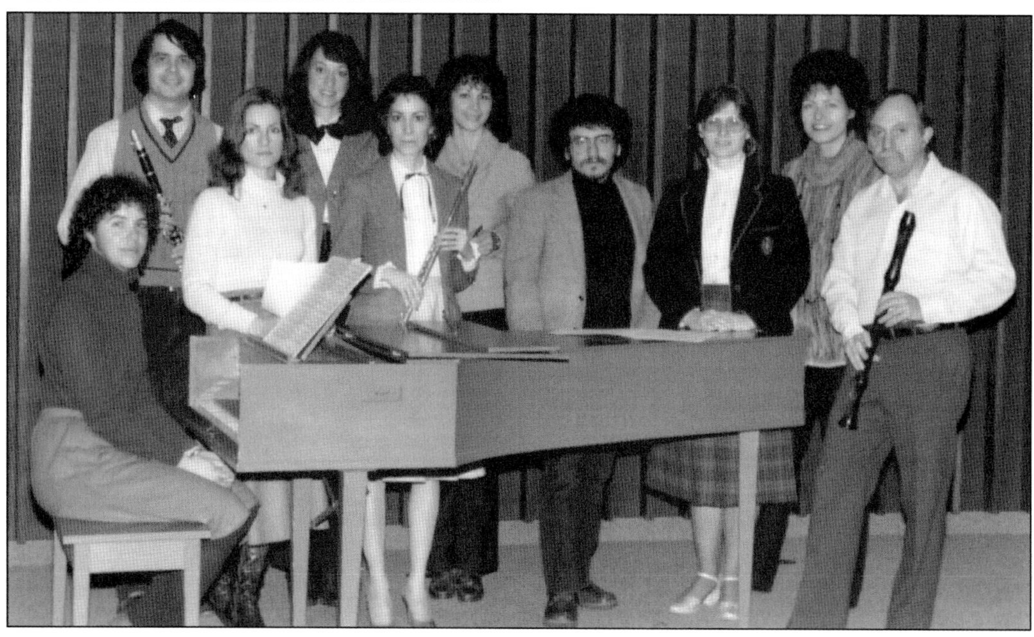

During the 1970s and early 1980s, Penn State Altoona faculty, staff, and former students performed in the amateur Pro Musica band. In this 1983 photograph are, from left to right, Sharon Plummer, Bill Balch, Teri Blasko, Rita Oliverio, Patty Brennan, Valerie Stratton, Gene Schlossberger, Cathy Whiteman, Annette Zalanowski (executive director), and Tom Russo (artistic director). The group specialized in early Renaissance and baroque music as their repertoire.

James A. (Jimmy) Duplass served as Penn State Altoona's chief administrator from 1983 to 1991. Duplass earned his doctorate from St. Louis University in 1974, and he later worked as associate provost at Wayne State University. In 1991, he left Penn State Altoona to accept an appointment at the University of South Florida's Fort Myers campus. Duplass currently serves as professor of education at the University of South Florida's Tampa campus.

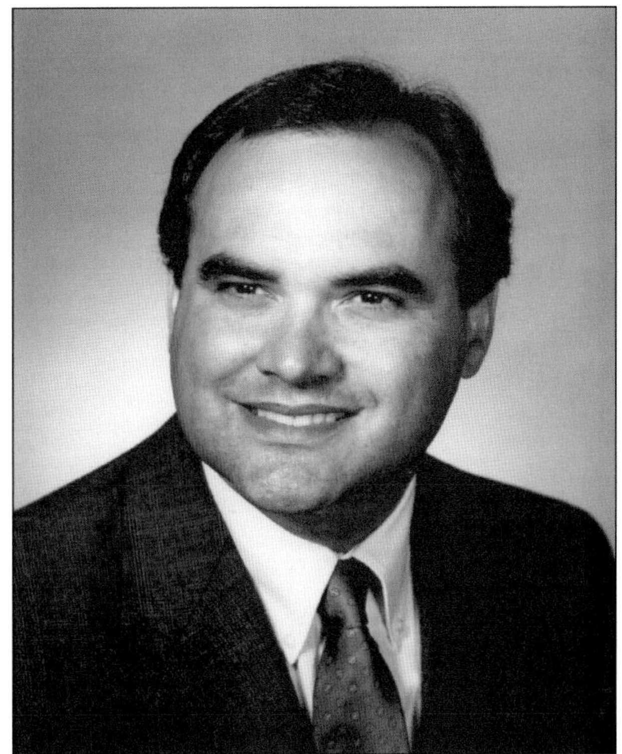

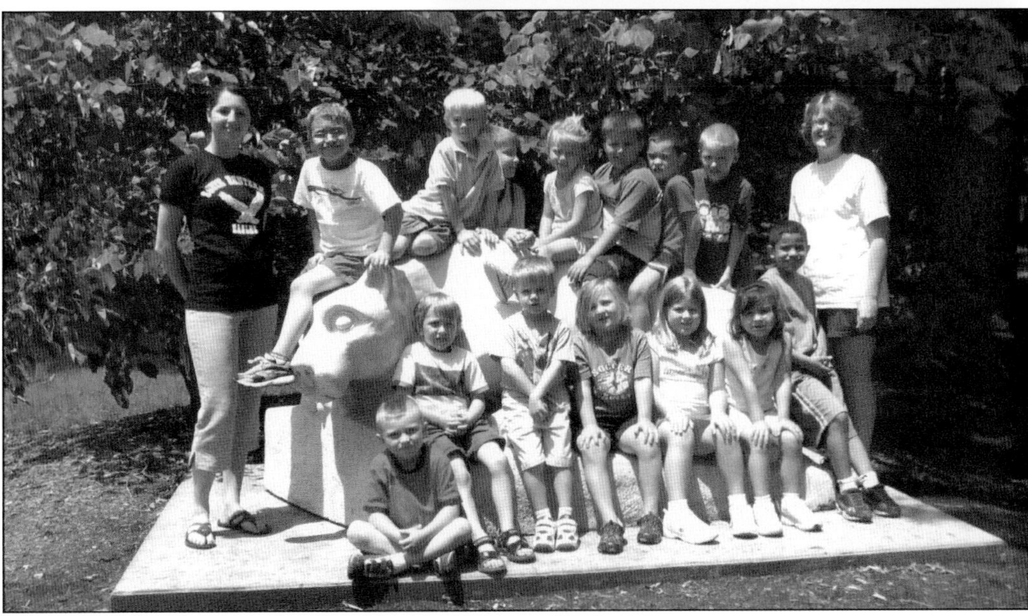

In the early 1980s, Penn State Altoona's office of continuing education and training opened Camp Nittany, a recreational sports day camp. Under the direction of Sherri McGregor, the program continues to be one of over 100 camps offered today through Summer Kids' College, which provides a fun and engaging array of educational and recreational programs for area youth. In 2005, Investment Savings Bank endowed scholarships in order to assist area children in taking advantage of Summer Kids' College offerings.

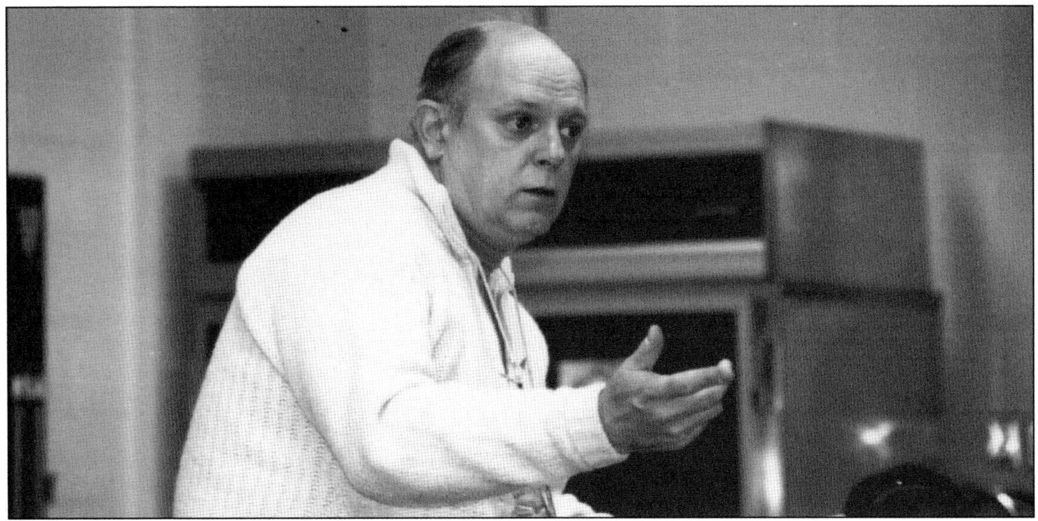

The George W. Atherton Award is presented annually to faculty from across the university who have developed a record of excellence in undergraduate teaching. Penn State Altoona award winners include John E. Lennox (pictured above), professor of microbiology (1984); William G. Engelbret, associate professor of accounting (1992); Lori J. Bechtel, professor of biobehavioral health (1993); Dinty W. Moore, professor of English and integrative arts (2000); Douglas K. Brown, associate professor of mathematics and science (1998); Lee Ann De Reus, associate professor of human development and family studies and of women's studies (2003); Roselyn Costantino, associate professor of Spanish and women's studies (2004); Michael Weiner, associate professor of mathematics (2004); Peter J. Shull, associate professor of engineering (2005); and Sandra Harbert Petrulionis, professor of English and American studies (2008).

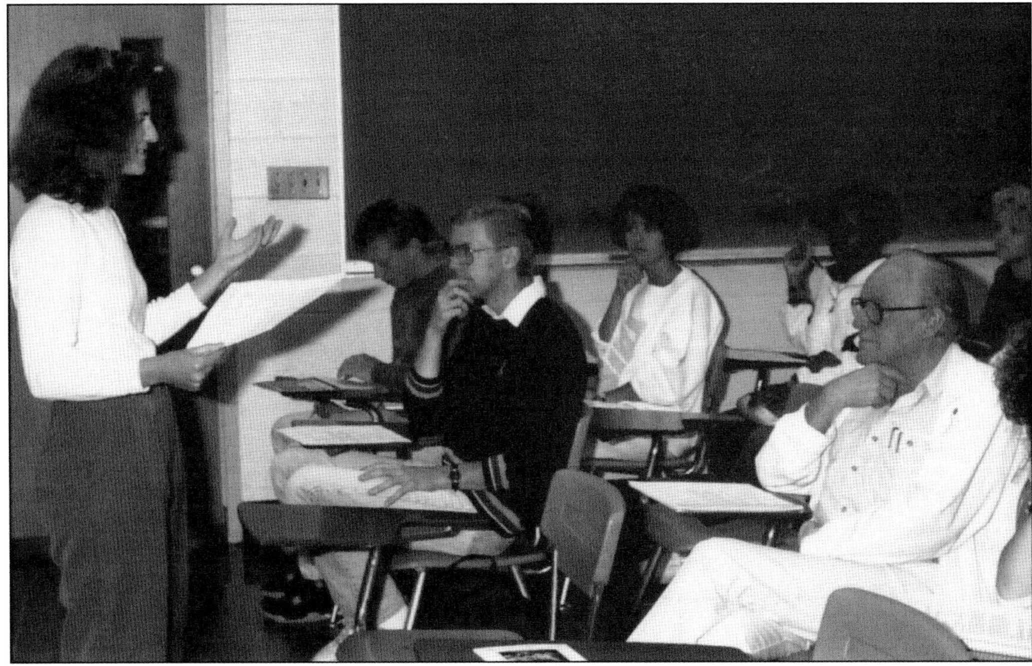

In this 1990 photograph, Lori J. Bechtel teaches a course in biobehavioral health.

A Chicago native, unrepentant Cubs fan, and ham actor, Thomas R. Liszka joined the Penn State Altoona faculty in 1984. A 1980 graduate of Northern Illinois University's doctoral program, Liszka serves as associate professor of English and coordinator of the college's English degree program. Liszka has lent his time and energy to a host of endeavors, including stints as assistant director of academic affairs and interim head of the Division of Education, Human Development, and Social Sciences. He is also rumored to be the mysterious "Dossier Fairy" who assists faculty with their promotion and tenure materials.

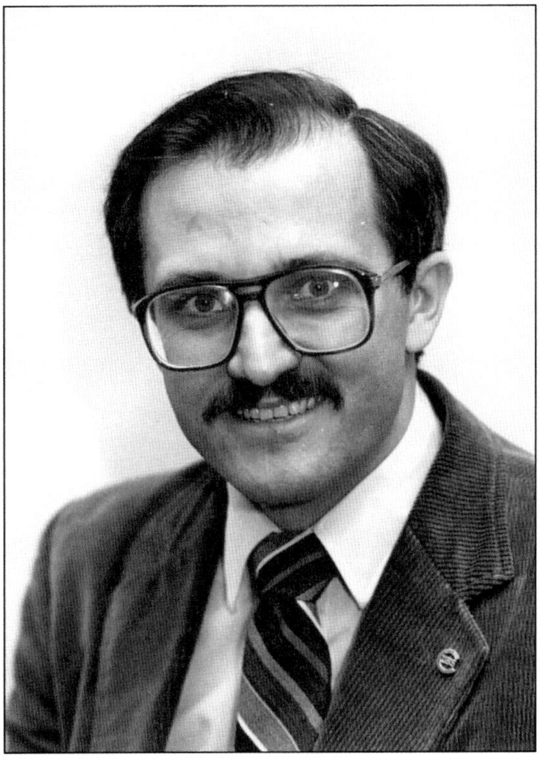

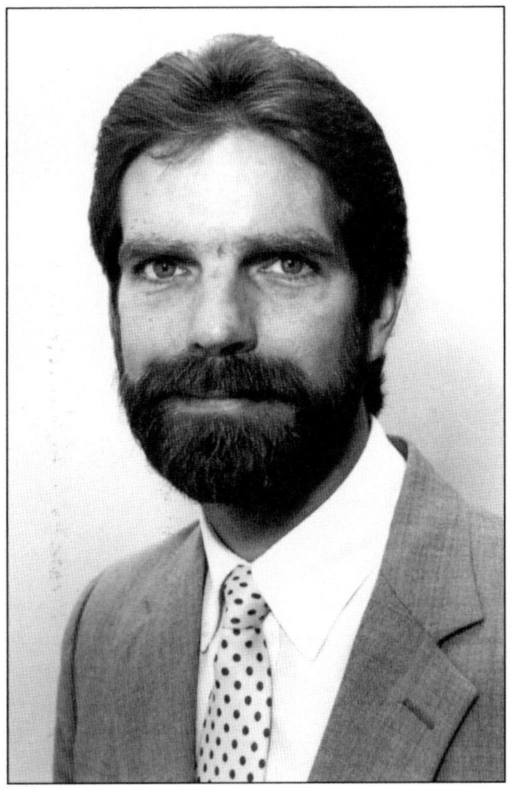

Western Pennsylvania natives Rick and Joann Shaffer joined the Penn State Altoona staff in 1984. Previously employed at Penn State's Delaware County campus (now Penn State Brandywine), the Shaffers have been an integral part of Penn State Altoona's admissions and advising missions for more than 25 years. Married in August 1975 and fellow graduates of Indiana University of Pennsylvania, Rick (pictured left) serves as director of admissions for Penn State Altoona and established the campus's adult center for nontraditional students, while Joann serves as senior programs coordinator for the Division of Undergraduate Studies.

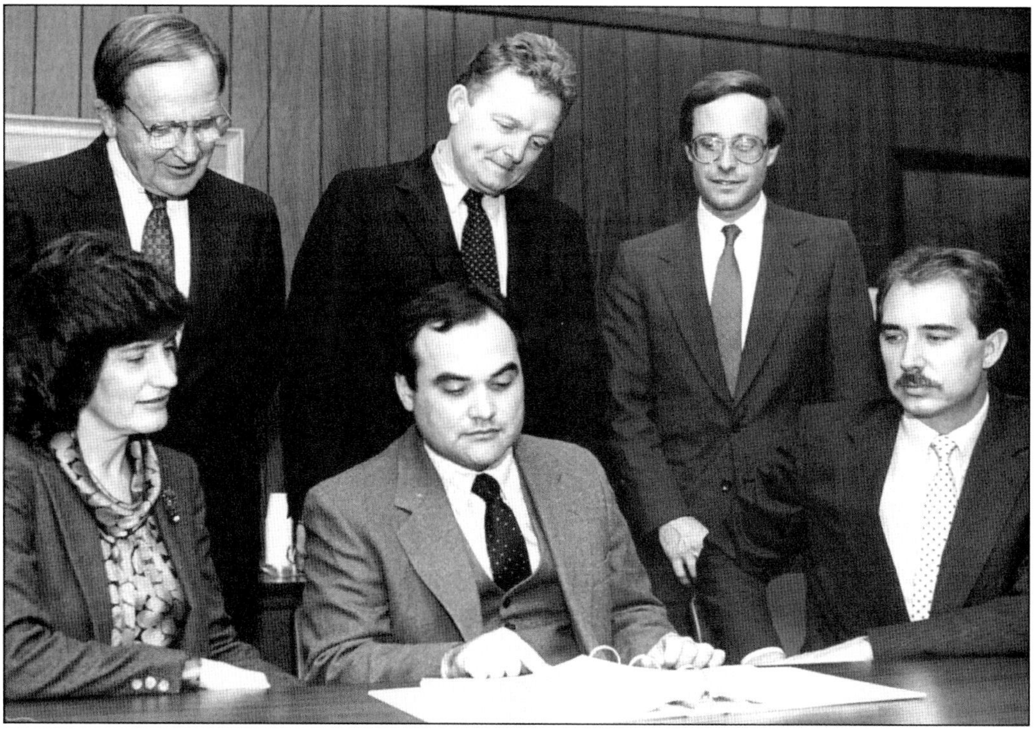

During the fall 1985 semester, Dean Duplass (center) welcomes new advisory board members to the campus. From left to right are Dolly Ickes, Ardie Dillen, John Kazmaier, George Sidney, and Richard Karcher.

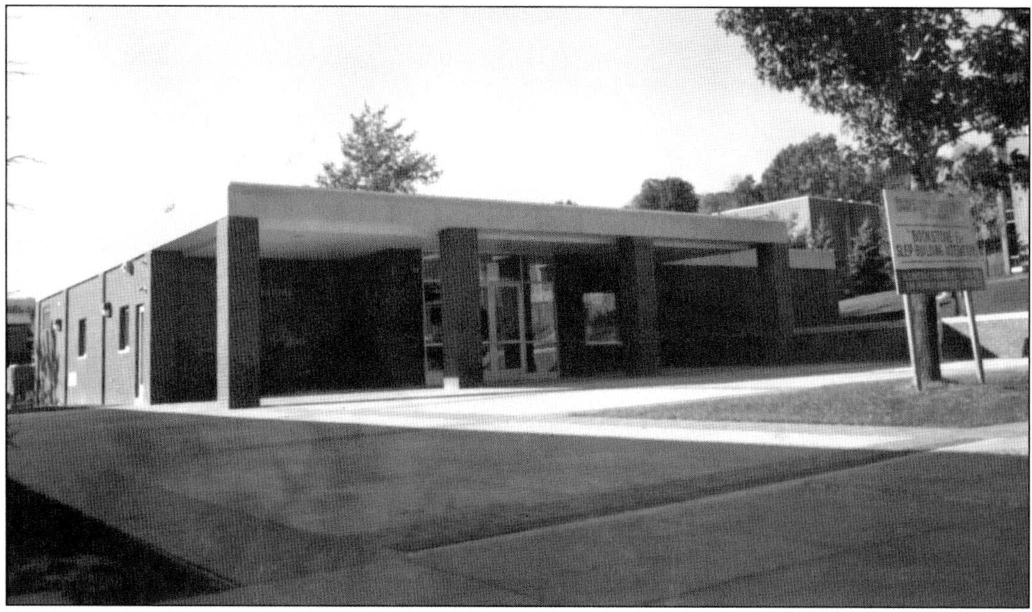

Completed in 1985, the campus bookstore provides students with textbooks, course materials, and supplies associated with their course work. The bookstore also offers officially licensed university apparel and various gift items. Operated by Barnes and Noble, the bookstore underwent an extensive renovation in 2004.

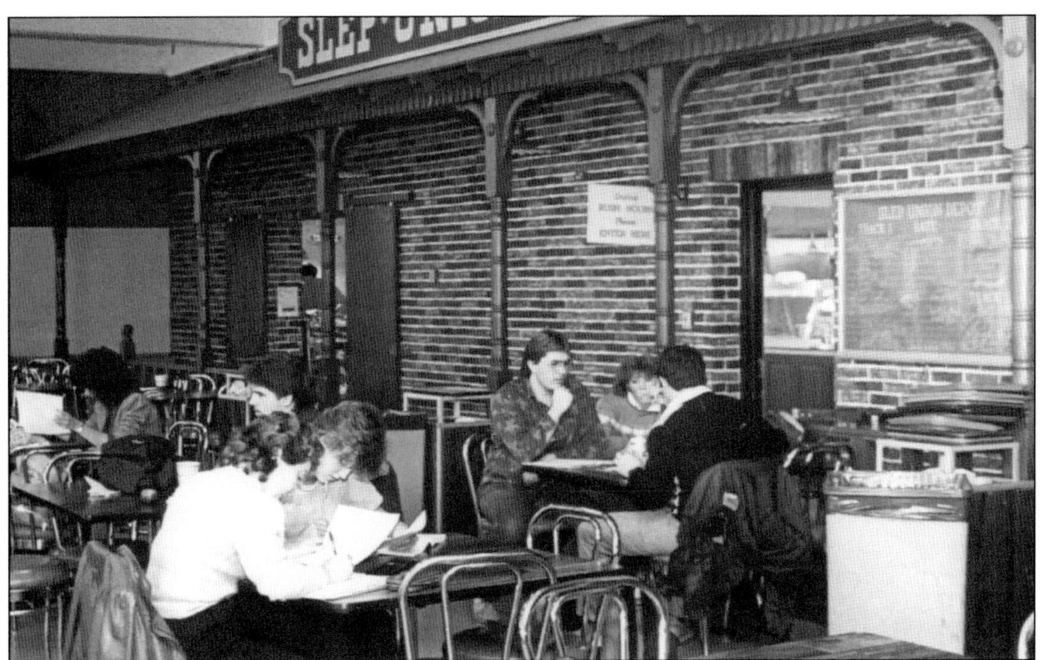

For many years, the Slep Union Depot served as one of the institution's primary eateries and social spaces. With its respectful nod to the campus's railroad heritage, the Slep Union Depot was replaced by study carrels in the 1990s, with the Hickory Court Café functioning as Penn State Altoona's principal dining facility.

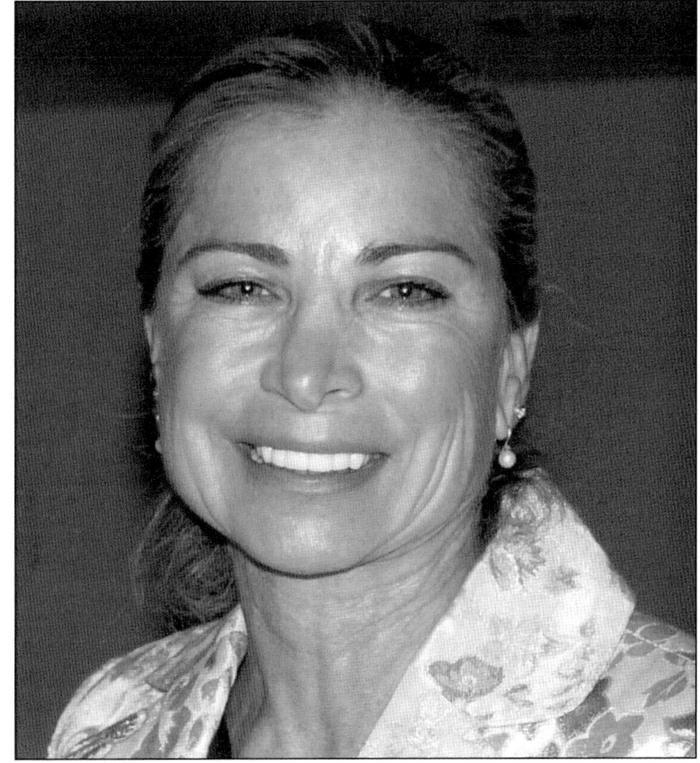

A veritable pioneer in the world of women's sports, Fredina M. Ingold was a member of the first women's varsity volleyball and basketball teams. In 1986, Ingold was appointed as director of intercollegiate athletics. She is credited with leading the college toward its current NCAA Division III membership. In 2004, she established the Fredina M. Ingold Intercollegiate Athletics Enhancement Endowment.

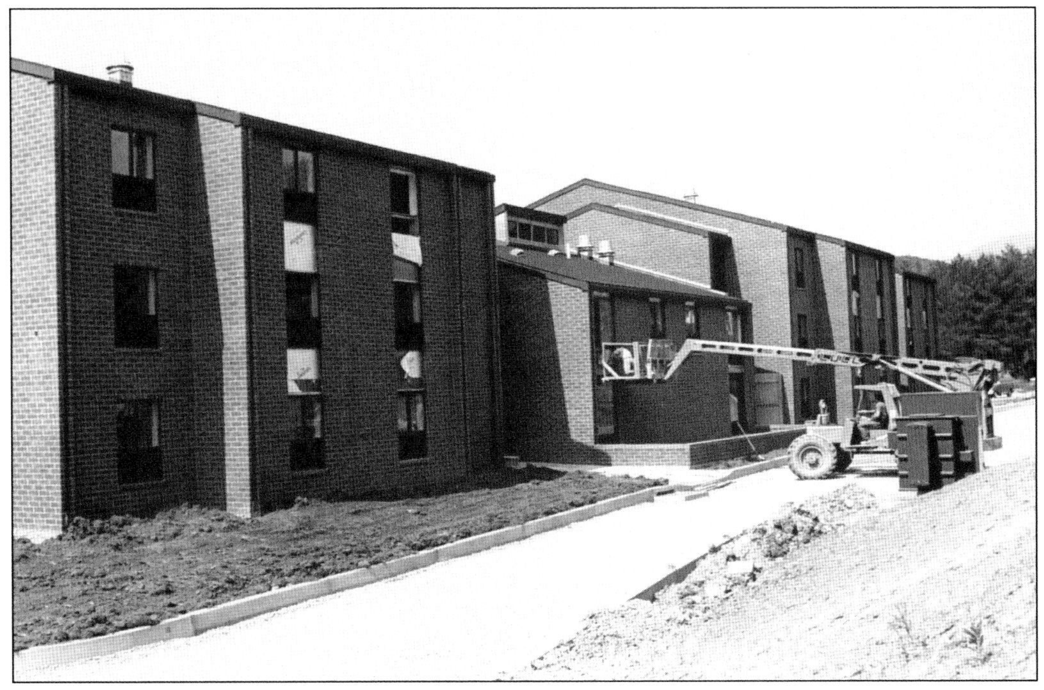

First occupied during the fall 1987 semester, Spruce Residence Hall houses some 141 students in suite-style rooms with adjoining bathrooms.

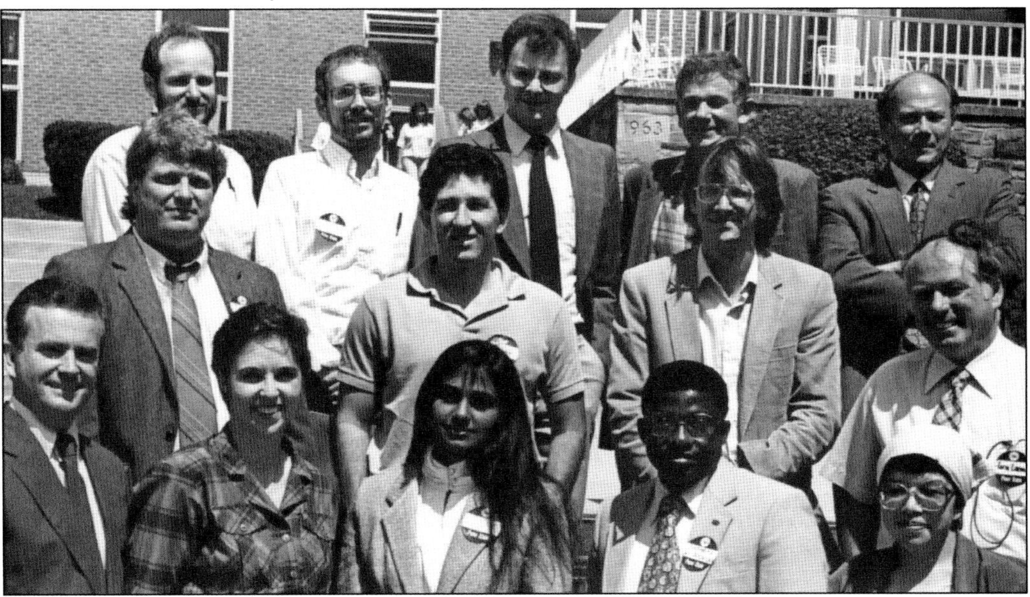

In this fall 1987 photograph, new faculty members pose in front of Oak Residence Hall: from left to right, (first row) Dan Wilshire (mathematics), Kammi Hefner (computer science), Padmasani Raghavan (computer science), Steven Fokuo (engineering), and Mila Su (university libraries); (second row) David Parry (philosophy), João Florencio (physics), Douglas K. Brown (mathematics), and Jack Larner (history); (third row) Keith Leggett (economics), Lawrence Connin (political science), Bruce Muller (engineering), Stan Phillips (mathematics), and Kjell Meling, director of academic affairs.

An Altoona native, Margery Wolf Kuhn was a lifelong supporter of the arts. In addition to sharing in the establishment of the Altoona Arts Society during the 1920s, Kuhn devoted her time and enthusiasm to a host of civic organizations, including the Railroaders Memorial Museum, the Southern Alleghenies Museum of Art, and the Bedford Springs Festival. In 1984, Kuhn created the endowment for the construction of the Community Arts Center, which later became the Misciagna Family Center for Performing Arts. Kuhn died in March 1988, scant months before the completion of the Community Arts Center. Her family's philanthropy is memorialized with the Paul R. and Margery Wolf Kuhn Theatre.

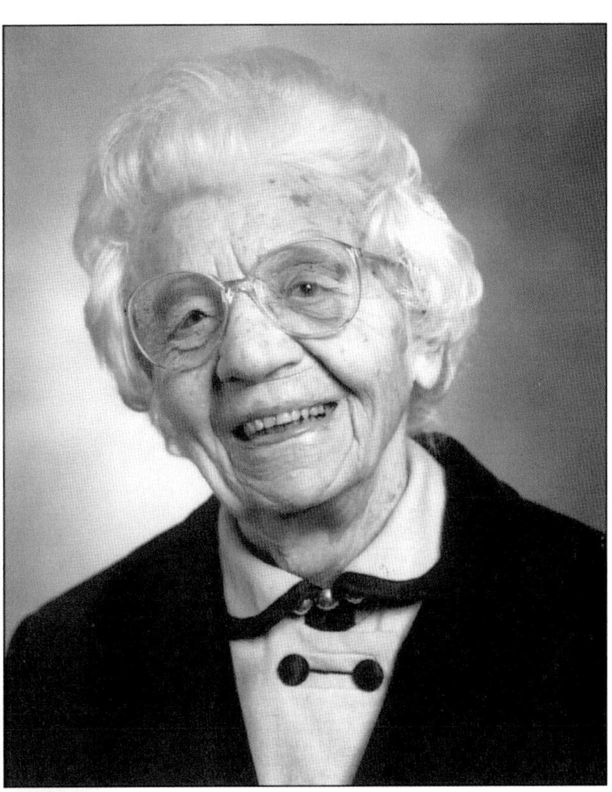

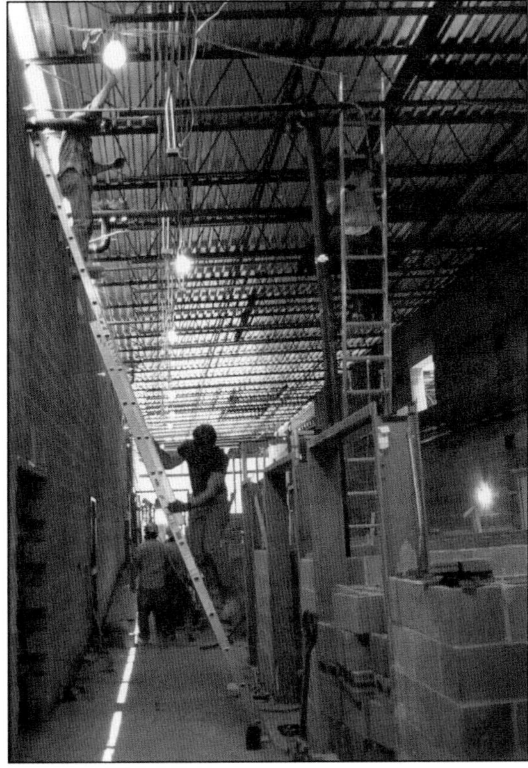

The Community Arts Center was funded through a combination of resources, including $1.4 million from some 800 local donors, as well as a million-dollar grant secured by Sen. Robert C. Jubelirer from the Commonwealth of Pennsylvania.

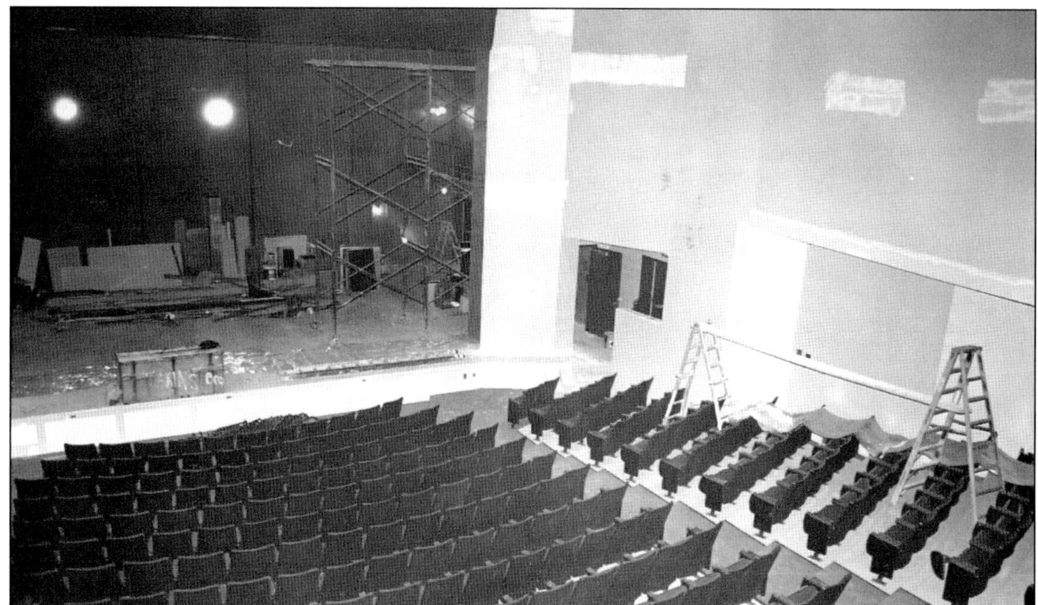

Named in honor of Paul R. and Margery Wolf Kuhn, the campus theater opened in 1988 with the completion of the Community Arts Center, later rededicated as the Misciagna Family Center for Performing Arts. In addition to being the regular home of Penn State Altoona theatrical productions, the 400-seat Wolf Kuhn Theatre hosts a number of greater Altoona cultural and performing arts series and special events throughout the academic year.

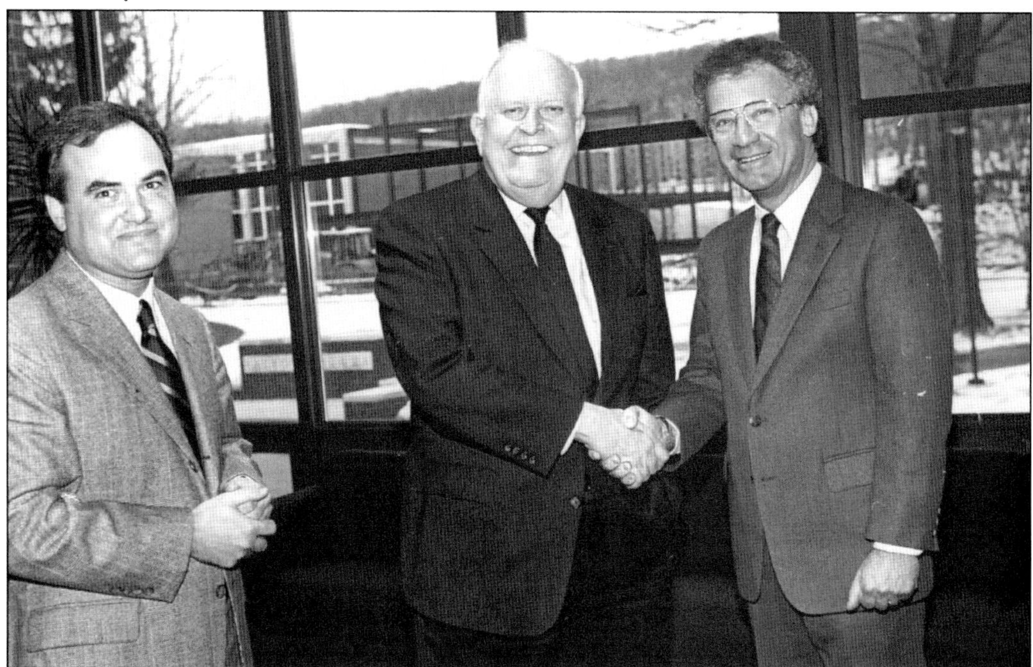

In this 1989 photograph, Bryce Jordan (center), president of Penn State University, joins chief executive officer and dean Jimmy Duplass (left) and Sen. Robert C. Jubelirer (right) to commemorate the opening of the Community Arts Center.

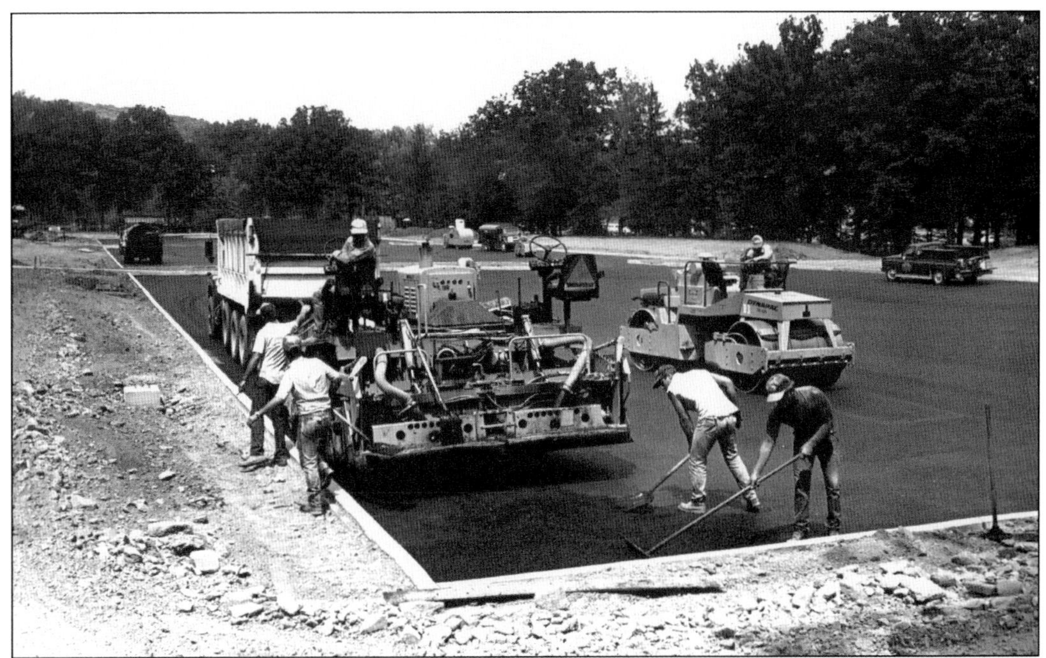

In this 1988 photograph, the former location of the Ivyside Recreation Park's world-famous swimming pool is transformed into a parking lot, bringing one of the last remnants of Penn State Altoona's amusement park origins to a close.

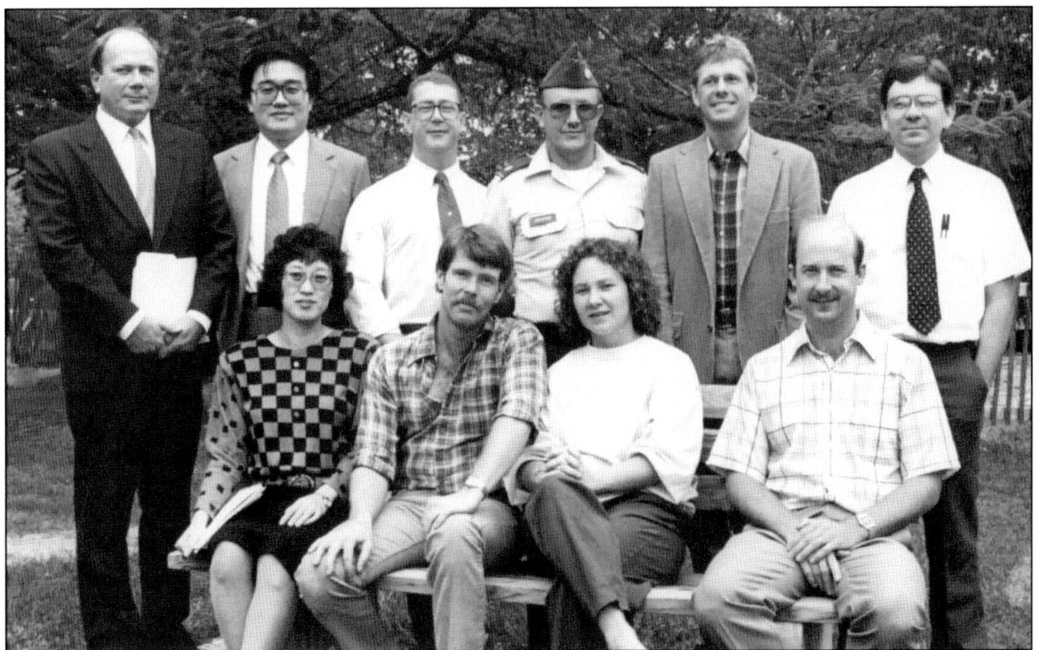

New Penn State Altoona faculty members pose together in this fall 1988 photograph. They are, from left to right, (first row) Connie Yu (mathematics); Jeff Kean (theater arts); Nona Gerard (theater arts); and Joe Conrad (mathematics); (second row) Kjell Meling, director of academic affairs; Alex Chen (business); Rick Stegman (student affairs); Maj. Albert Sheaffer (ROTC); Ian Marshall (English); and Kevin Leddy (undergraduate studies).

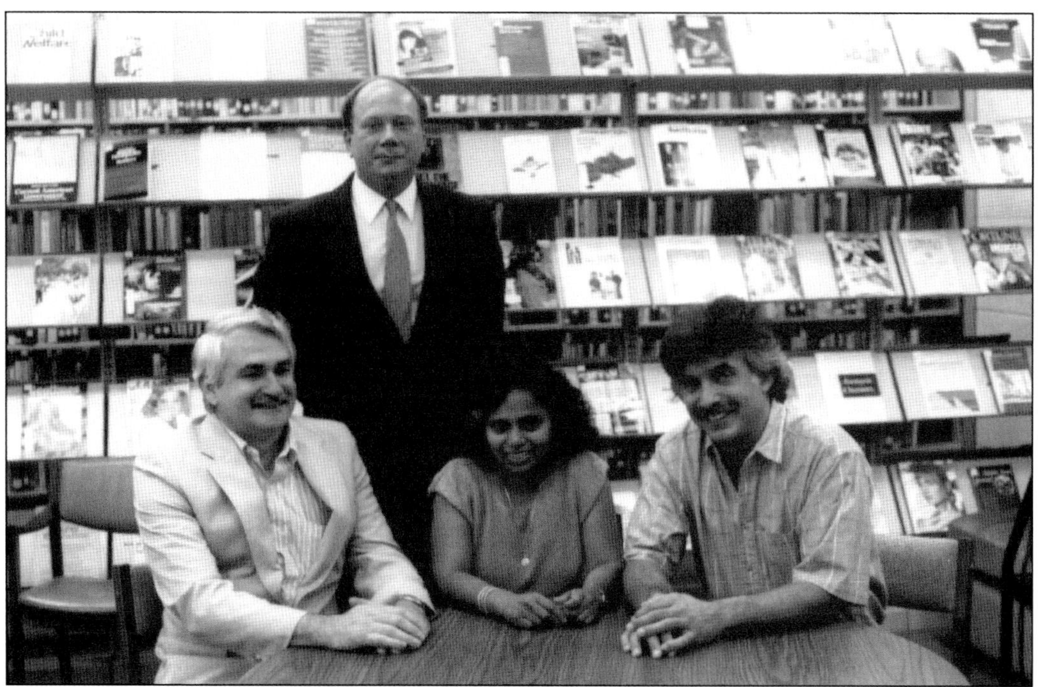

In this fall 1988 photograph, newly tenured faculty members pose with Kjell Meling, director of academic affairs. Seated are, from left to right, Lawrence J. Pilione (physics), Mary Menachery (chemistry), and Jerry Zolten (communication arts and sciences).

BROADWAY REVIEW

Two of Broadway's star leads, Laurie Beechman from Cats and Lee Roy Reams from 42nd Street, and their piano accompanist will present a performance of song and dance from Broadway's hit shows. Laurie Beechman made her Broadway debut in the original cast of Annie, and has just finished her fifth year as the lead in Cats. Lee Roy Reams also known as "Mr. Broadway," has performed the male lead in 42nd Street for seven years. The Broadway Review is being planned exclusively for the Altoona Campus by Broadway producer Terry Hodge Taylor and will contain hit songs from Broadway shows, such as Hello Dolly, Applause, 42nd Street, and "Memory" from Cats.

Celebrating

50

Years

PENNSTATE

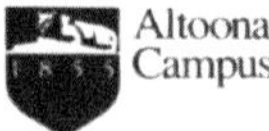

Altoona
Campus

Penn State Altoona celebrated its 50th anniversary with a gala September 1989 celebration at the newly completed Community Arts Center. Guests were treated to dinner and a Broadway review featuring theatrical stars Laurie Beechman from *Cats* and Lee Roy Reams from *42nd Street*.

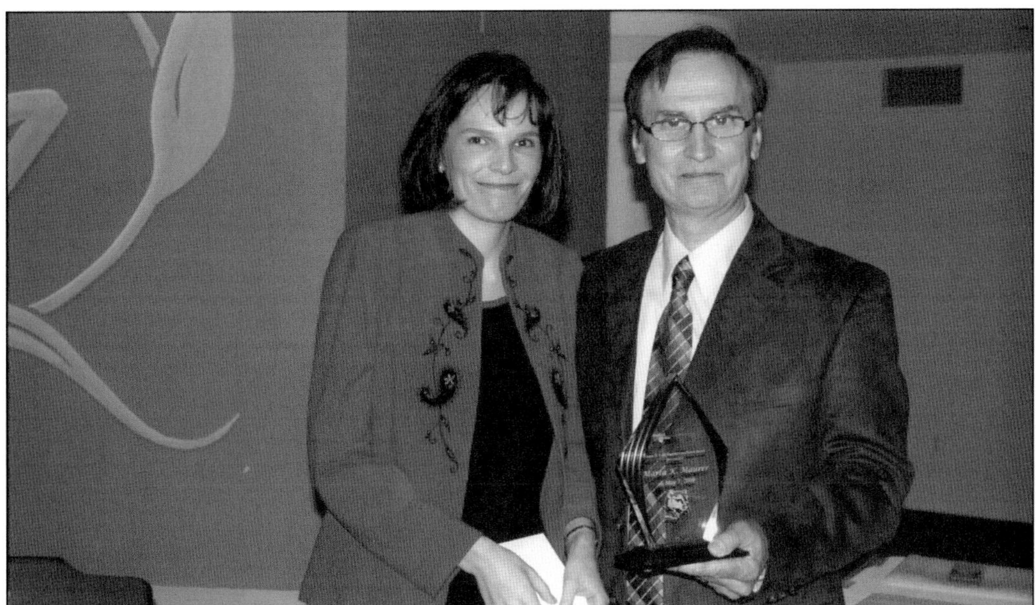

The Ted J. and Grace D. Long Awards were established in 1990 to recognize faculty and staff professionalism, dedication, and enthusiasm in support of the college. In this 2009 photograph, Marta Maurer (left), assistant professor of chemistry, is presented with the Grace D. Long Award by Nicholas M. Miskovsky (right), head of the Division of Mathematics and Natural Sciences.

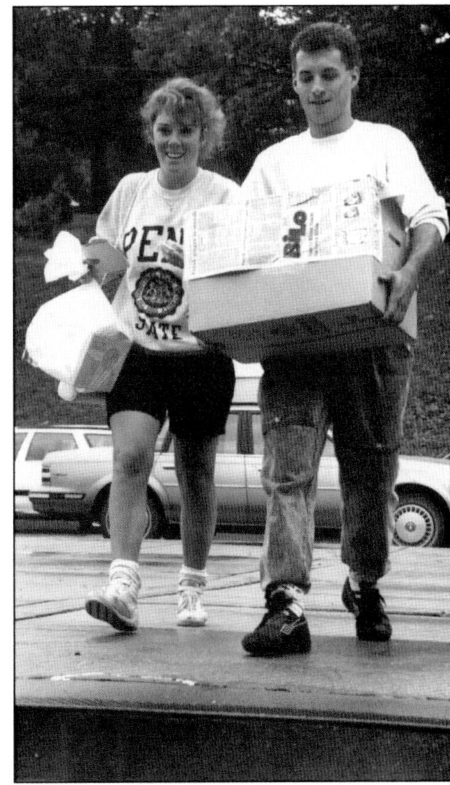

In this fall 1990 photograph, student Sue Crone of Harrisburg moves into her dorm room at Penn State Altoona with assistance from her friend Tony Kline.

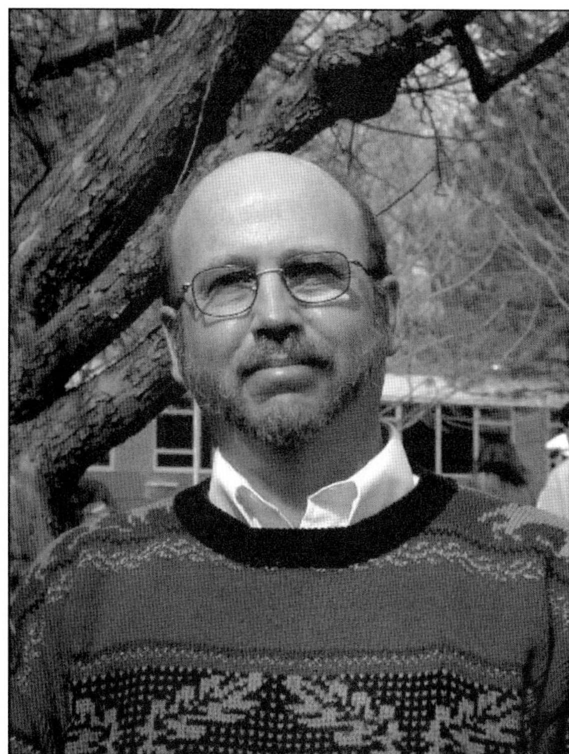

Michael W. Wolfe served as the college's inaugural head of the Division of Arts and Humanities. Having completed his doctorate at Johns Hopkins University in 1985, he earned the rank of professor of history at the college. Wolfe currently serves as associate dean of graduate arts and sciences at St. John's University.

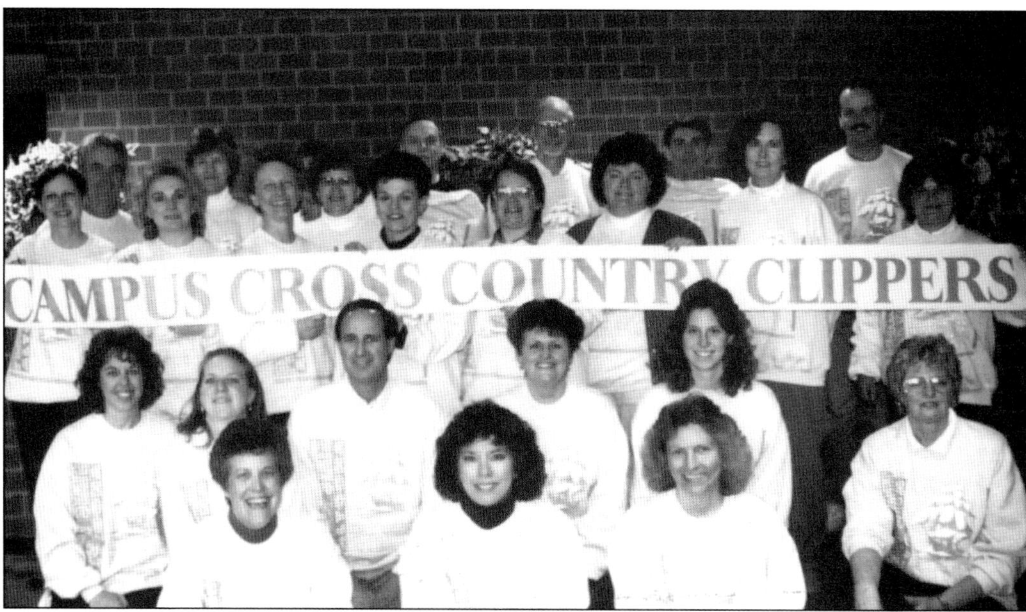

Organized by Lori J. Bechtel as part of a university-wide health promotion effort, the Campus Cross-Country Clippers involved a group of faculty and staff devoted to promoting the value of healthy living and exercise at Penn State Altoona. The Cross-Country Clippers collectively accrued enough individual mileage to have walked across the United States twice over—a statistic that they carefully measured using stickpins and a map of the nation.

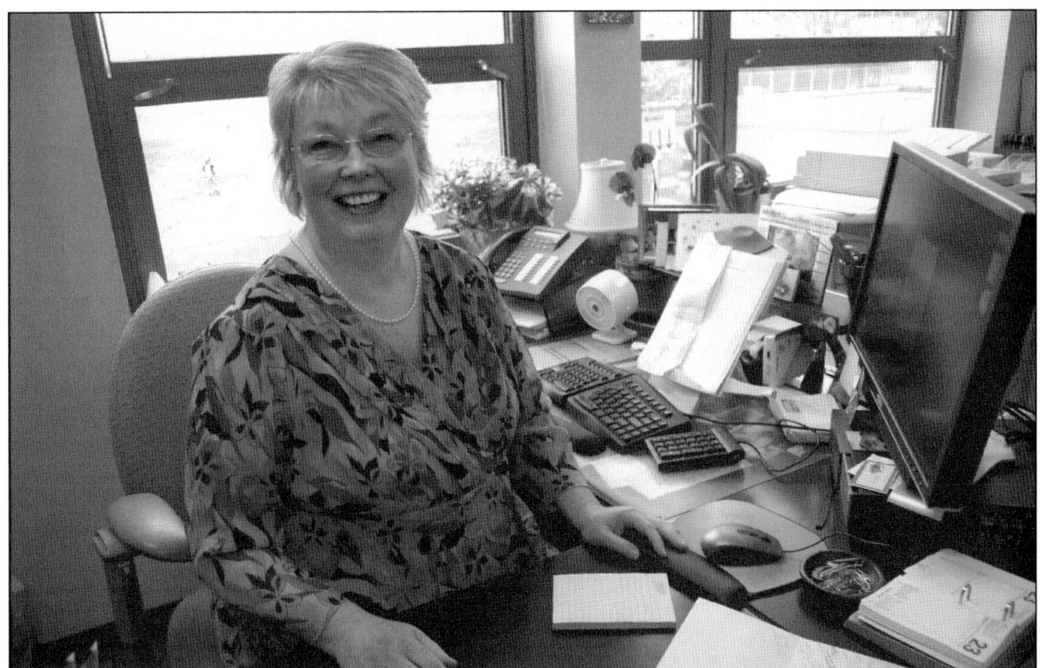

One of the college's most distinguished and beloved faculty administrative assistants, Molly J. Slep first joined Penn State Altoona in 1993. In 2002, her efforts on behalf of the institution were rewarded with a Ted J. Long Staff Excellence Award. She is married to Harry E. Slep IV, whose great-great-grandfather founded the *Altoona Mirror* and for whom the Harry E. Slep Student Center is named.

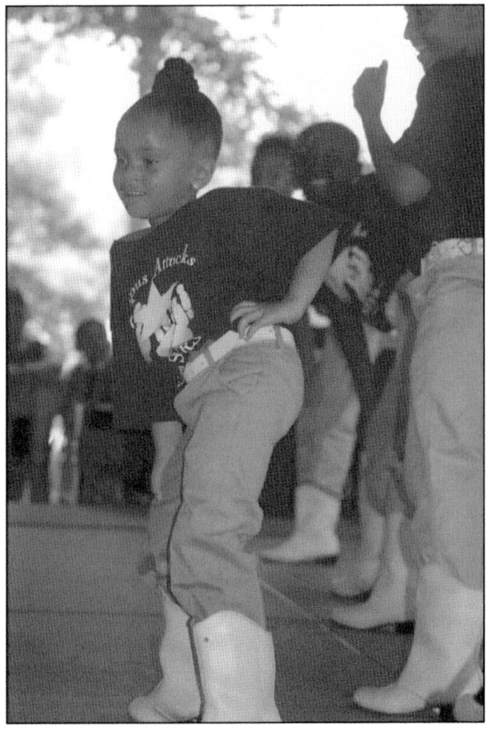

First held in 1993, the African American Heritage Festival has become an integral part of the college's diversity efforts. The festival celebrates African American performing arts in the genres of dance, music, and storytelling. In addition to an array of food and crafts, the festival features a host of musical acts. In this 2005 photograph, a children's dance troupe performs in the Laurel Pavilion.

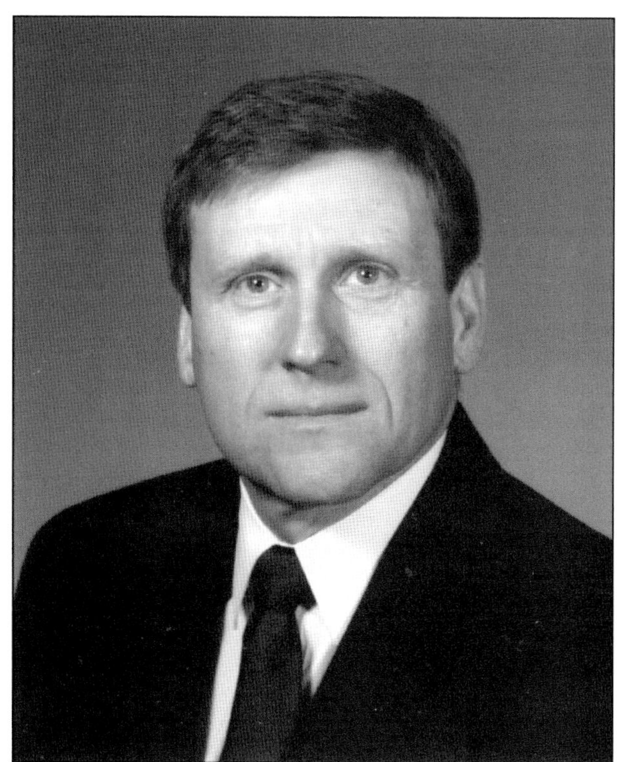

Allen C. Meadors served as Penn State Altoona's chief executive officer and dean from 1994 to 1999. Before joining Penn State Altoona, he worked as professor and dean of the College of Health at Eastern Washington University, as well as dean of the College of Public Health at the University of Oklahoma. In July 1999, he was appointed as chancellor of the University of North Carolina at Pembroke. In 2009, he was appointed as president of the University of Central Arkansas.

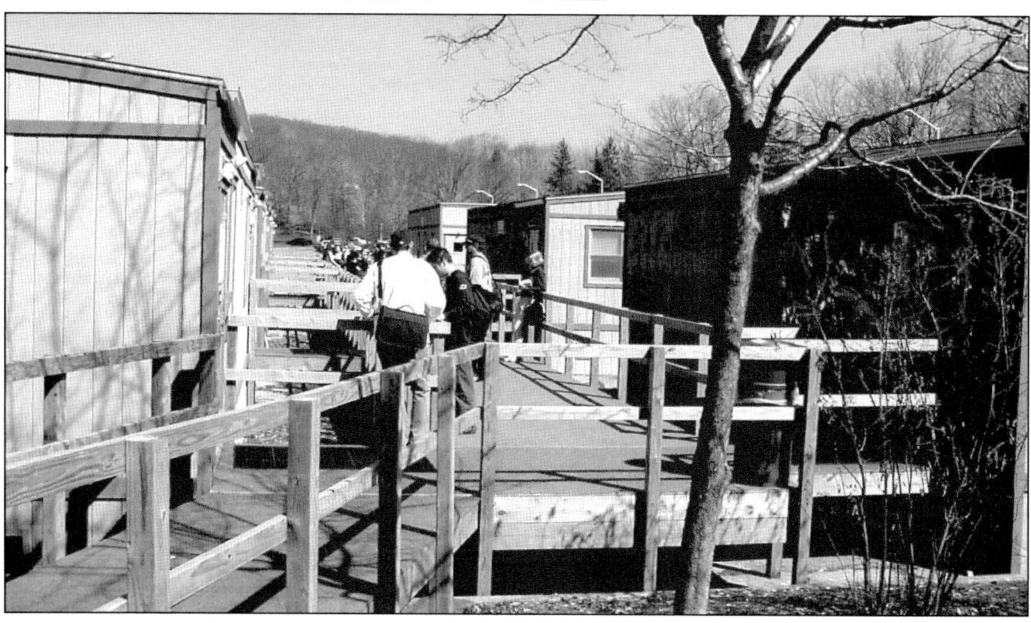

The college's phenomenal growth during the 1990s led to the establishment of temporary facilities using a set of six portable trailers. Known as the Birch Complex, the trailers were originally situated near the site of the current Hawthorn Building, only to be relocated to the southern end of the Misciagna parking lot during the building's construction. With the completion of the building in 2005, the Birch Complex was dismantled—much to the delight of the campus population.

Installed in 1996, the railroad clock overlooks the central academic quad on the Penn State Altoona campus. The clock was built in order to celebrate the region's railroad heritage.

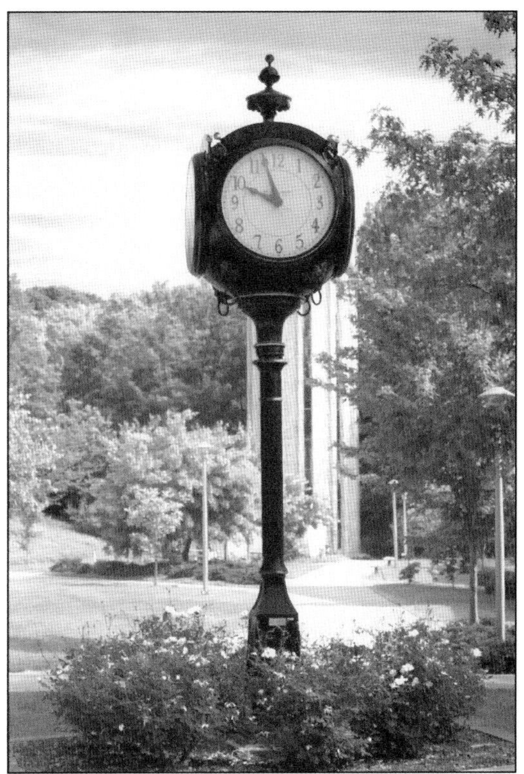

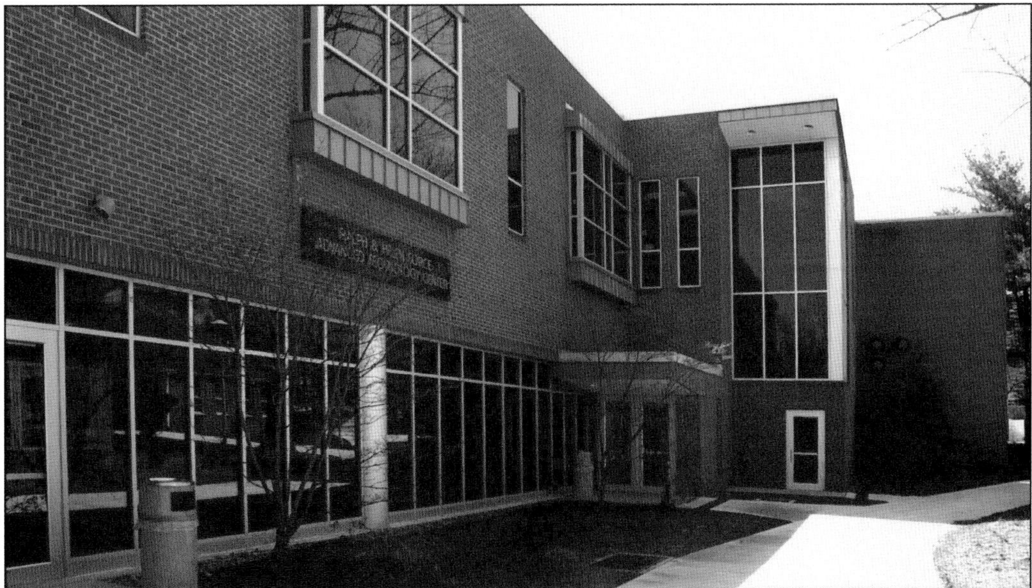

Completed in 1996, the Force Advanced Technology Center was named in honor of Ralph and Helen Force, who celebrated the legacy of their successful electric motor company with a gift that led to the construction of a permanent home for the college's electromechanical engineering technology program. The building houses several engineering laboratories as well as a machine shop, a chemical laboratory, a manufacturing laboratory, a controls laboratory, and faculty office spaces.

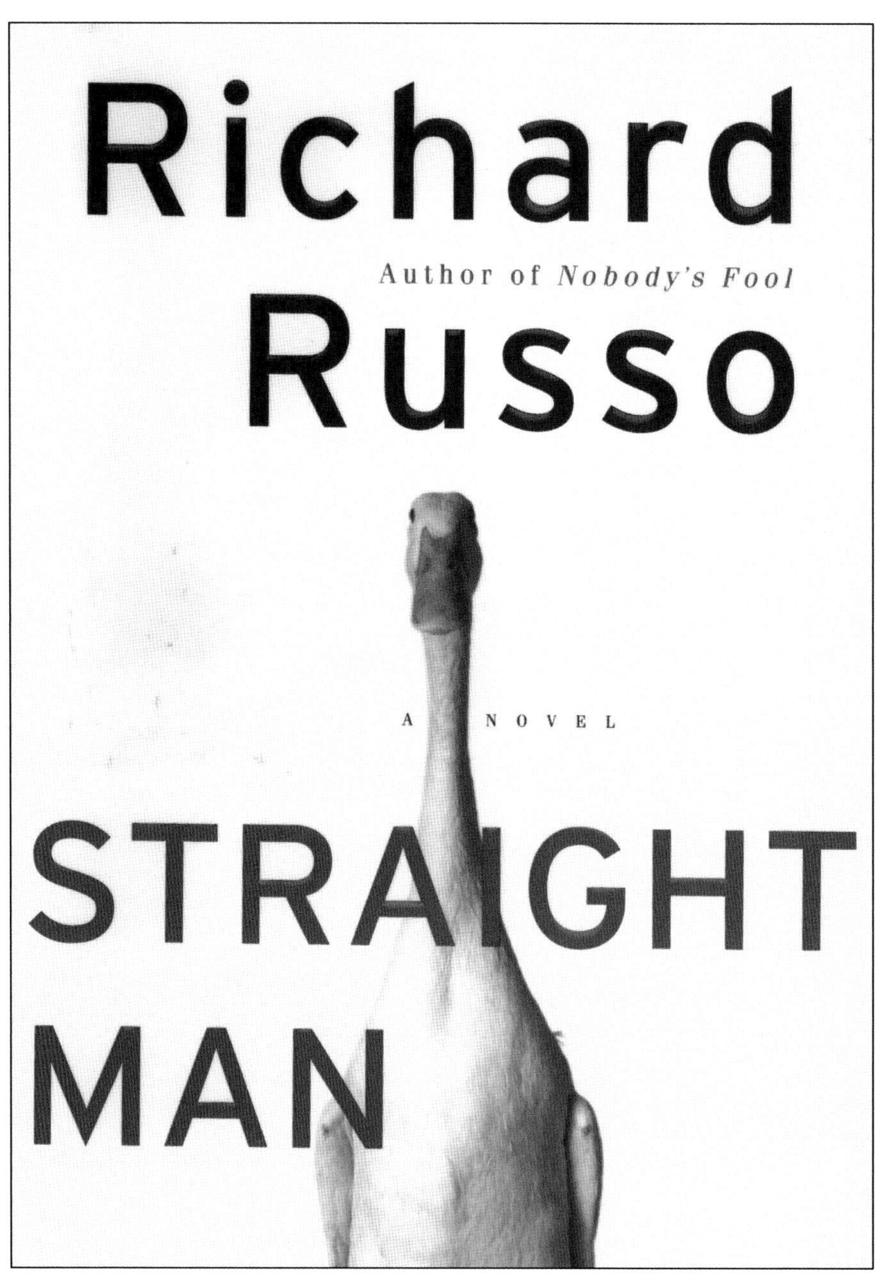

Set in thinly veiled Railton, Pennsylvania, Richard Russo's tragicomic novel *Straight Man* (1997) traces the life and times of fictional West Central Pennsylvania State University, a small, bucolic college with a duck pond gracing its interior. Narrated by interim English department chair William Henry Devereaux Jr., *Straight Man* focuses a sharp, satirical eye upon the scholarly rites and interpersonal crises of academe. With his budget in tatters, Devereaux famously threatens to kill a duck a day until the college ratifies the department's budget request. An academic roman à clef, *Straight Man* was a *New York Times* best seller. In May 2000, Russo delivered the spring commencement address at Penn State Altoona. In 2002, Russo won the Pulitzer Prize for fiction for his novel *Empire Falls*.

Four

The Old College Try

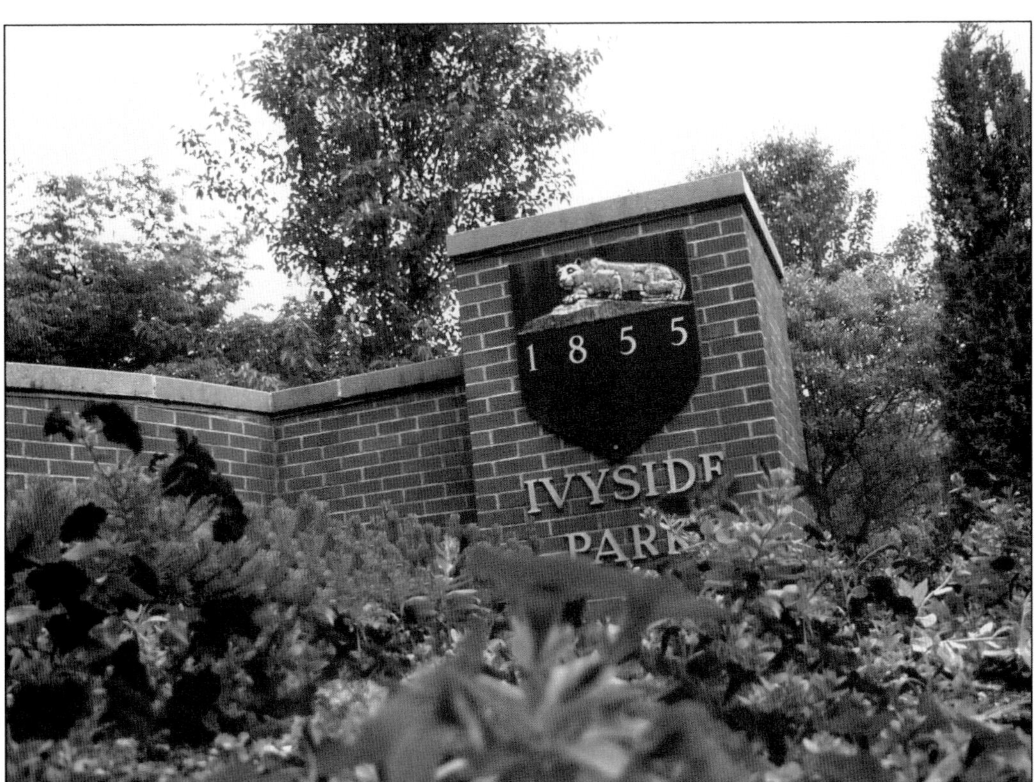

On July 1, 1997, the Altoona campus was rechartered as a four-year, degree-granting institution in the Penn State University system, thus ending its tenure as a member of the university's commonwealth educational system. In the ensuing years, Penn State Altoona's faculty and staff have grown in number precipitously, along with the addition of some 20 academic majors, ranging from business and criminal justice to history, communications, and environmental studies, among others.

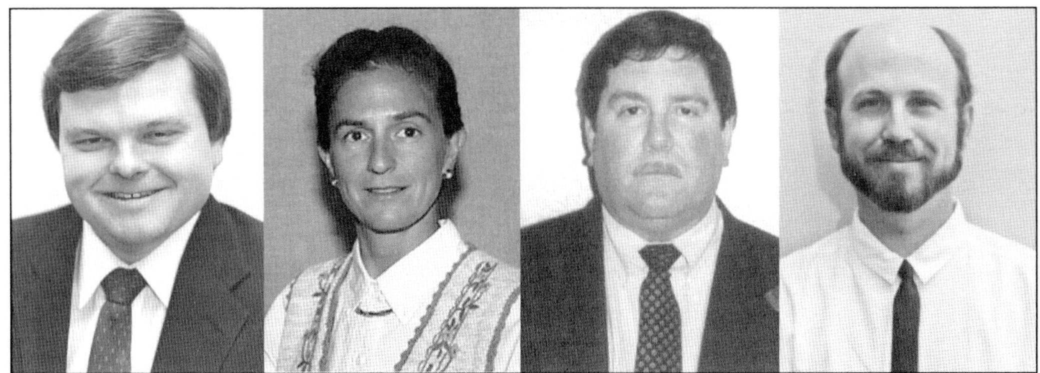

With its transition into becoming a four-year institution, Penn State Altoona slated its inaugural group of division heads. From left to right are William G. Engelbret, head of the Division of Business and Engineering; Lori J. Bechtel, head of the Division of Education, Human Development, and Social Sciences; James A. Winsor, head of the Division of Mathematics and Natural Sciences; and Michael W. Wolfe, head of the Division of Arts and Humanities.

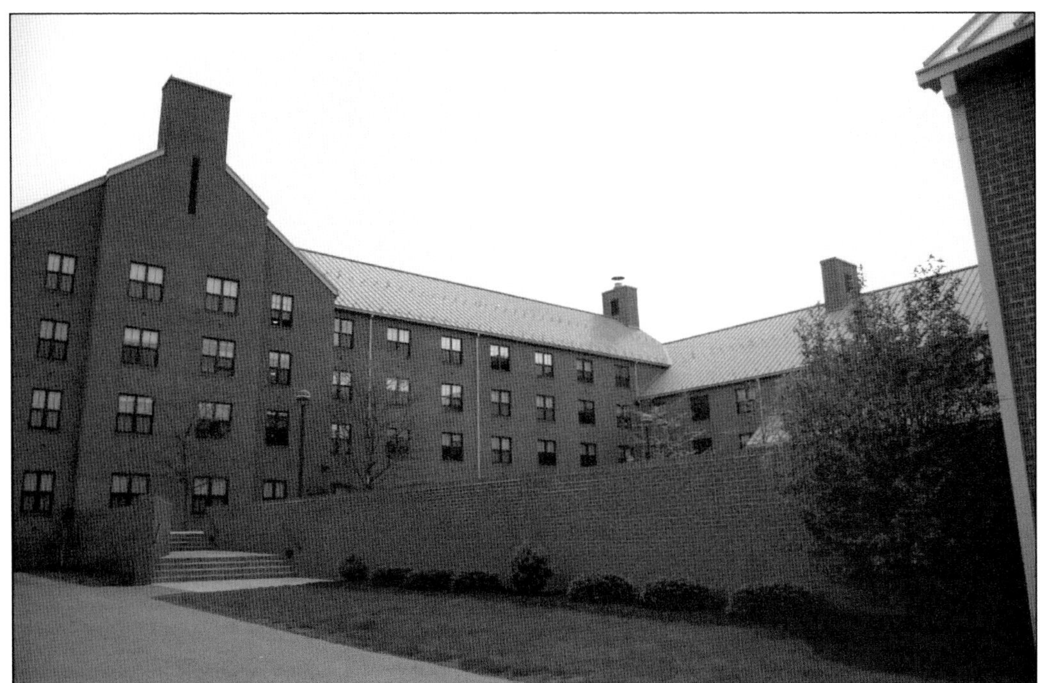

First occupied during the fall 1997 semester, Cedar Residence Hall houses some 320 students in suite-style rooms with adjoining bathrooms. Cedar Residence Hall features a number of study and television lounges.

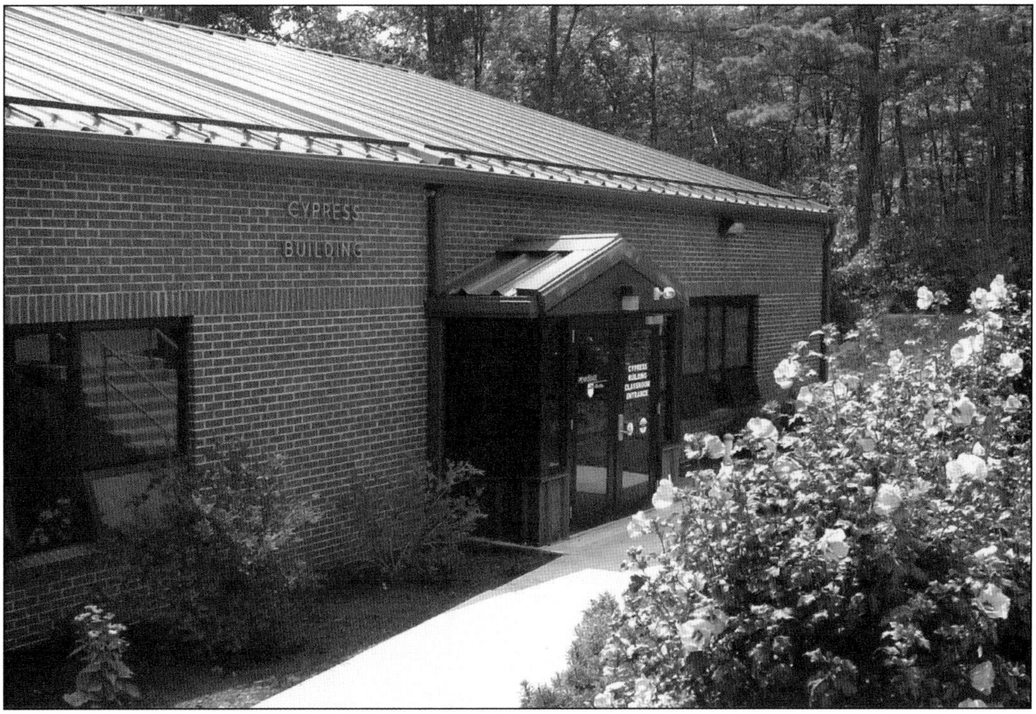

Completed in 1998, the Cypress Building was initially slated to be the home of the college's office of continuing education and training, which relocated to the Devorris Downtown Center. The building features classroom facilities and faculty offices. In January 2010, the Cypress Building will become the home of the college's childcare center.

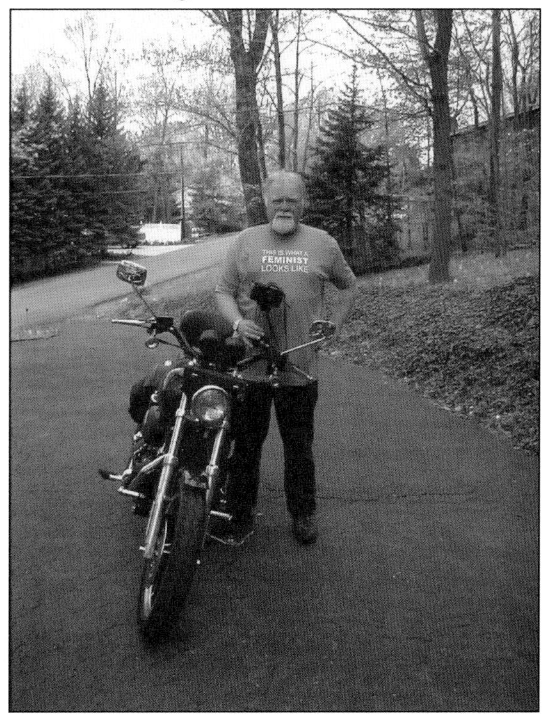

In 1998, L. A. Wilson II joined Penn State Altoona as assistant dean for research and sponsored programs and as associate professor of political science. Wilson has enjoyed a long and distinguished career as faculty and administration at such institutions as the University of Nevada, Las Vegas; Arizona State University; and the University of Alaska Southeast, where he served as dean of the School of Business and Public Administration. Under Wilson's tutelage, the college has seen a dramatic increase in external funds and grantsmanship.

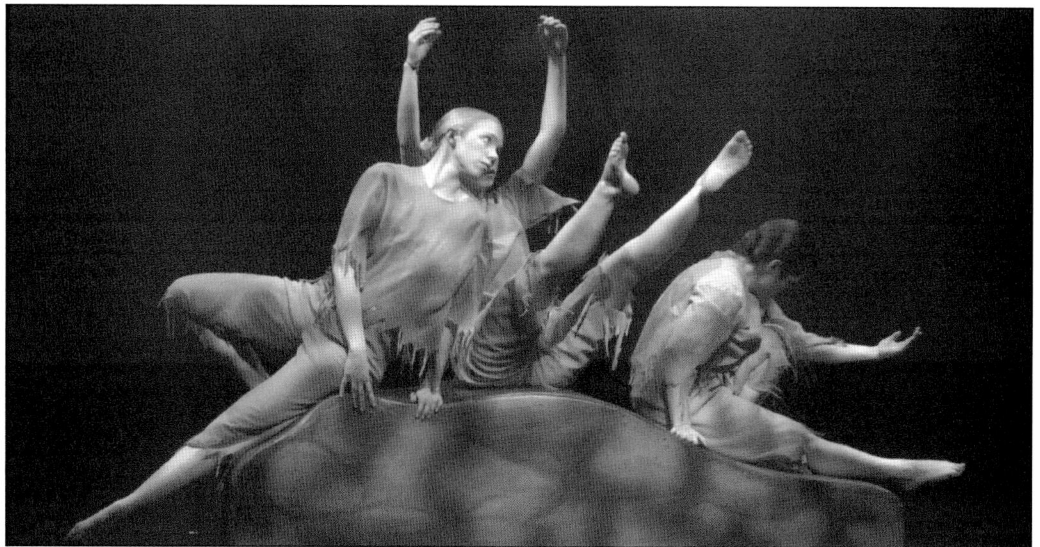

Under the direction of KT Huckabee, assistant professor of dance and integrative arts, Allied Motion offered formal productions of original works each semester, often in collaboration with artists, musicians, actors, and poets. Although Allied Motion performed its final concert in February 2008, its outreach program, the Children's Dance Theatre Project, provides some 20 children with the opportunity to experience dance each semester. The Penn State Altoona Dance Program currently sponsors the activities of a student dance company, the Ivyside Dance Ensemble.

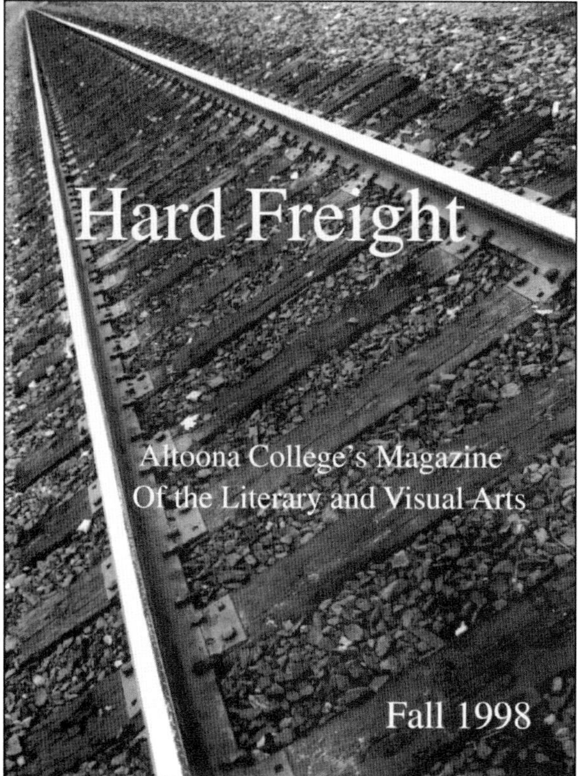

The student literary magazine was known as *Nous* until February 1967, when its name was changed to *Ylem*, connoting the primeval substance from which all other elements form, under the leadership of editor Richard Delozier and associate editor Timothy L. Wherry, the college's current head librarian. During the mid-1970s, the magazine was known as *The Altered View*. Following Penn State Altoona's new charter as a four-year college in the late 1990s, the magazine was rechristened as *Hard Freight* to reflect the region's railroad heritage.

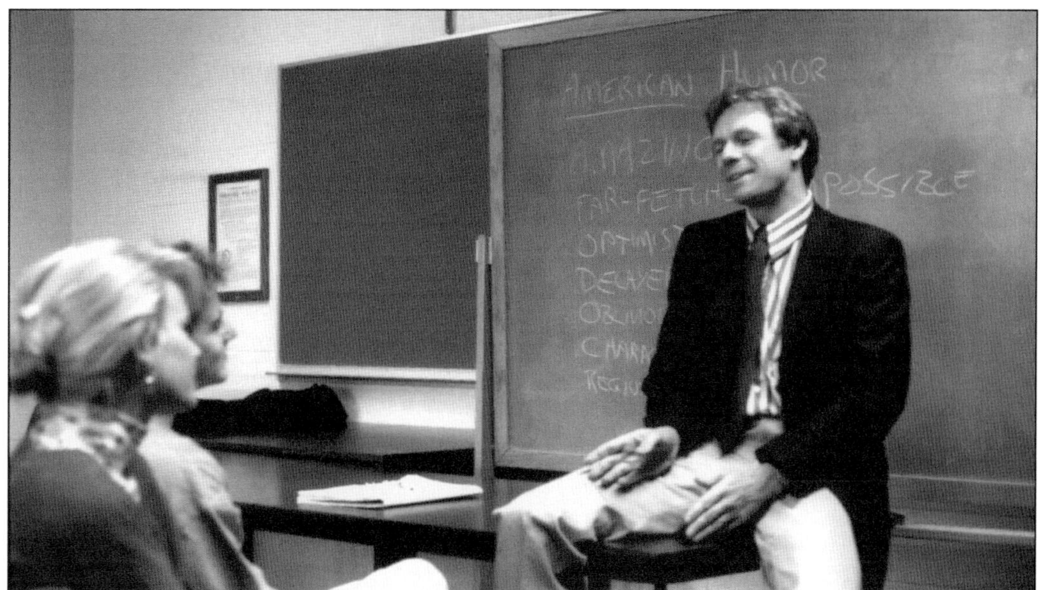

Established in 1986, the Alumni Teaching Fellow Award is sponsored by the Penn State Alumni Association, the undergraduate student government, and the graduate student association. The award is presented annually to three faculty members from across the university who have developed a record of distinguished teaching. Penn State Altoona has garnered three Alumni Teaching Fellows, including Ian Marshall (pictured above), professor of English and environmental studies (1999); Kenneth Womack, professor of English (2006); and Rebecca Strzelec, associate professor of visual arts (2009).

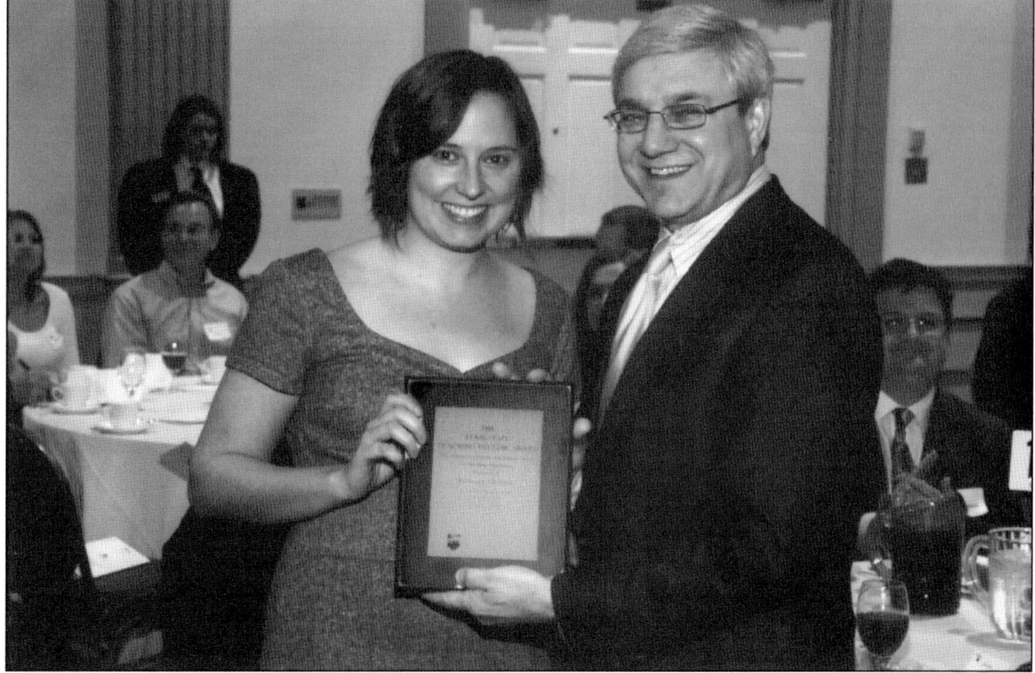

In this photograph, Rebecca Strzelec receives the Alumni Teaching Fellow Award from Penn State president Graham B. Spanier.

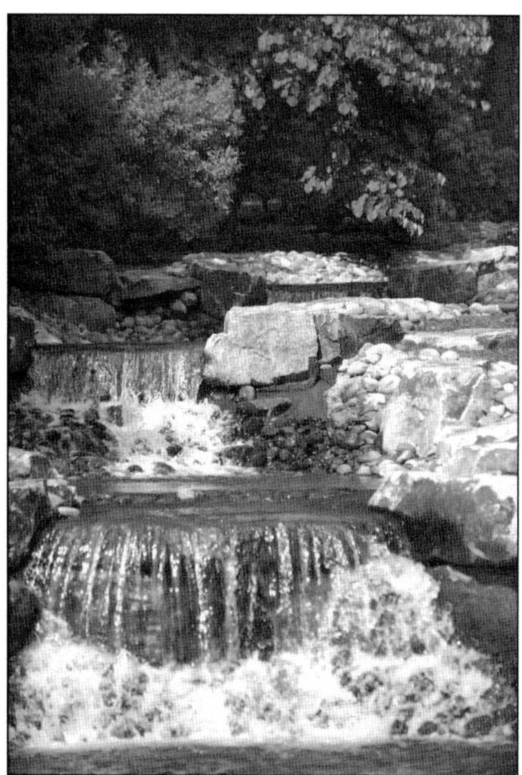

Located at the northeastern edge of the reflecting pond, the waterfall was constructed in 1999 at the behest of Dean Allen C. Meadors, who wanted to create an additional water feature to accent the pond's natural beauty.

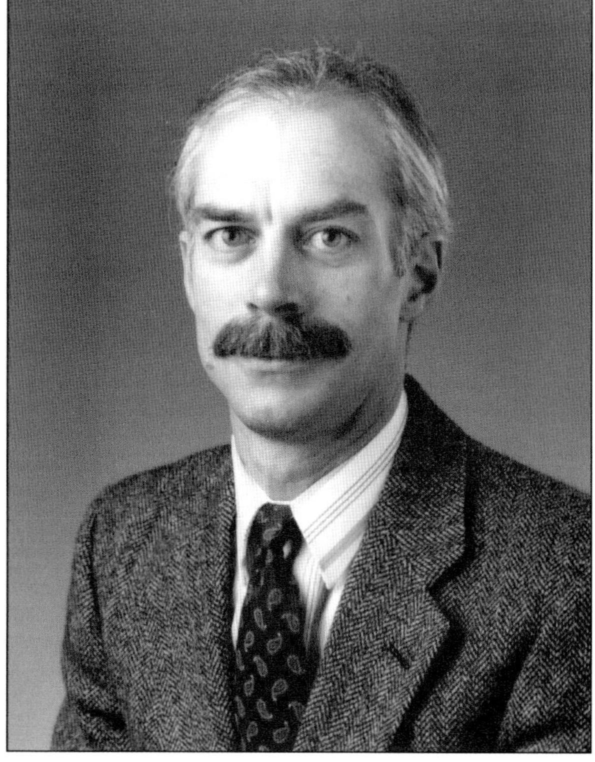

Robert N. Pangborn served as the college's interim chief executive officer and dean during the 1999–2000 academic year. Pangborn earned his doctorate from Rutgers University in 1979. In addition to serving as professor of engineering mechanics, he served as associate dean for undergraduate studies in Penn State University's College of Engineering. In January 2006, he was appointed vice president and dean for undergraduate education.

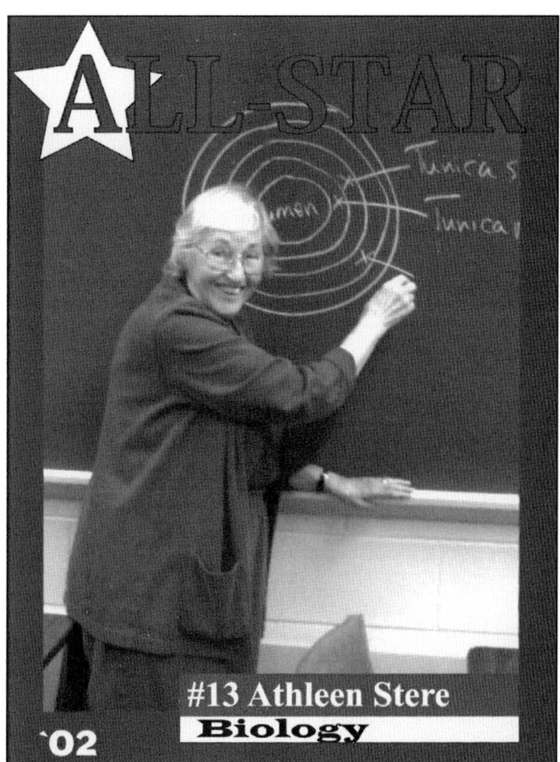

The brainchild of James A. Winsor, professor of biology, Penn State Altoona's faculty trading cards were brought to life by Mike Weiner, associate professor of mathematics. Each card highlights the faculty member's professional accomplishments, as well as their teaching effectiveness in the classroom.

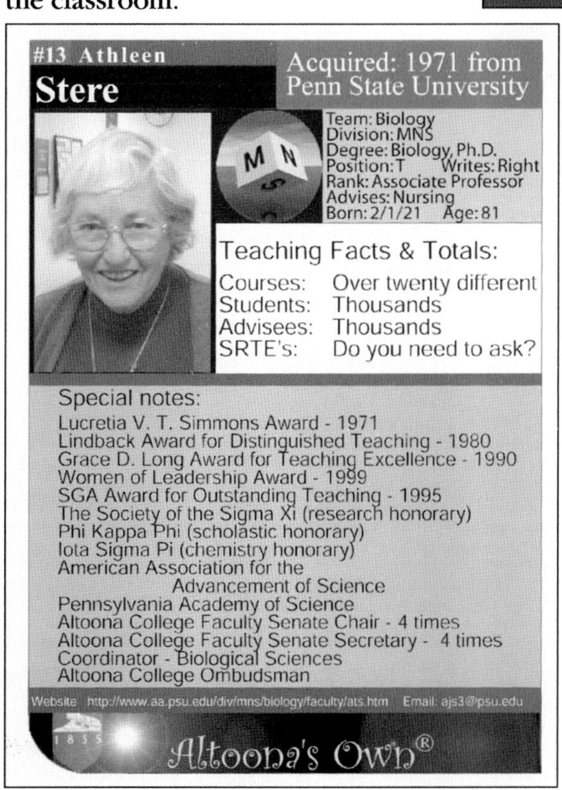

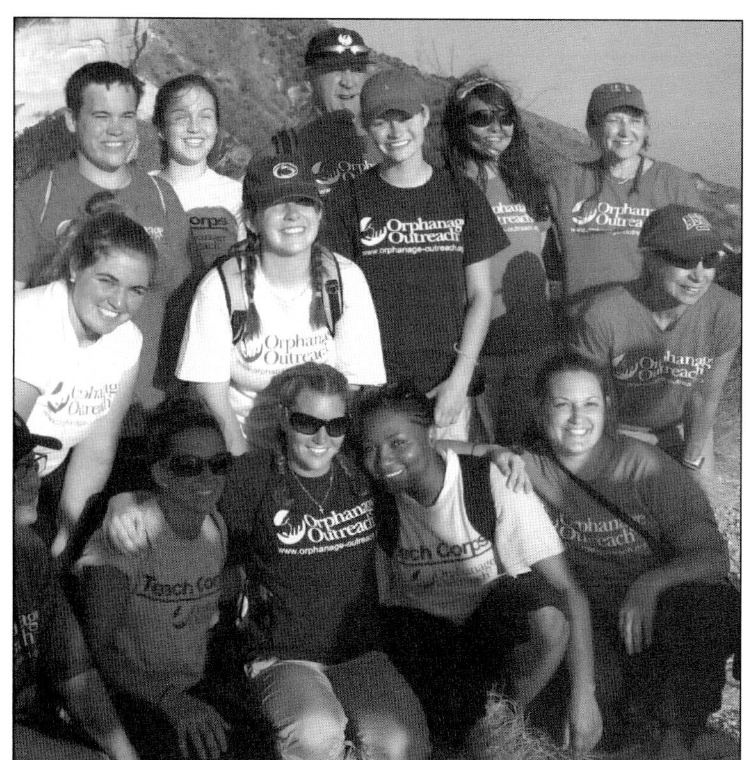

The brainchild of Lee Ann De Reus, associate professor of human development and family studies and of women's studies, and freshman Rebecca Moore, Penn State Altoona has hosted an annual "Alternative Spring Break" since 2000 at an orphanage in the Dominican Republic. Now in its ninth year, the program challenges students to engage in service learning by helping children in need while others across the nation engage in more traditional, beach-oriented spring break experiences.

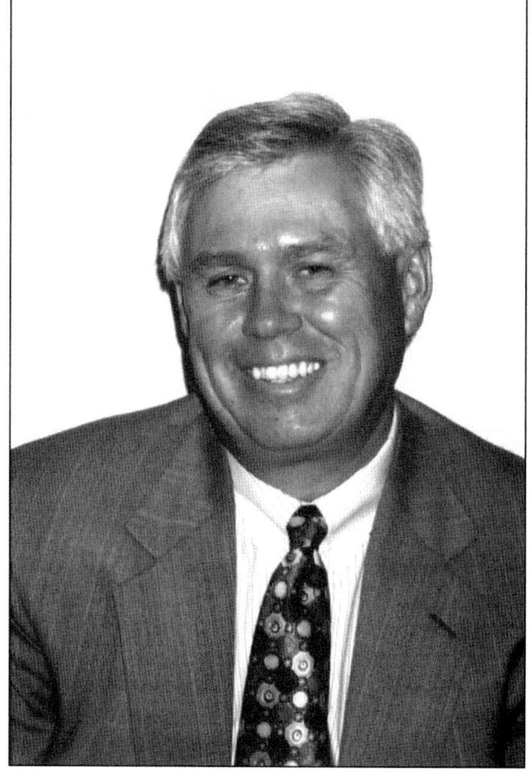

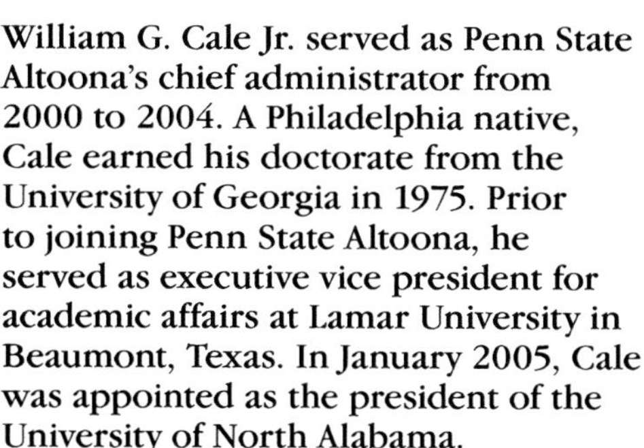

William G. Cale Jr. served as Penn State Altoona's chief administrator from 2000 to 2004. A Philadelphia native, Cale earned his doctorate from the University of Georgia in 1975. Prior to joining Penn State Altoona, he served as executive vice president for academic affairs at Lamar University in Beaumont, Texas. In January 2005, Cale was appointed as the president of the University of North Alabama.

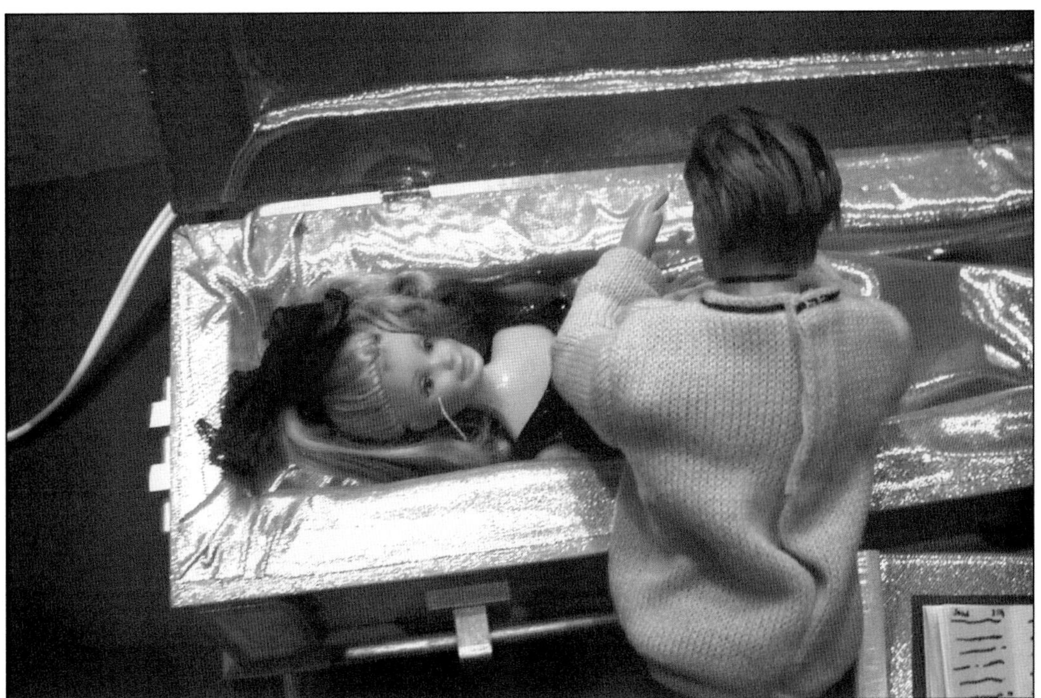

During the fall 2000 semester, Penn State Altoona faculty sponsored a festival devoted to addressing the culture of Barbie dolls and their iconic significance in American life. Barbie 2000 afforded particular emphasis to attendant issues concerning body image, popular culture, and other subjects related to women's health. Barbie 2000 featured art exhibits, interactive theater productions, health screenings, book displays, guest lectures, and panel discussions. (Dinty W. Moore.)

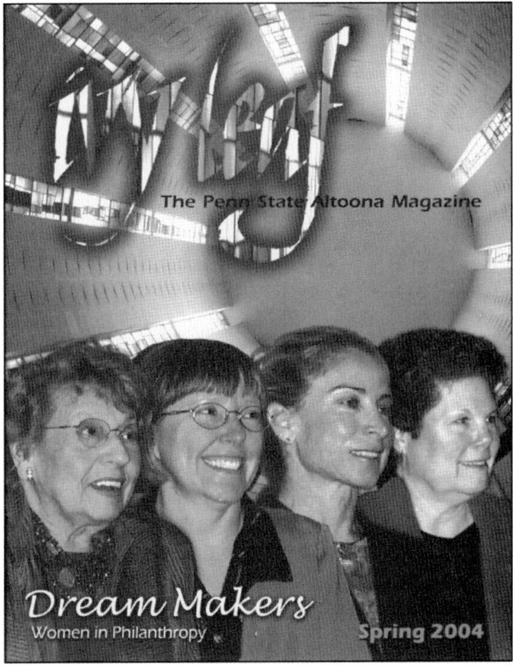

Edited by Shari Routch, director of university relations, the *Ivy Leaf* alumni magazine began production during the fall 2000 semester. The magazine includes feature stories about student and alumni accomplishments, as well as information and updates regarding faculty and staff news. In addition to the alumni magazine, the *Ivy Leaf* has served as the title of a campus newsletter (1953–1955) and the campus yearbook (1966–1972).

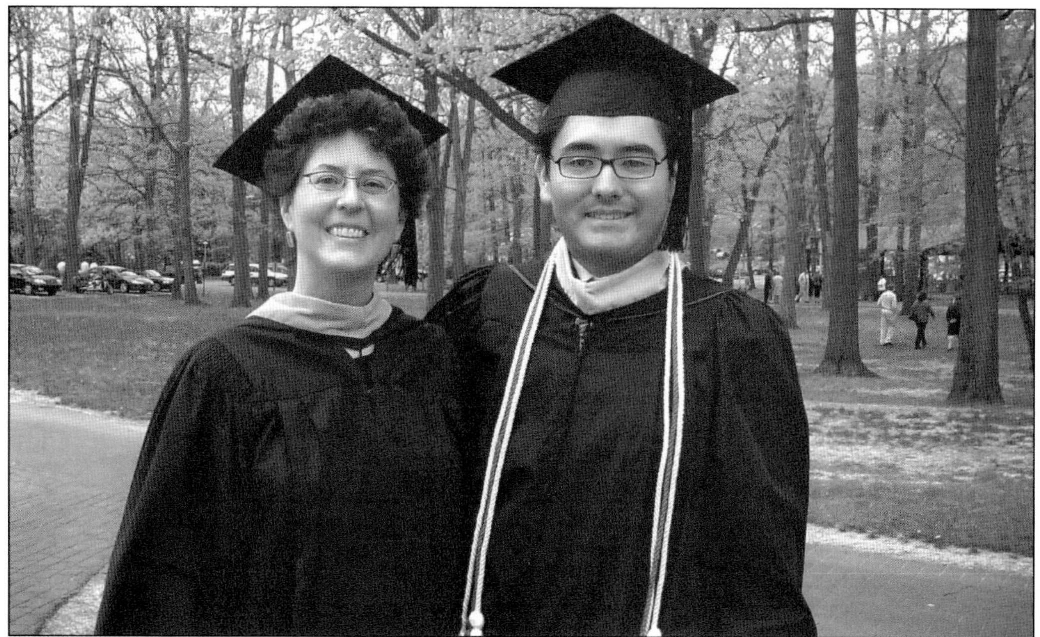

A member of the Penn State Altoona staff since 1989, Maggie McNulty was promoted to college registrar in 2001. Having earned a master's degree in adult education in 2006, McNulty's tenure as registrar has been distinguished by her reorganization of a key student-services unit, as well as her enhanced deployment of technology in the registrar's office. In this photograph, McNulty and her son Hiro receive their master's degrees during spring 2006 commencement exercises.

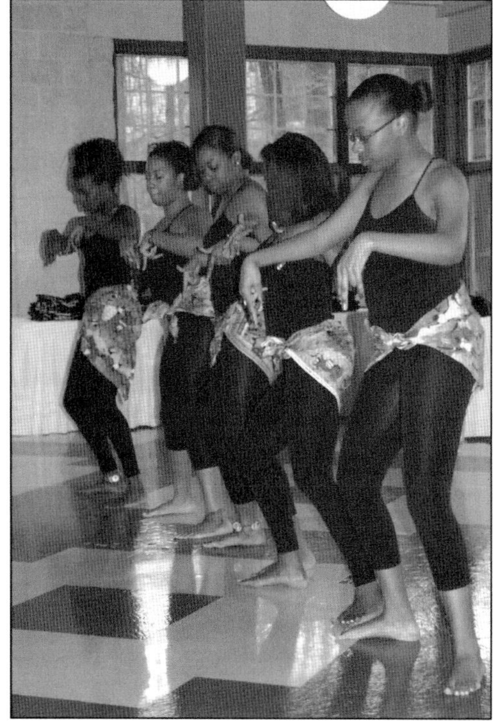

Under the leadership of Megan Simpson, associate professor of English and women's studies, the African American Read-In has been celebrated since 2003 at Penn State Altoona. The two-day event includes a Sunday community dinner program, an all-day Monday Marathon open mike reading and performance venue, a visiting featured author, a local secondary or elementary school writing project tie-in, and a "design-a-tee-shirt" art contest open to all Penn State Altoona students. Pictured are performers from the African Student Association Dance Group.

In April 1970, students joined in inaugural Earth Day festivities with discussion about local air pollution issues and a campus-wide cleanup effort. In 2001, Earth Day returned with an annual celebration involving yoga, canoe races, kickball games, live music, and children's activities designed to spread awareness about environmental issues. In this April 2008 photograph, a cleanup crew from maintenance and operations joins in the festivities. From left to right are Tim Bruce, Bob Rossman, Brad Long, Russell Bruce, Mike Baronner, John-Michael Werking, and Steve Rossman.

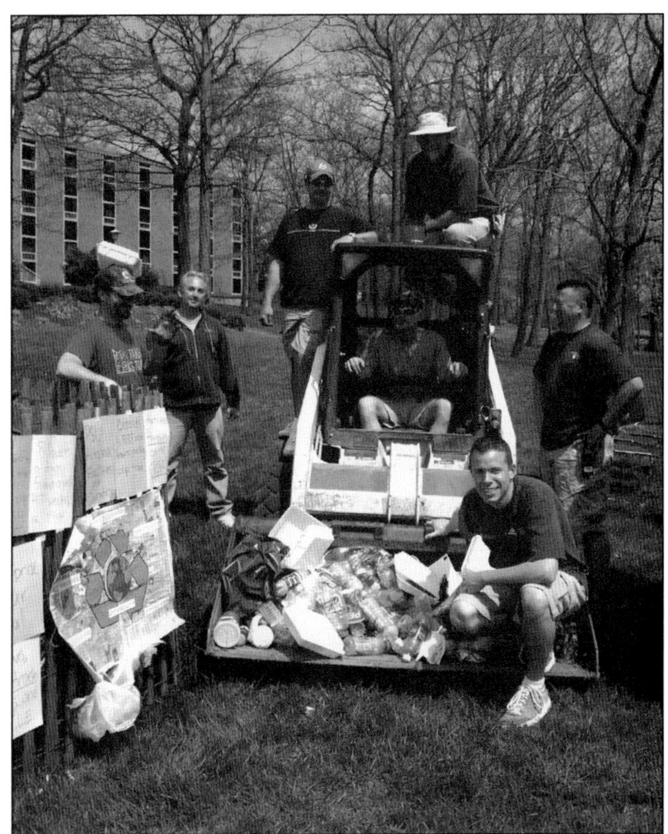

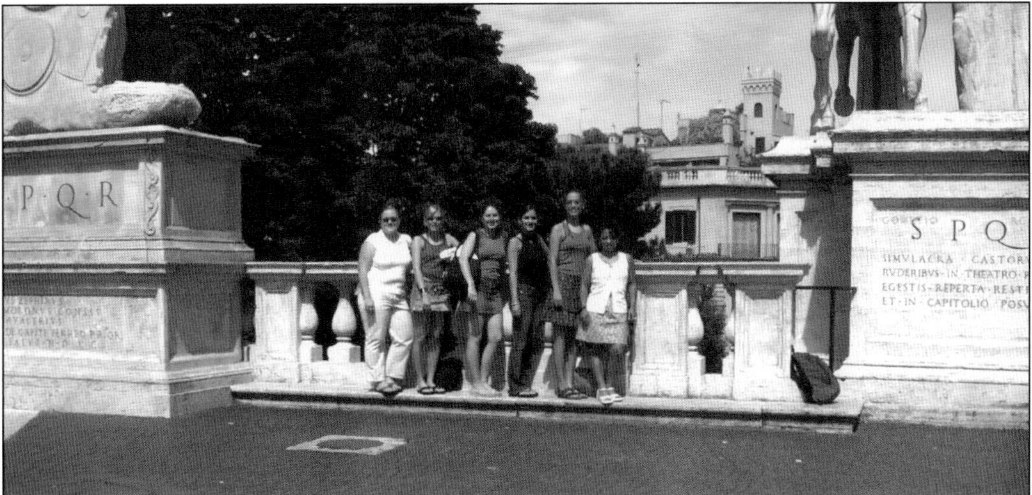

In 2001, the human development and family studies degree program began sponsoring a study abroad program in Rome. Under the leadership of Margaret Benson, assistant professor of human development and family studies, the summer semester in Italy challenges Penn State Altoona students to gain international perspectives and global contexts for the study of human development and family dynamics. Field trips include expeditions to Pompeii, Ercolano, Florence, and Venice, as well as visits to Italian day care centers, preschools, and an orphanage. (Margaret Benson.)

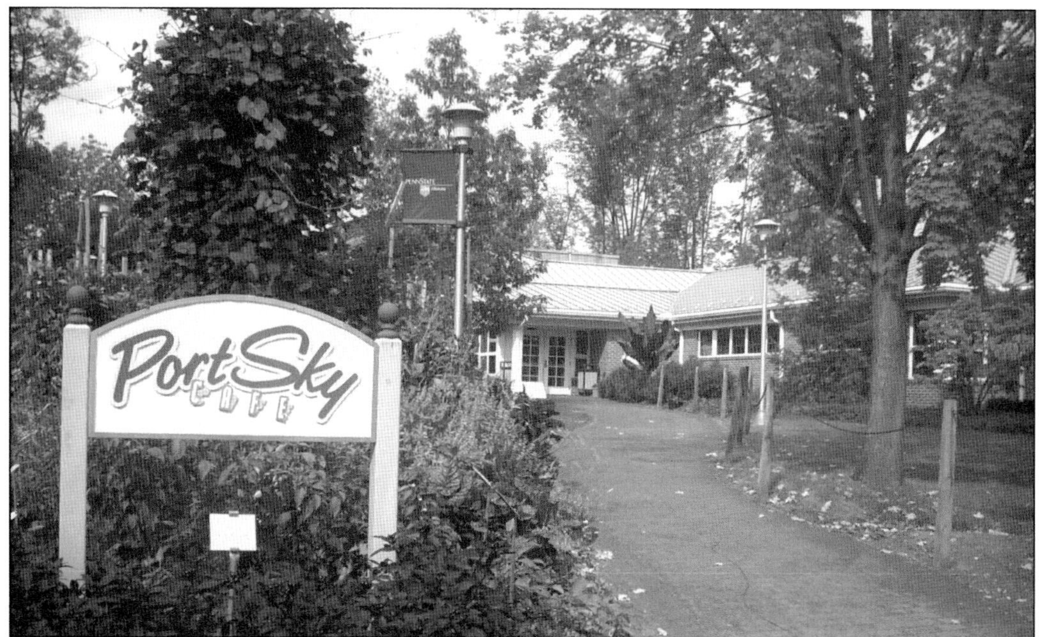

In 2001, the Hickory Court Café was rededicated as the Port-Sky Café in honor of the generous gifts to the campus from Neil and Marilyn "Mickey" Port and Phil and Rosalind "Roz" Sky, respectively. The Port and the Sky families made their name in the local food service industry, and their long-standing commitment and philanthropy were celebrated in the rededication of the college's central dining facility.

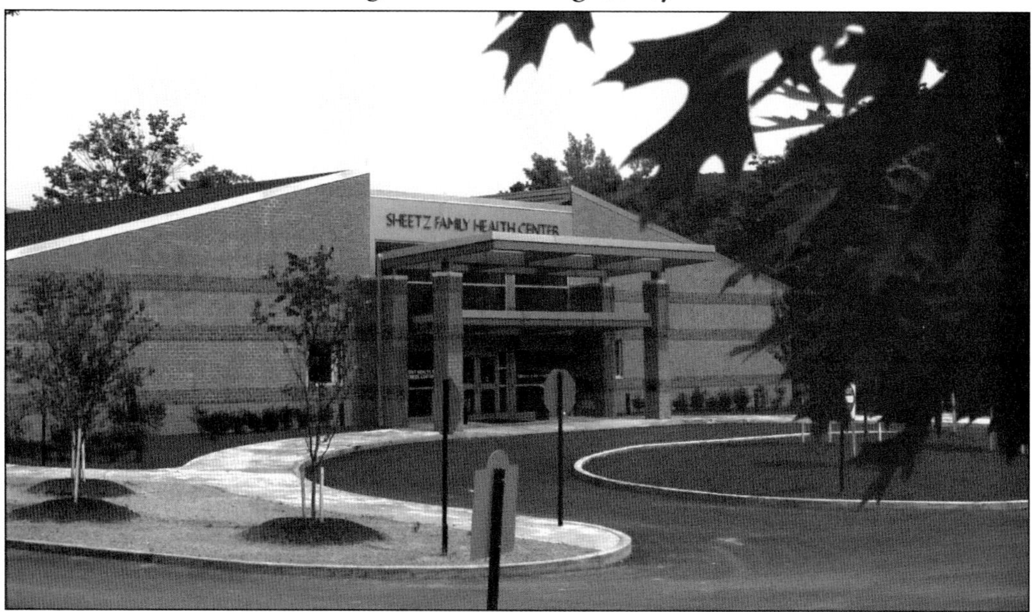

Named in honor of one of Altoona's most successful entrepreneurial families, the Sheetz Family Health Center was completed in 2002. The building houses the college's health and wellness center, while also serving as home to Penn State Altoona's nursing program. The facility features classroom spaces, clinical laboratories, and faculty offices, as well as personnel and equipment suitable for providing routine medical care.

The Spooktacular Science Show affords the local community a "Day of Play" associated with experiential learning. The brainchild of Richard Flarend, associate professor of physics, Spooktacular Science Show's attractions include exploding balloons, flying pumpkins, Ping-Pong balls ejected from a giant bazooka, and the ever-popular haunted physics laboratory, where kids fashion orange juice clocks, fizzy bombs, and crystal stencil stars.

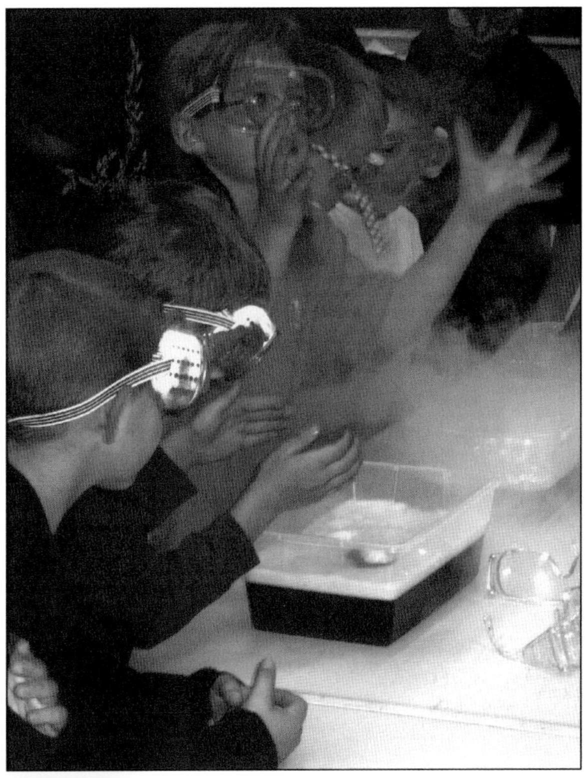

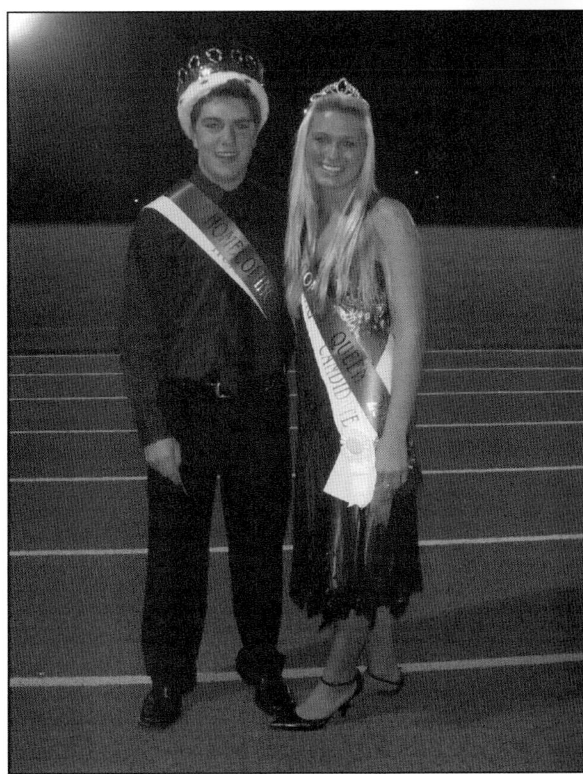

After a 20-year absence, homecoming returned to Penn State Altoona as a regular campus tradition in 2003. As part of the festivities, the college held a homecoming carnival outside the Harry E. Slep Student Center, as well as a number of sporting events, concerts, guest lecturers, and even a canoe race around the reflecting pond as a nod to the activities associated with Penn State Altoona homecomings past. Pictured are 2007 homecoming king and queen Connor Polcari and Katherine Paseka.

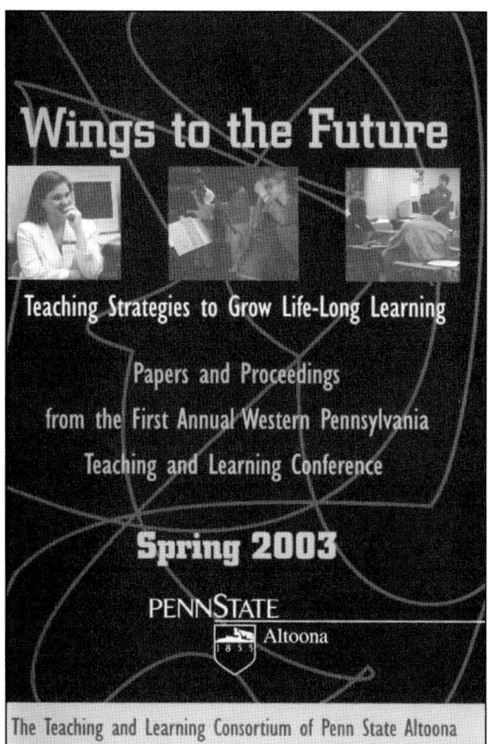

The Penn State Altoona Teaching and Learning Consortium (TLC) was established to facilitate communication about the improvement of teaching and learning throughout the university. The TLC hosts an annual Free University Series, as well as brown-bag luncheons designed to assist faculty in exploring various aspects of their teaching. In March 2003, the TLC sponsored an academic conference entitled Wings to the Future: Teaching Strategies to Grow Lifelong Learning. The conference resulted in the publication of an edited anthology (pictured left).

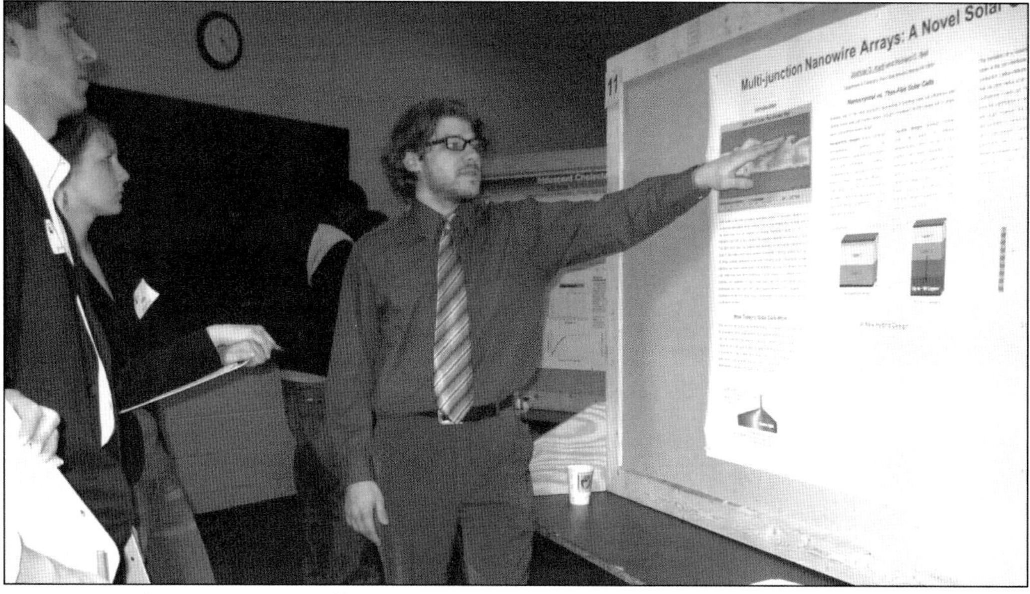

Inaugurated in 2003 in an effort to celebrate honors education and to promote student research, the Penn State Altoona undergraduate research fair was established by honors coordinator Lee Ann De Reus. In the annual research fair held each spring, students working in a variety of different academic disciplines share the results of their research through poster displays. In this photograph from the 2007 fair, student Joshua O. Karli demonstrates his work.

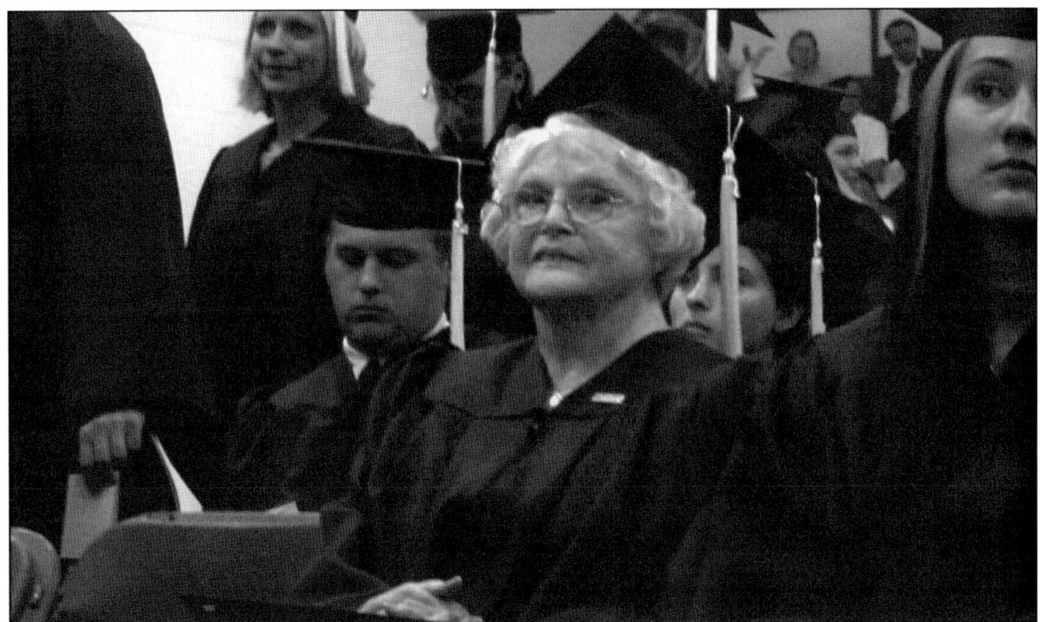

In May 2003, Mildred Turner graduated from Penn State Altoona at the age of 80 with an associate's degree in letters, arts, and sciences. Turner completed the degree in 2000 at the age of 77, although family obligations and illness forced her to delay commencement exercises until 2003. After retiring in 1990, Turner pursued her studies at Penn State Altoona on a part-time basis through the college's GO-60 program that allows Pennsylvania residents over 60 to attend select courses on a tuition-free basis.

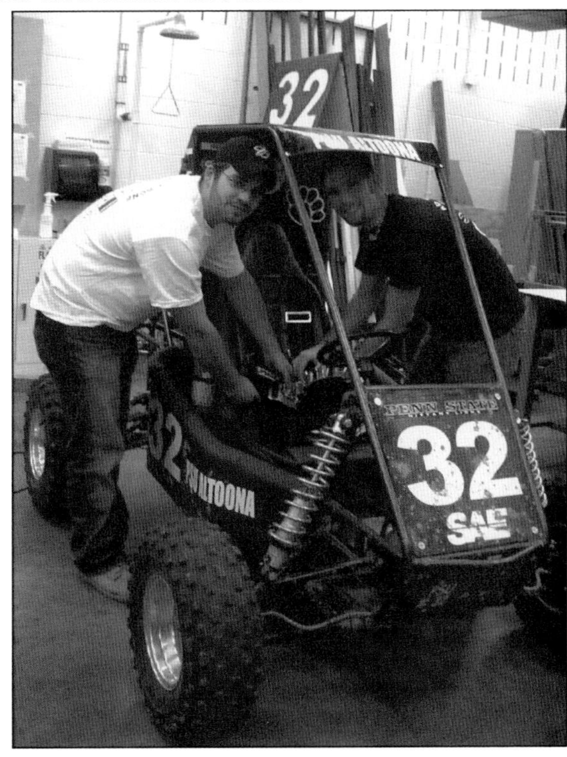

A complex of three regional competitions held annually across the United States, Mini Baja challenges engineering students to design and build off-road vehicles that simulate real-world engineering design projects and specifications. Each car must meet stringent cost, safety, and performance goals. Local advisors have included Andrew Vavreck, associate professor of engineering; John Sjolander, engineering laboratory coordinator; and Eric Granlund, instructor in engineering. Pictured are electromechanical engineering technology students Will Fedun (left) and Brett Johnston (right).

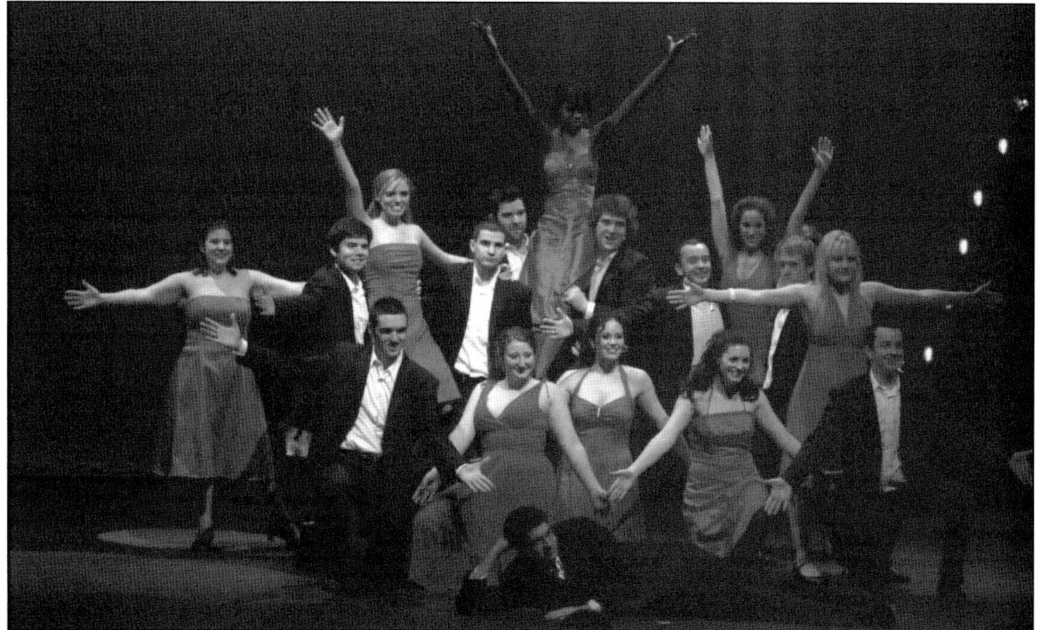

Founded in 2004, Ivyside Pride is Penn State Altoona's resident song-and-dance troupe. Over the next four years, the ensemble performed tributes to Stephen Sondheim, George Gershwin, Cole Porter, Irving Berlin, and the Beatles. In 2008, the troupe was refashioned as a vocal ensemble under the direction of Bonnie Cutsforth-Huber, assistant professor of music. In this photograph, Ivyside Pride poses during its fall 2006 tribute to Jerome Kern.

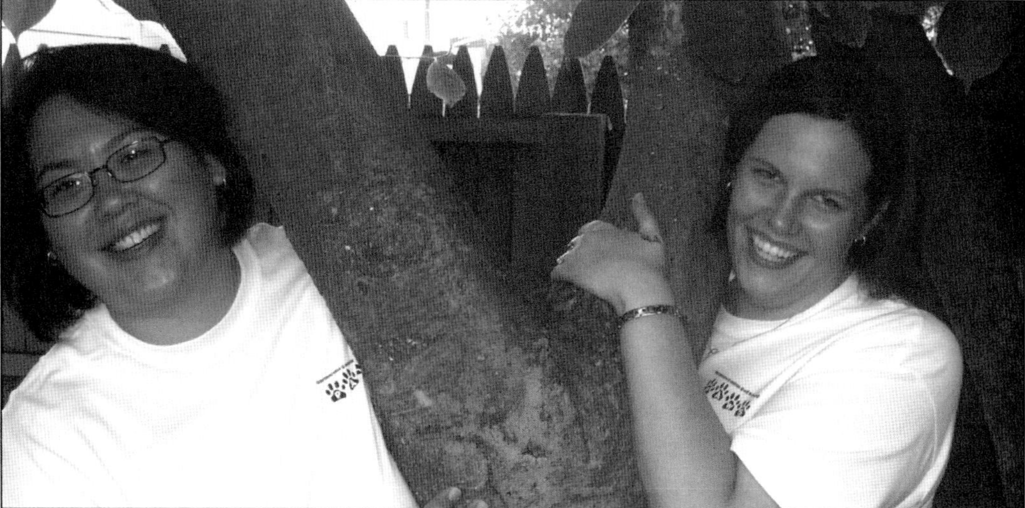

Led by Dan Lago, assistant professor of human development and family studies, Penn State Altoona established the Center for Community Based Learning and Research in 2004 through the auspices of a $300,000 Housing and Urban Development Community Outreach Partner Center (HUD COPC) grant. The center has afforded nearly 1,000 students the opportunity to engage in community-based learning activities. Pictured are students Christina I. Frantz (left) and Amanda Neff (right), key members of the grant's initiative to assist public-housing residents in pursuing opportunities in higher education.

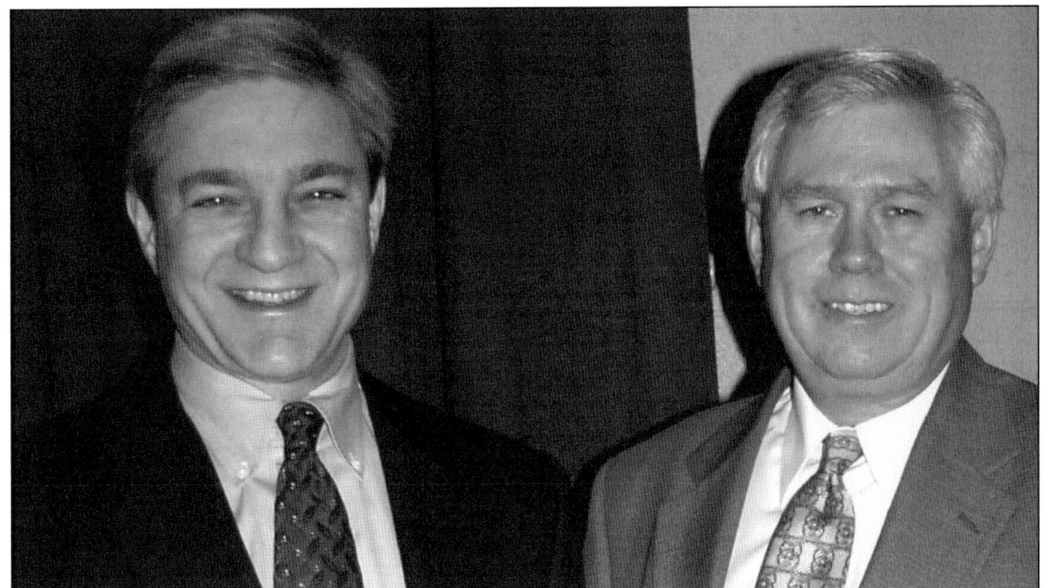

On December 16, 2004, Penn State president Graham B. Spanier (left) joined Penn State Altoona chief executive officer and dean William G. Cale Jr. (right), for the Hawthorn Building's official groundbreaking. Also in attendance were Pennsylvania state senator Robert C. Jubelirer and associate dean for academic affairs Kjell Meling.

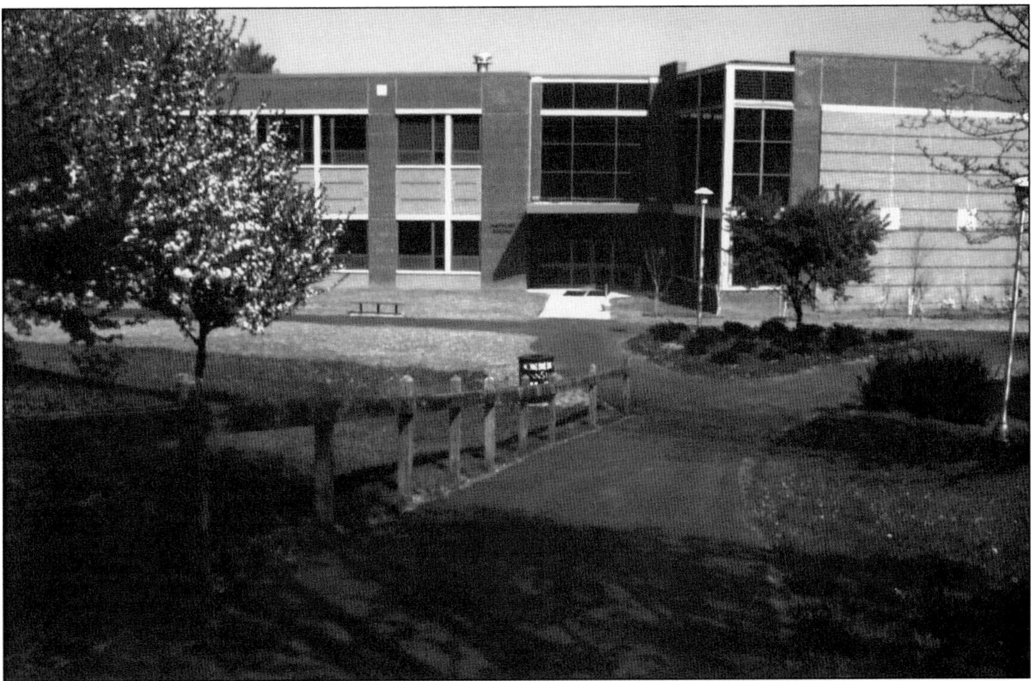

Completed in 2005, the multipurpose Hawthorn classroom building added nearly 60,000 square feet to the college's existing teaching facilities. The building features 24 classrooms, 56 faculty offices, computer laboratories, and three dedicated computer classrooms. In addition to a theatrical-style teaching auditorium, the building includes small seminar classrooms and a café.

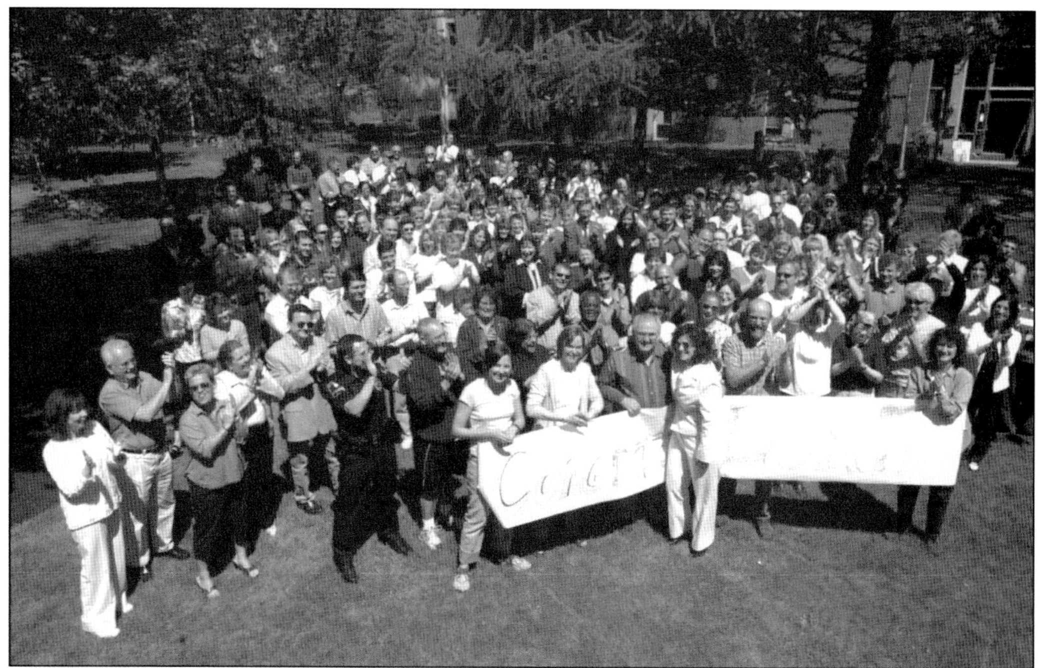

In May 2005, Lori J. Bechtel-Wherry was appointed as the college's first female chancellor. Having joined the campus faculty in 1985, Bechtel-Wherry earned her doctorate from Penn State University in 1987.

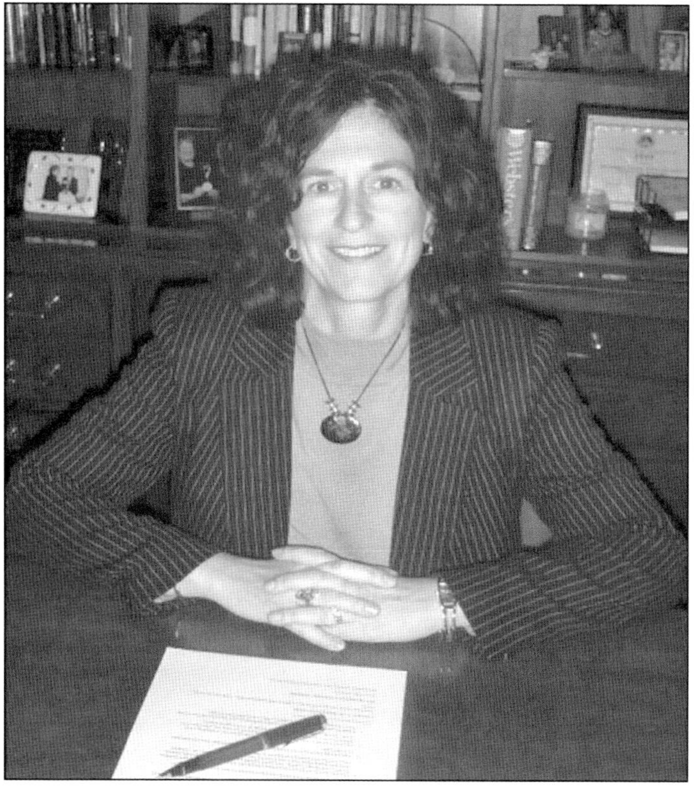

In addition to serving as a professor of biobehavioral health and women's studies, Chancellor Bechtel-Wherry had previously served as one of the college's inaugural division heads and as the successor to Associate Dean Kjell Meling. She has received numerous awards for her teaching, research, and service to the university and the community.

Under Bechtel-Wherry's leadership, Penn State Altoona expanded its facilities considerably, continuing to improve its services both to its student body and the greater Altoona community beyond the college. In addition to providing leadership for several record fund-raising efforts, Chancellor Bechtel-Wherry expanded the college's facilities, particularly in terms of establishing a key revitalizing effort in downtown Altoona.

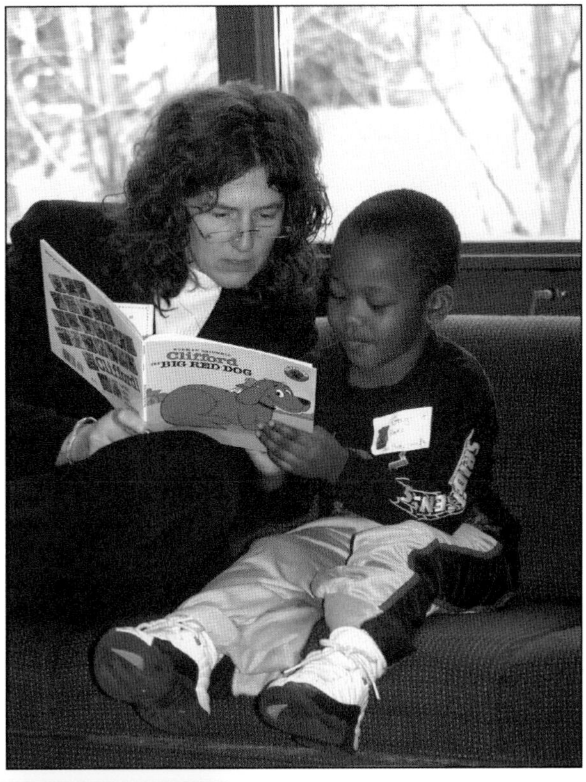

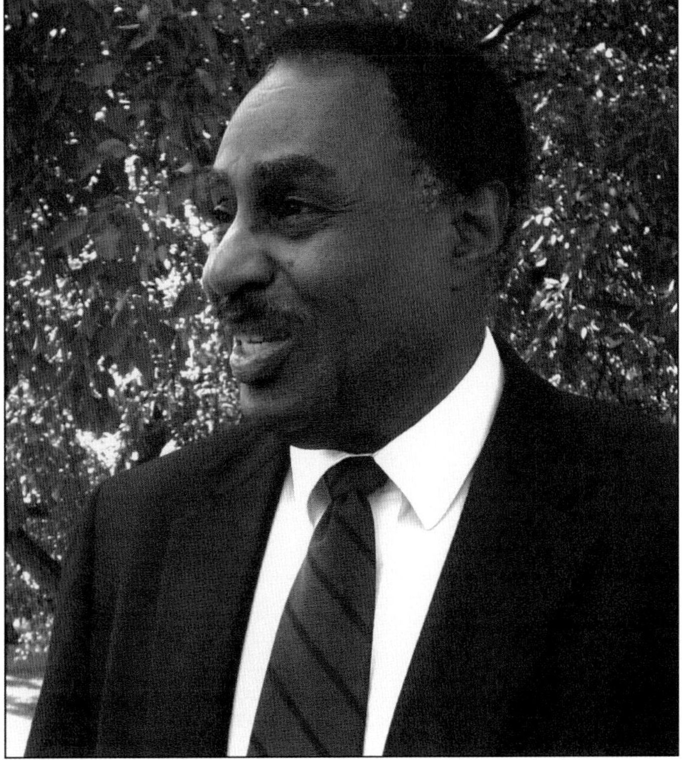

As the inaugural recipient of Penn State Altoona's Outstanding Alumni Award and a Penn State University Alumni Fellow, Ronald L. Mallett has distinguished himself as one of the institution's most celebrated and accomplished graduates. Having begun his academic career as a Penn State Altoona undergraduate in 1966, Mallett has devoted his research to addressing the possibilities of achieving time travel. Mallett is the author of *Time Traveler: A Scientist's Personal Mission to Make Time Travel a Reality* (2006), a bestselling memoir in production with director Spike Lee.

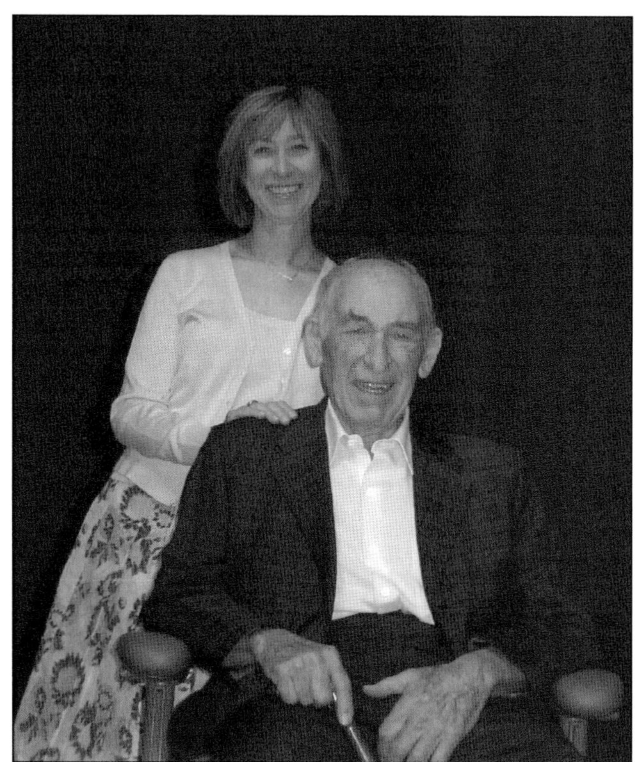

Anthony (Tony) Misciagna committed $1 million in 2006 toward the expansion of the former Community Arts Center, which was renamed as the Misciagna Family Center for Performing Arts. The retired Hollidaysburg stockbroker's gift afforded the college the opportunity to expand the facility to include a dance studio, a black-box theater, and vital theatrical spaces, including a set-building shop. In this photograph, Misciagna poses at the dedication with his daughter, Dr. Marianne Misciagna Young.

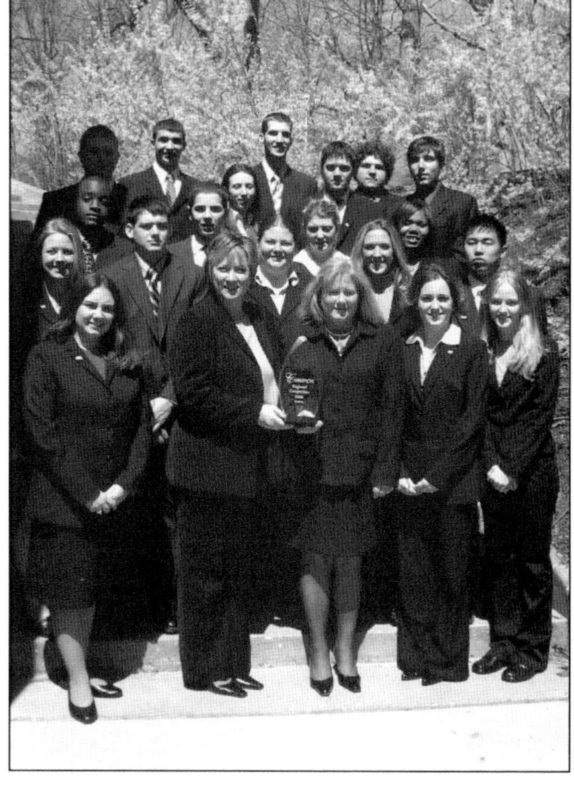

Established in 2006, the Students in Free Enterprise (SIFE) team earned Rookie of the Year honors at the SIFE USA National Competition in Kansas City, Missouri. SIFE is an international, nonprofit organization that gives students the tools to learn the free enterprise system in a real working situation. Under the leadership of sponsors Cynthia Wood (center left) and Donna Bon (center right), the SIFE team was recognized as regional champion during its second year of competition.

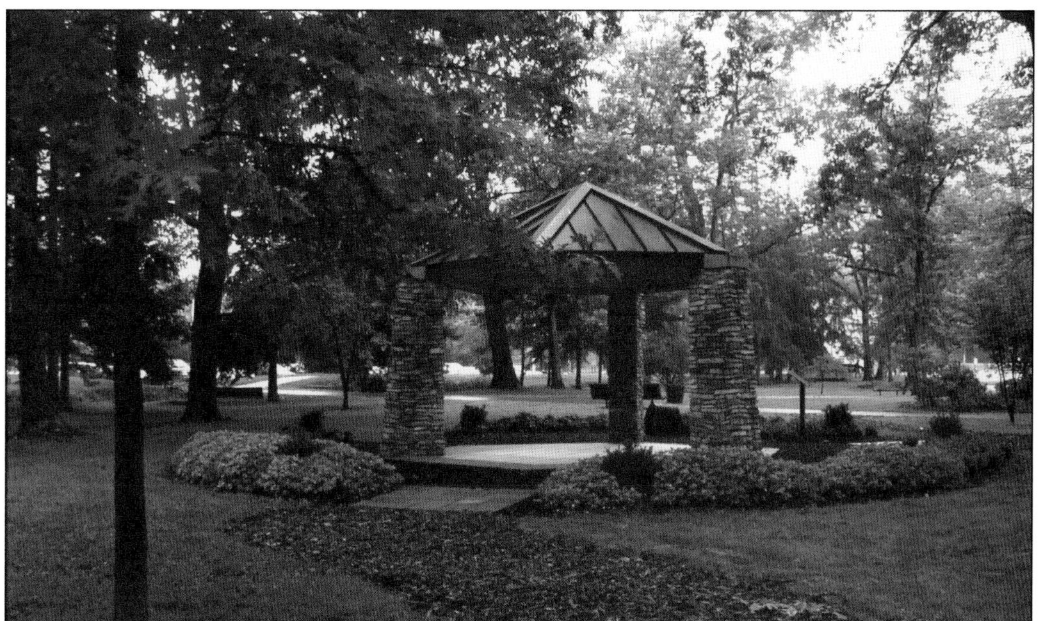

Designed in 2003 by Laurencio Carlos Ruiz, instructor in theatre arts, the Adam and Mary Christodoulos Gazebo was dedicated in September 2006. Penn State Altoona alumna Helen M. Christodoulos established the outdoor gazebo in order to honor the memory of her father and mother, who were immigrants from Cyrus and Lebanon, respectively.

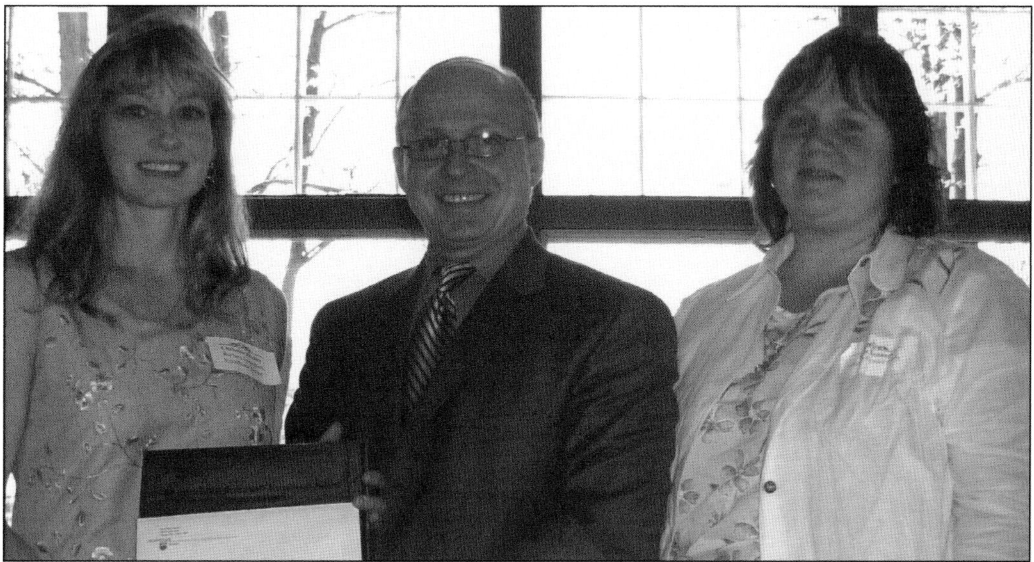

The Barbara Long Beck Endowed Excellence Award was established in 2006 to honor and recognize outstanding achievement by a faculty member and staff member of Penn State Altoona who represent the field of nursing. This award was established by Kimberly M. Kennedy in memory of her mother, a loyal friend and devoted supporter of Penn State Altoona. The award celebrates Beck's commitment to higher education and the nursing profession. In this 2006 photograph, award-winner Christine Ritchey (left), nurse practitioner, poses with David Shields (center), director of student affairs, and Kennedy (right).

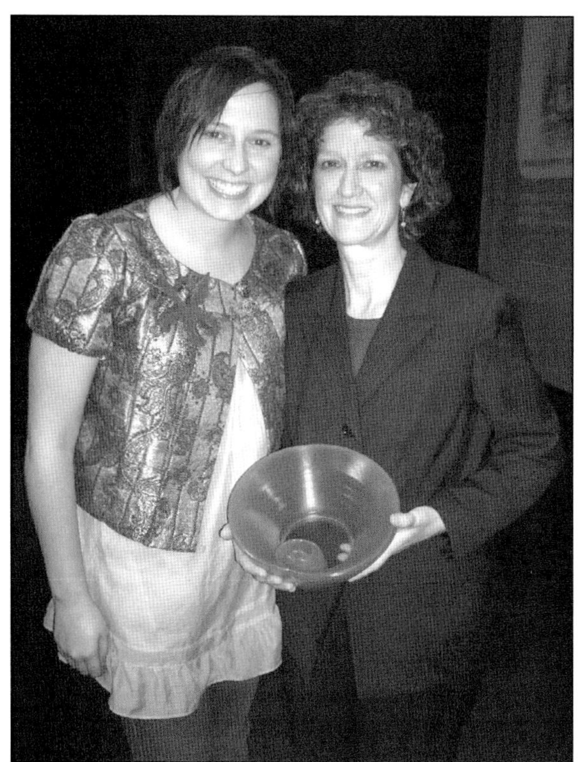

Endowed in 2006 by Diane Meling, the Kjell Meling Award for Distinction in the Arts and Humanities honors the life and work of the late associate dean for academic affairs. Past speakers include Pulitzer Prize–winning novelist Richard Russo, musicologist Walter Everett, Disney imagineer MK Haley, and Penn State Altoona scholars Sandra Harbert Petrulionis (right), professor of English and American studies, and Ian Marshall, professor of English and environmental studies. Honorees receive a ceremonial bowl designed by Rebecca Strzelec (left), associate professor of visual arts.

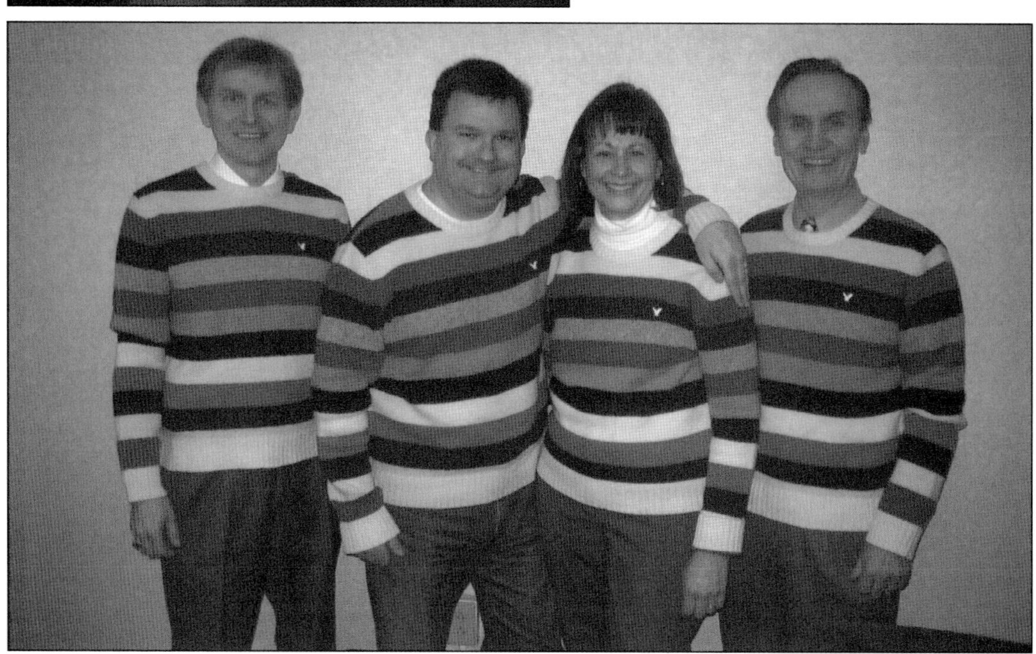

In this 2007 photograph are, from left to right, Andrew N. Vavreck, head of the Division of Business and Engineering; Kenneth Womack, head of the Division of Arts and Humanities; Valerie N. Stratton, head of the Division of Education, Human Development, and Social Sciences; and Nicholas M. Miskovsky, head of the Division of Mathematics and Natural Sciences.

Sponsored by the Teaching and Learning Consortium, the Free University Series affords Altoona area residents with a lecture series designed to establish vital interconnections between the community and the college. During its 2007 inaugural season, the Free University Series featured talks by Brian Black, professor of history and environmental studies, and Jerry Zolten (pictured right), associate professor of communication arts and sciences.

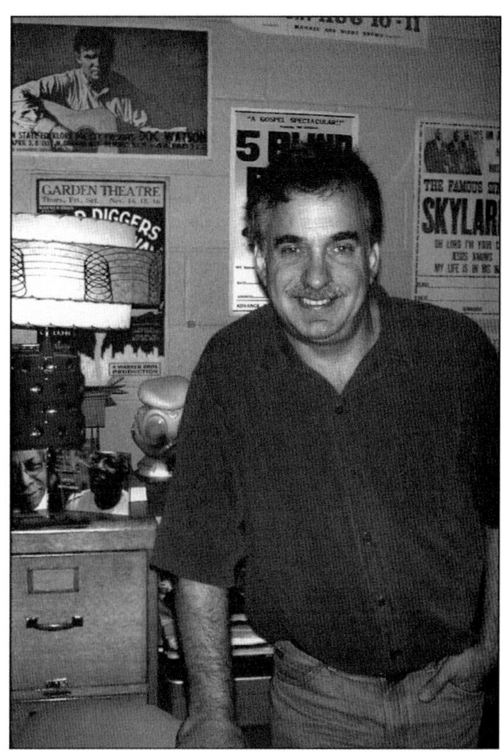

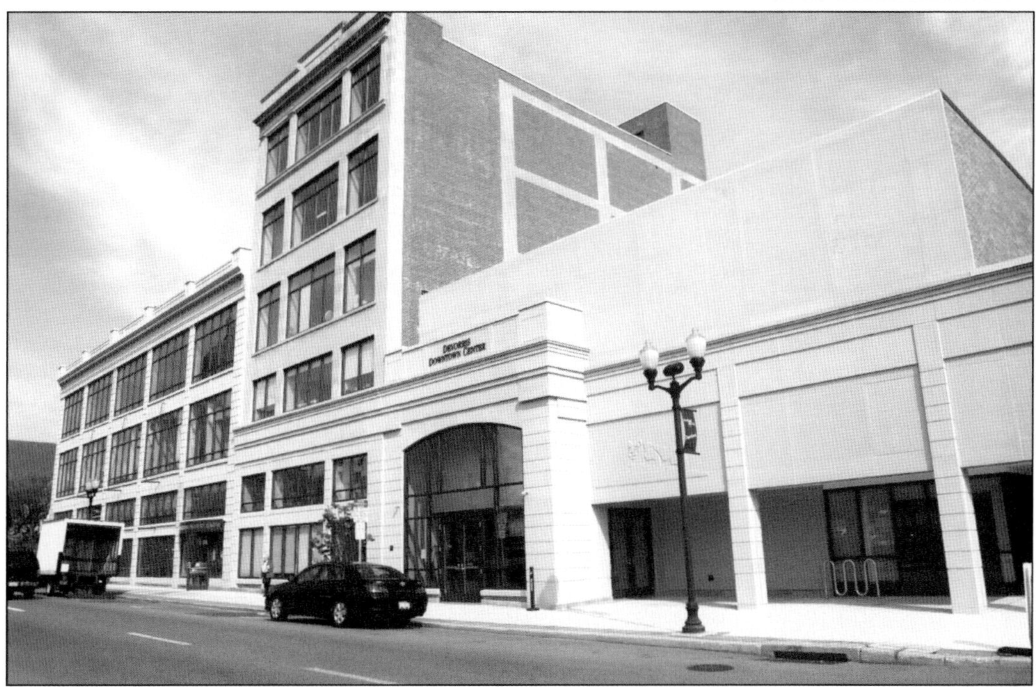

Dedicated in 2008 for the philanthropy of local entrepreneur Donald Devorris and his wife Nancy, Penn State Altoona's Devorris Downtown Center houses the institution's office of continuing education and training, as well as a suite of classrooms and a 370-seat auditorium and theatrical space.

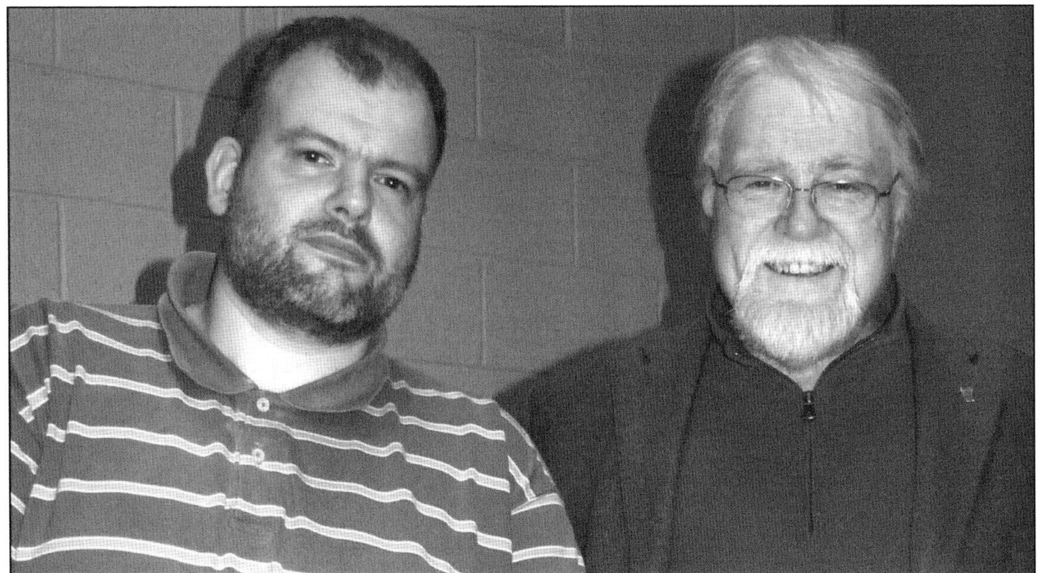

Established in 2008 in order to recognize distinguished research, scholarship, and creative contributions by the college's faculty, the inaugural Outstanding Achievement in Research and Creative Activity Award was presented to Thomas Krainer, assistant professor of mathematics. Krainer's innovative work considers partial differential equations and their role in the modeling of various phenomena in science and engineering. Krainer is pictured (left) with L. A. Wilson II (right), assistant dean for research and sponsored programs.

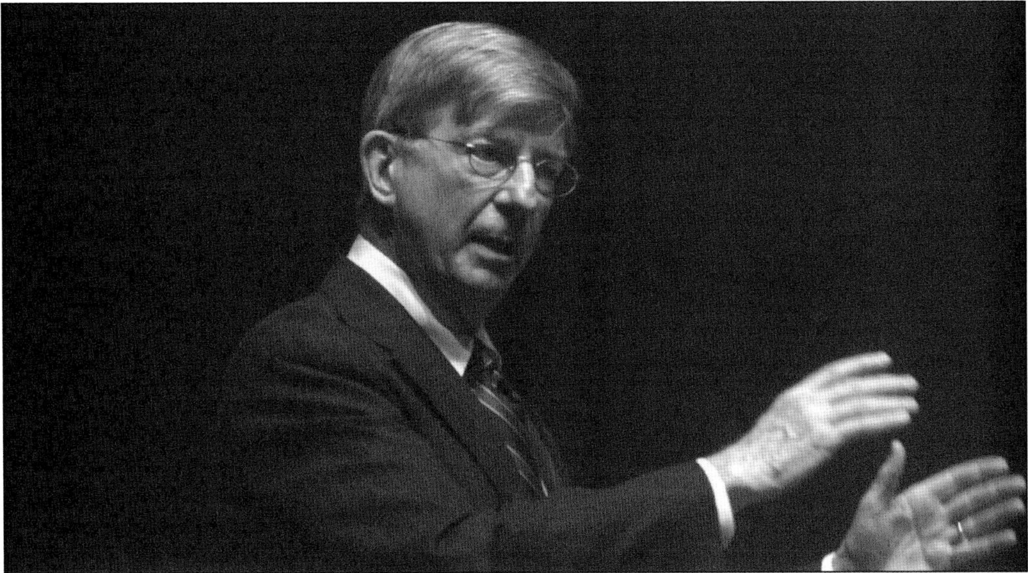

Established in order to benefit the Penn State Altoona Future Fund, the Distinguished Speaker Series hosted its inaugural speaker, conservative commentator and Pulitzer Prize–winning author George Will (pictured above) in November 2008. The second speaker in the series, former United States secretary of state Madelyn R. Albright, visited the college in April 2009. The Future Fund provides funds for academic and cultural enrichment programs on campus and in the community, while also offering emergency scholarship assistance to students undergoing financial crisis.

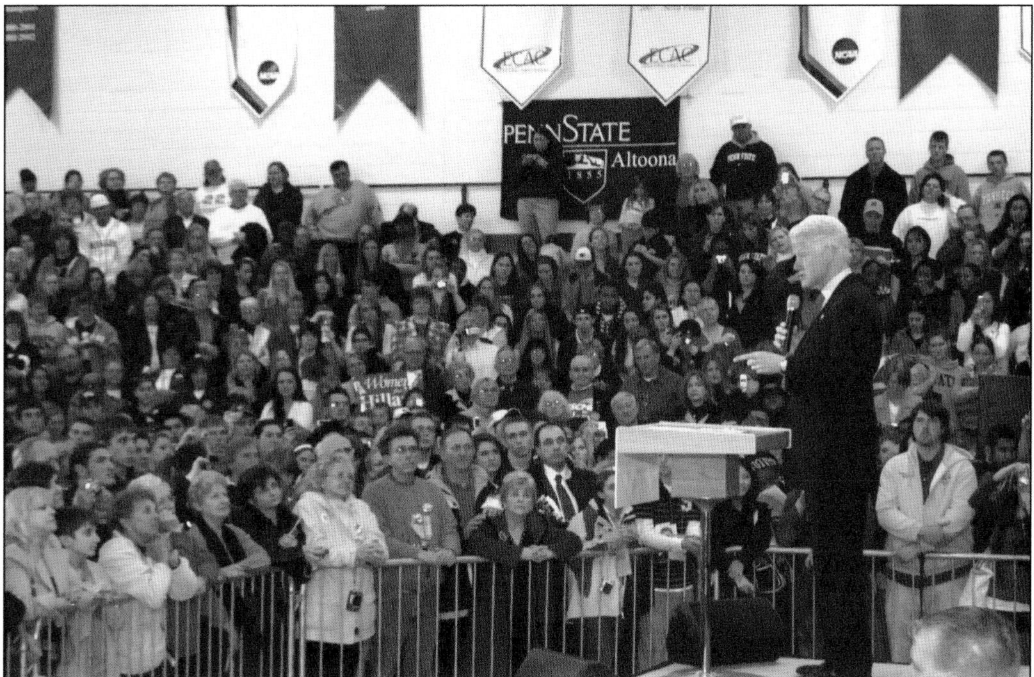

On April 3, 2008, former president Bill Clinton delivered an address in the Steven A. Adler Athletic Complex in support of Sen. Hillary Rodham Clinton's bid for the Democratic Party's presidential nomination. After speaking in front of a capacity crowd, President Clinton signed autographs before departing in his motorcade.

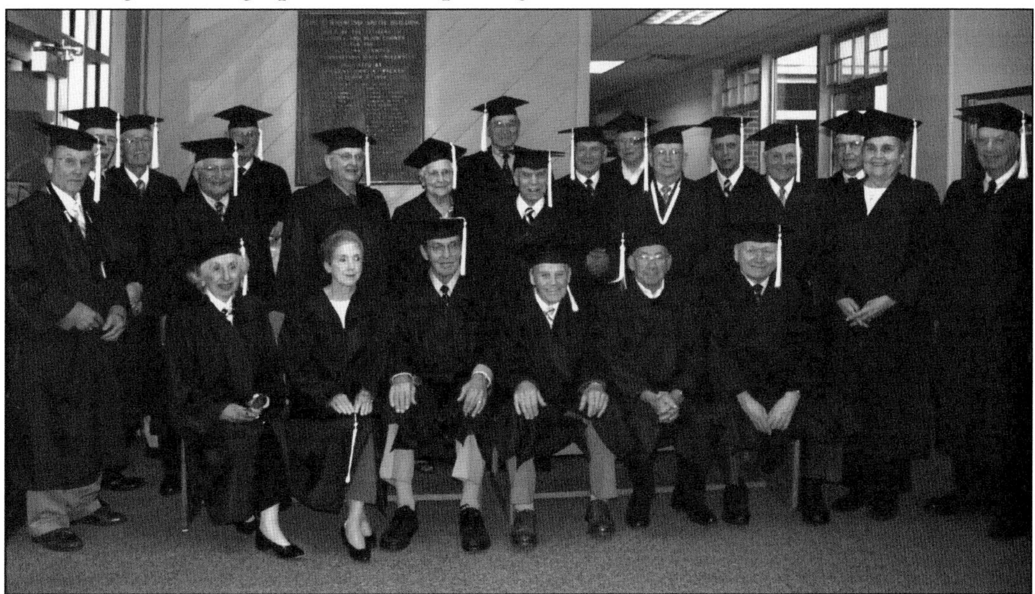

In May 2008, the college held its inaugural Pioneer Reunion in which some 30 former students who attended Penn State Altoona between 1939 and 1958 returned to the campus to celebrate their legacy. Five of the pioneers, including John E. Boyd III, Victoria F. Lee, James B. Miller, John E. "Ted" Mock, and Bernard G. Monahan, endowed a $50,000 Trustee Scholarship in order to commemorate the reunion.

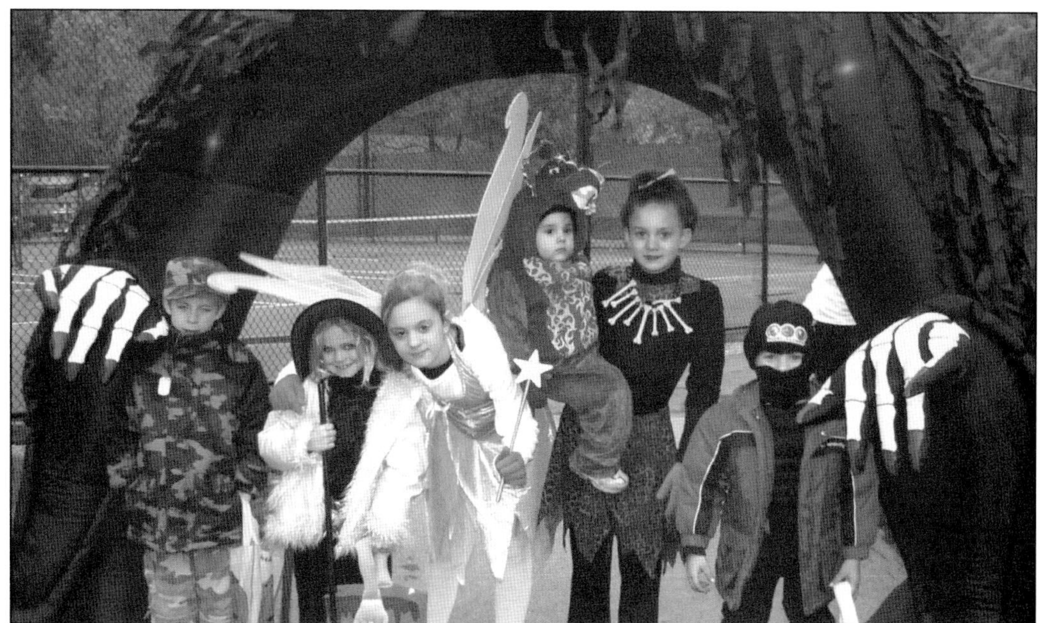

Sponsored by the student life office, Operation Safe Trick-or-Treat affords area children and their families a safe alternative to traditional Halloween activities. Each October, numerous student organizations invite children from the community to dress up in their Halloween finery, receive candy, play games, and participate in a wide variety of interactive displays.

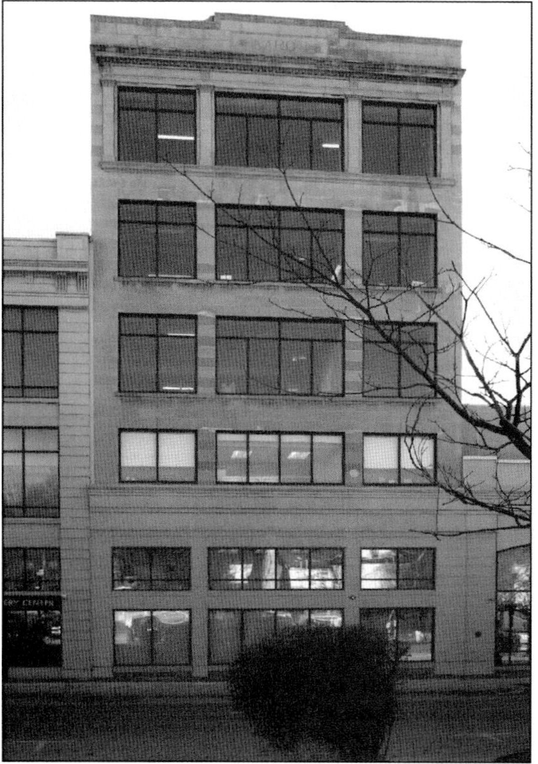

As the central foundation in Penn State Altoona's creation of a downtown campus, the purchase of the Aaron Building under the leadership of Chancellor Lori J. Bechtel-Wherry paved the way for the college to provide multicampus course offerings. In addition to the creation of the Dining Car, a first-floor eatery, the Aaron Building houses key facilities devoted to the nursing and communications programs, as well as to the office of continuing education and training.

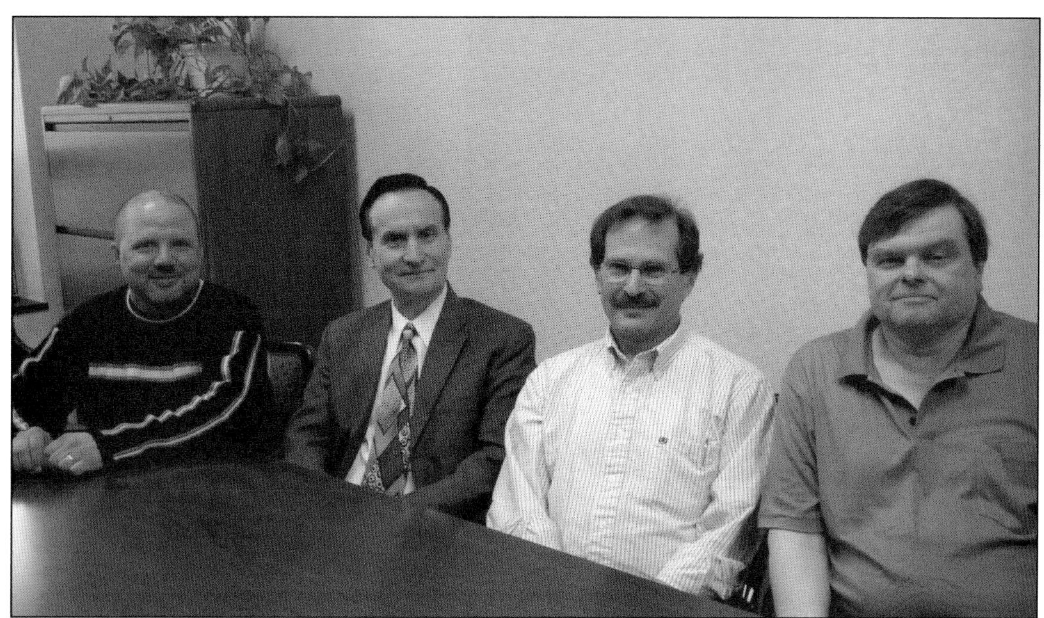

In this 2009 photograph are, from left to right, Timothy D. Slekar, head of the Division of Education, Human Development, and Social Sciences; Nicholas M. Miskovsky, head of the Division of Mathematics and Natural Sciences; Marc L. Harris, head of the Division of Arts and Humanities; and William G. Engelbret, head of the Division of Business and Engineering.

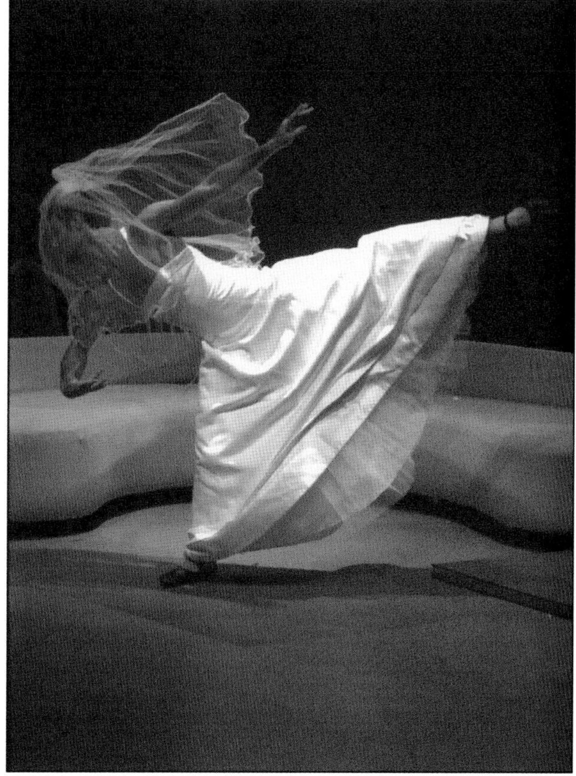

Directed by Robin L. Reese, assistant professor of theater arts, the Penn State Altoona theatrical production of Charles L. Mee's *Big Love* received high honors from the Kennedy Center American College Theatre Festival, which was held at the University of the Arts in Philadelphia in January 2009. Several individual students received accolades for their performances, including Mallorie Halsall, Michael Makin (pictured), and Megan Marcaurelle, who received nominations for the Irene Ryan National Acting Scholarship.

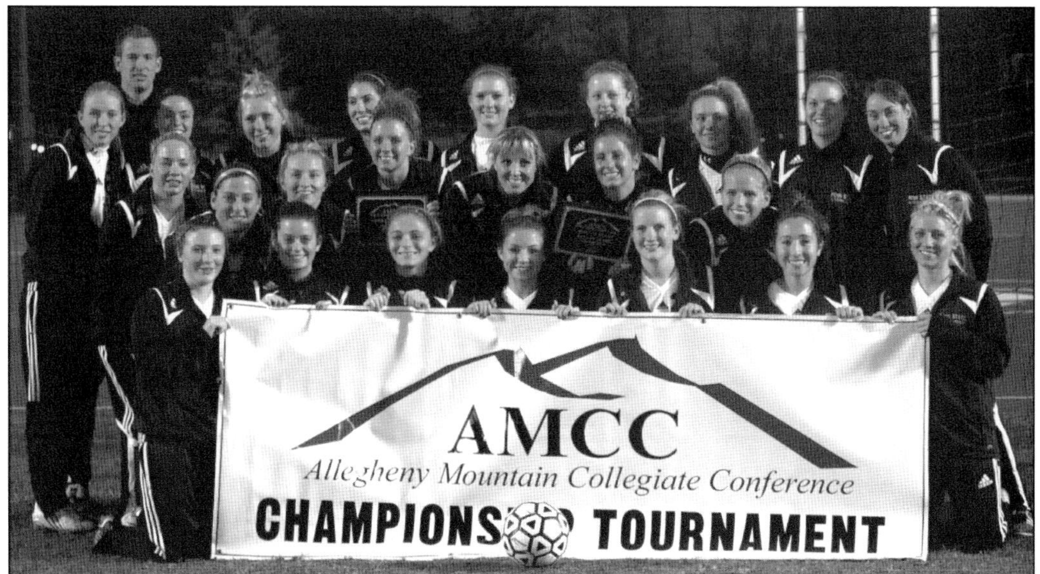

During the 2008–2009 campaign, the Penn State Altoona women's soccer team won the Allegheny Mountain Collegiate Championship, as well as an appearance at the NCAA Division III tournament. Under the leadership of head coach Tim Wassell, the Lions turned in an undefeated season. In January 2009, the squad received a coveted Silver Team Ethics Award for their good sportsmanship.

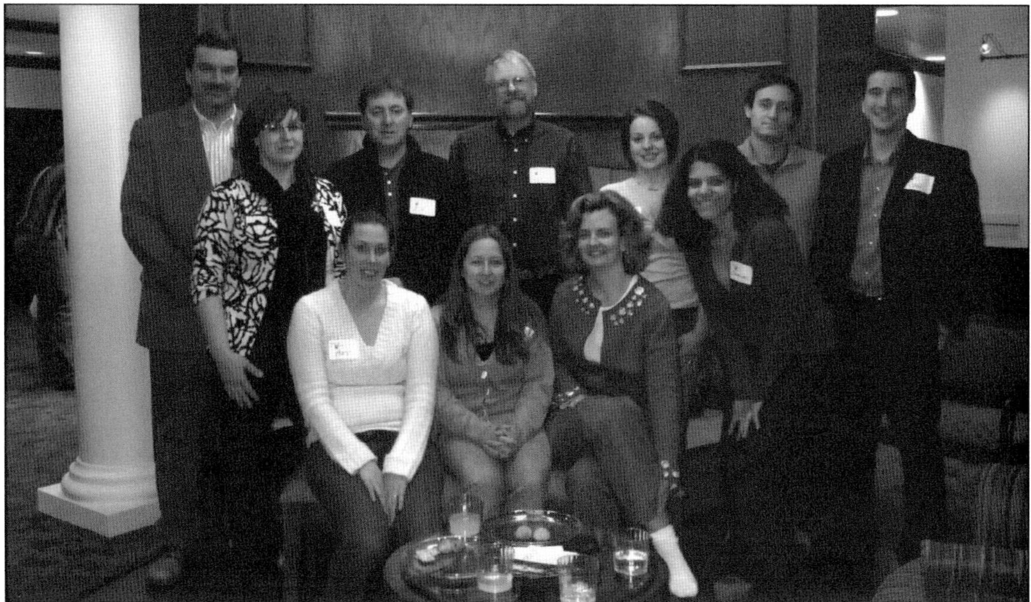

In February 2009, the environmental studies program celebrated its 10-year anniversary with an alumni reunion. Graduates have gone on to careers in public policy, education, environmental law, environmental planning, conservation biology, and environmental engineering. Pictured are, from left to right, (first row) Mary Moore Feerrar, Mindy Wilkins, and co-coordinator Carolyn Mahan; (second row) co-coordinator Brian Black, Mary Helsel, William Hollern, former coordinator Ian Marshall, Amie Myers, Jasmine Almonte, Eliot Levine, and Dan McCombie.

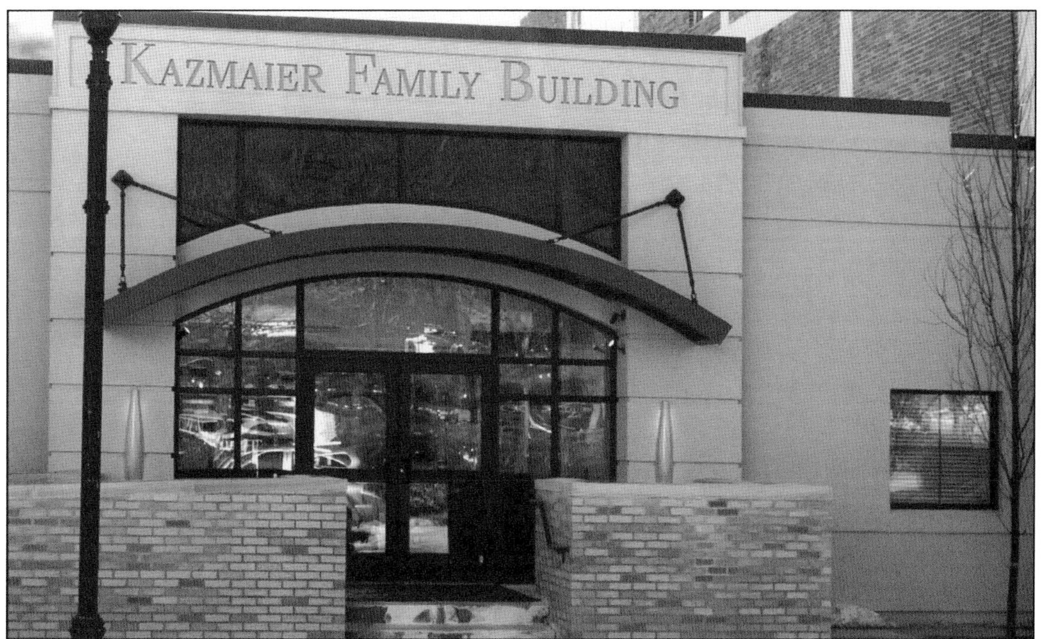

Formerly the WRTA radio broadcast facility, the Kazmaier Family Building in downtown Altoona affords the college a dedicated center for Penn State Altoona's alumni and development initiatives. Under the leadership and expertise of N. Susan Woodring, director of development and alumni relations, the college has seen its private donations grow considerably in recent years. The Kazmaier Family Building was made possible by the philanthropy of former Mid-State Bank executive John Kazmaier; his wife, Dede; and his mother, the late Jane Patterson Kazmaier Lower.

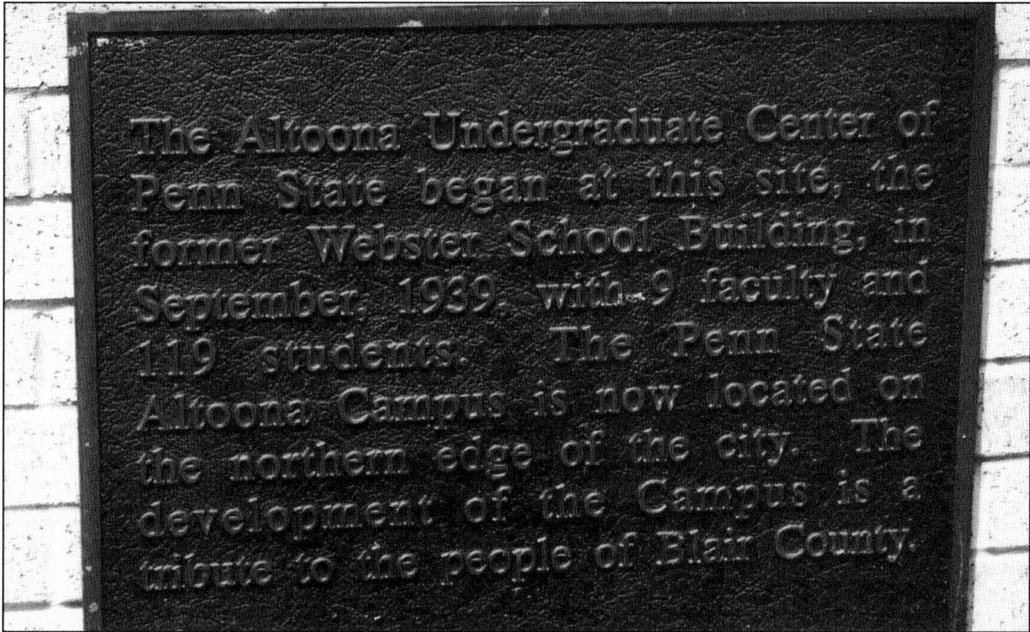

A bronze plaque now commemorates the former location of the Webster School building at Lexington Avenue and Tenth Street in downtown Altoona.

Consistent with our mission to preserve history on a local level, this book was printed in South Carolina on American-made paper and manufactured entirely in the United States. Products carrying the accredited Forest Stewardship Council (FSC) label are printed on 100 percent FSC-certified paper.

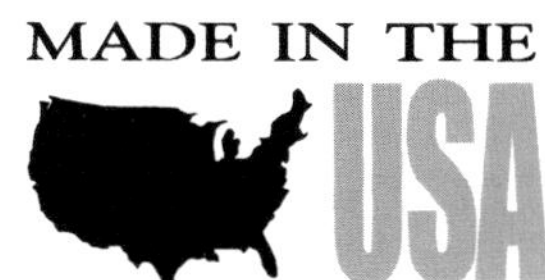